T0368219

Ministers of Vengeance

God's Rules Of Engagement

D.H. PENNY

WestBow Press books may be ordered through booksellers or by contacting:

WestBow Press
A Division of Thomas Nelson & Zondervan
1663 Liberty Drive
Bloomington, IN 47403
www.westbowpress.com
1 (866) 928-1240

ISBN: 978-1-9736-2975-7 (sc)
ISBN: 978-1-9736-2976-4 (hc)
ISBN: 978-1-9736-2974-0 (e)

Library of Congress Control Number: 2018906380

Print information available on the last page.

WestBow Press rev. date: 10/3/2018

From Psalm 122:6

שׁאלו שׁלום ירושׁלם ישׁליו אהביך:

Pronounced

Aw-habe Shaw- lav Yer-oo-shaw-lah-im Sha-lome Shaw-ale

Translated from Hebrew to English

Pray for the peace of Jerusalem, those who love you shall prosper

It is my prayer the contents of this book minister to those who willingly endure hardships, risking life, body, and soul to secure our freedom, provide safety, and seek justice. Those whose lives are on the line each day, behind the scenes, on our streets, during a crisis, and serving abroad.

To the family members of military and sister organizations. Thank you for your extraordinary sacrifices and support. Your labors are mission essential, yet mostly unseen, and often unacknowledged. You are not taken for granted. You are greatly appreciated. You are worth fighting for. The Lord Jesus loves you, and so do we whom you support.

Thank you for your service. What Jesus says applies to you all. 'Greater love hath no man than this, that a man lay down his life for his friends' Lord Jesus the Christ, Gospel of John 15:13

Acknowledgments

A special thank you to my lovely wife Linda, who helped in editing, accuracy, and critiquing stages.

Quotes are from the King James Bible unless specified. Other Bibles quoted: **The American Patriots Bible** (APB), **One New Man** (ONM), **John Maxwell Leadership Bible** (MLB), **John Hagee Prophecy Bible** New King James Version (NKJV), The New Jewish Publication Society **Tanakh** (TNK)-, **The Amplified Bible** (AMP), **The Geneva Bible** [the Bible of the American Revolution](GB), **Young's Literal Translation** (YLT), **Literal Translation** [Green's] (LTB), **Modern King James Version** (MKJV), and **New International Version** (NIV).

Note: Western Bibles list the salutation or to whom or by whom a psalm is written but did not give it a verse reference. Therefore some Old Testament verse references of ONM and TNK have a one verse number difference due to the Jewish custom of counting the salutation as part of inspired scripture. Example: Psalm 19:15 in the ONM is 19:14 in the King James.

Contents

Prologue

(I often skip these myself, but really, read this first)

I make no apologies for the extent of spiritual counseling and advice I am giving. There are plenty of honest, competent, and helpful books and caregivers whose primary methods and approach are in the natural. The natural approaches are needed, no doubt about it. There is no sense in writing a book or warfare manual which says all the same things others have said. The gap in the literature which needs filling is consolidated in this book, direct answers to turn formally morally gray actions, into black and white issues- in the supernatural.

Having a moral and spiritual understanding of violence helps you maintain your humanity and sanity in the face of inhumanity and insanity. Supernatural, or as it also called, spiritual help is always a good thing to have. We are not in the business of dealing death, but of preserving life. The harsh reality is often someone must kill, injure, or imprison one or more people, to preserve and safeguard the lives of those they threaten. In a warrior's desire to defend peace, they must be willing to punish those who threaten peace, to keep the peace. No one appreciates peace more than those who fight and sacrifice to preserve it.

Warriors are those commissioned and authorized to do violence to another human being under exceptional circumstances. I use the term warrior and soldier a lot. I am not only referring to the military forces, but also law enforcement, and intelligence community personnel, both male and female; for all are warriors serving in one capacity or another. This book's content is a foundation for the *Doctrine of Violence.*

Border Patrol: Federal Republic of Germany

While guarding a ground surveillance radar (GSR) position overnight, this Private was a little nervous. Everyone heard the stories of Russians or East Germans coming across the East German and Czech borders to harass, hurt, or kill American soldiers. The rules of engagement were simple. Don't do anything on the long list of actions on the Border test. If the enemy sees or photographs any unauthorized activity considered an act of aggression or war it can cause problems for the US (and that soldier) if broadcast on the news.

Two magazines containing thirty rounds of ammunition each are carried in a cargo pocket, or one already inserted into the magazine well, but not charged (a bullet in the chamber ready to fire) with the weapon on safe. There are many DO NOT's which are considered an act of war if done. We are not to insert a magazine into a weapon in sight of the enemy on the Border. We are not supposed to charge the weapon to fire in view of the enemy and to avoid an accidental discharge. The practice of many was to keep both mags with the tape over them (so as not to lose any bullets) out of the rifle unless needed; this is stressed as highly unlikely despite the stories. The Private follows his directives and heads out for the night watch.

He settles in on a partly cloudy, moonless, typical clammy night, for some good old infantry guard duty. Of note, the soldier in question is not a practicing or self-identifying Christian, far from it as a matter of fact. The sergeant and specialist have the night-vision equipment. They are down the side of mountain path guarding the GSR (ground surveillance radar) site some little ways away. The private's guard post is the entrance to the location up the hill. To the right is a road that bends around out of sight continuing into East Germany, now fenced off. To his left is the route down and back out of the 1K zone (a one-thousand-meter area next to the Border with restricted access). It led back to Coburg Harris Barracks, our base of operations. The Lieutenant (LT), as he dropped us off at our position, said: "No one should be approaching from the northeast road." The road leading to the Border.

Later that night he heard what sounded like footsteps of two or three people approaching from the direction of the Border! In the still of the night, the guard saw no flashlights or headlights. The private stopped walking his post, to listen and look. His nerves got edgy; the one pair of night vision is with the Sergeant and Specialist at the GSR site. As he listened, he thought; *Maybe that's not an enemy, maybe its a wild dog, boar, or --- nope, it's someone walking...more than one someone.* He called out, halt! Which means the same in English as it does in German. They didn't stop. He had expected them to stop. He naively, nervously thought, *They always stopped in training.* He calls out again, louder. No answer and the footsteps kept getting closer. Suddenly, the soldier realized how vulnerable he was. Fear crept into his thoughts. *Am I about to become a Border story? What if they have night vision? 'I'm an easy target. If I cry out, they'll know I'm alone... What do I do?"*

It does not haunt him, but the significant emotional impact lasted decades. To this day the incident is easy to vividly recall. His thoughts kept going for what seemed a long time but must have only been seconds. The reality of possibly being hurt, captured, that the Army really isn't the boy scouts, and maybe not seeing his twenty-second birthday was a wakeup call. "One moment," he said, recounting the story, "you take your life and future for granted. Then you're reminded of your mortality." The next thing he does, somewhat panicked, is call out a third time, his heart racing. Halt! Advance to be recognized! The challenge and password should be given, and that after halting, but nerves will do that. His voice cracked like a little boy's, revealing his fear and lack of experience.

It was crazy. In an instant, he thought about the length of time, and steps, it would take to unbutton a cargo pocket, reach in and grab a magazine of ammo. Then take the tape off and insert into the magazine well of an M16A2. Charge the weapon chambering a round, then maybe fire a warning shot, or hope the clouds break so he can see farther than six feet from some starlight. Those thoughts came suddenly, and the time to lock and load a round now seemed like a very long time—too long. *If they have night vision they will see me go for the mag* (a hostile act)- *so what! They're already hostile. They didn't stop! They haven't said anything. They heard me! They can't be friendly!* The footsteps are almost upon him.

Without another thought, he reacted by John Wayneing his weapon. Pulling the charging handle back, thumb on the magazine well button, released the charging handle. The bolt slid forward as if chambering a round with a Cha-Ching ringing out loudly in that night. The universal sound of imminent lethal force about to be unleashed was a bluff. The assailants stopped in their tracks.

A split-second later a voice calls out from the dark. "Private (his last name is called out) there better not be a round in that chamber!" It was the familiar voice of the Lieutenant. Our platoon leader was making the rounds checking up on our various guard points. Red lensed flashlights turn on, and assurance is made—no round in the chamber ready to be fired. After the inspection, the LT returned to the barracks.

After the LT left, the private's thoughts went back to earlier that day. He woke up in the late afternoon for the night detail, his first Border assignment. After eating and laughing during dinner with his friends, he sets out with his fellow guards, nothing out of the ordinary. Then five or six hours later, he believes he could be killed or captured by East German troops. From then on, the Private kept one mag in the cargo pocket, and one in the magazine well; weapon on safe, and no round in the chamber,but there could be one quick enough now. No wild dog, boar, or East German would catch him off guard again. He was glad the threat wasn't as real as it felt.

Incidentally, after that night the LT always radioed ahead he was coming to inspect, during the rest of our Border mission. No one snuck up on any guards. Good choice not to scare the inexperienced or any warrior with live rounds on a hostile border...Just saying. That soldier never forgot how scared, mentally unprepared, and foolish he was. He joked about it later, but still remembers it in technicolor. You don't forget the day you realize you will die, and that it might be that day. Even when, thankfully, you end up not being killed.

The flow of this book assumes the reader has little or no Biblical knowledge, or in-depth thinking about warfare from a Biblical perspective. My approach is not to demean the reader's knowledge base or status. Instead, it is to assure the development of a common point of reference, between the author and the reader, following a specific train of thought. For those with strategic training, and or extensive Biblical study, you should still find most of the book thought-provoking, and informative, adding a new dimension to thinking strategically, and in applying God's word in war and law enforcement.

What you see is what you believe

As I'm sure you've already guessed, the Private on the Border is me. The point of my experience is, even though my perception was wrong, I was never in real danger at all. But, the feelings and thoughts experienced were very real. Perception is critical. Your perception is your reality. Your perception is not necessarily reflective of an understanding of true reality but is the reality on which we base our thoughts, beliefs, feelings, and actions. A limited, warped, or confused sense of understanding is reflected in our incorrect thoughts, beliefs, feelings. Lousy information (incorrect thoughts, feelings, beliefs) leads to bad decisions and unwise actions. Good leaders still make bad choices if based on unknowingly flawed or deceptive intelligence.

My view radically altered of how quick and easy your life can change or end causing a reality check on the seriousness of my job as a soldier. Awareness and maturity come in leaps and bounds, or over time, but perception can be altered in an instant. An instant which can help or hurt the person whose views are changed. It's time to re-train how you believe, think, and feel. Then you will make better decisions.

Welcome to an ancient and still operational dimension of warfare: the supernatural, often neglected, and extremely powerful. The spiritual has a tangible influence on the quality of life, safety, and security of people, families, and nations. The spiritual, as you will soon discover, is a reality which supersedes and can superimpose itself over our perceived physical reality. Think of the difference between true north and magnetic north. Both are north, but only one is true north. Time to follow true North. Time to gain an unfair advantage. Fair means you give the enemy an equal chance to win. War is not about fighting fair. War is fighting honorably and dominating totally.

2008-09 Task Force Phoenix VIII

Before leaving for mobilization, I realized I did not know a lot about warfare in the Bible. Now the war is staring me in the face. An old event rose up from the well of my memory. I joined the Infantry back in 1984. After returning home from Ft. Benning a close friend, who is not a Christian, asked me a question. "If you are a Christian how can you kill someone when the Bible says killing is a sin?" I was not a follower of Christ back then, just a believer, who practiced things he shouldn't have. A high holiday Christian, sort of, going to Easter and Christmas services, maybe. And sometimes saying a customary grace at some meals, maybe, depending on the company I kept.

I didn't really have an answer to this my friends question back then. Assuming there was one (which was good enough for me) I kept on soldiering figuring it was ok. I heard about David and Goliath, so it must be ok somewhere, even though the commandment read "Thou shalt not kill." Honestly, back then, I didn't much care. My spirituality is simple.

- I'm saved in Sunday school as a boy
- Jesus is good. Satan is bad...got it
- I'm basically a good person, so I'm not going to Hell; no problem

My spiritual journey is not uncommon having its ups and downs.

✓ Went through some tough times and made some bad choices
✓ I believed in the supernatural and experimented with it.
✓ Bounced back sometimes serving the Lord, sometimes not
✓ Drifted in and out of service and relationships
✓ Finally found peace in the Lord, a great wife, got back in service
✓ Once on my feet and stable went back to school, got ordained
✓ With a heart for finding answers to questions and problems I experienced, were asked, and saw; I prayed, researched, and now present to you this book.

Detective Frank Serpico suffered dearly after blowing the whistle on corruption within part of the New York City Police Department. During his testimony in front of the Knapp Commission detective Serpico said, "We must create an atmosphere where the crooked cop fears the honest cop and not the other way around." Those within the ranks who put at risk or seek to tarnish the personal and professional reputations of law enforcement agents, intelligence community operatives, and military personnel should not feel safe in doing so.

COVENANT MINDSET

CHAPTER 1

What is Covenant (a brief overview)

You recognize who you are as you learn who God is. God is personal and wants to show Himself personally to you. Sure, I could just list a bunch of do's and don'ts in a pamphlet twenty pages long, but that wouldn't help you understand and apply what God has for you in the way of supernatural resources. We can know about God through studying the Word, but still not know Him as a person. What is immediately known about others is known because we are all people through what we commonly experience. All have curiosity, imagination, needs, ability to learn, reason, and feel. However, this still does not reveal who we are, how we think or feel, or what we imagine.

We can understand things about God based on what we are, the things around us, all creation. Someone can tell you about others, or you can read an autobiography about them. However, just as we must interact to know each other, who is trustworthy, funny, mean, or whatever. We must also interact with the Holy Spirit to learn and experience who He really is for ourselves.

We are created in God's image, from His imagination to reflect and relate to Him on His level, but have fallen terribly short of our intent and potential through sin. We are created for relationship with God the Father through His Son Jesus, by the Holy Spirit interacting with and through our spirit. There are things you cannot learn about someone except through fellowship with them, where they reveal themselves to you.

For example, people lie, but does God lie or can He lie? Good question since all relationships are based on trust. We know people lie because all of us have lied or been lied to. We learn who to trust and under what circumstances. God cannot lie because when you're all powerful and all knowledgeable, you don't need to, wouldn't, and cannot. God cannot lie because if He speaks it, it must become since He is all-powerful. Hint, He wants us to develop our faith (a substance and a force), and understanding of Him. Then when we speak, it happens, through our faith, just as it does for Him.

But, what is familiar to all people, is what we generally know about other people. This general knowledge only partially translates to knowledge about God. We must learn from Him, of Him, through the word of the Bible and the life Jesus lived. Where do we start; God created our physical bodies with all their attributes, our emotions, intellect, unlimited personalities, and imagination. So, we can assume God has a body of some kind, emotions, intelligence, personality, imagination, and the power to create or nothing would be. It's a start. God relates to us through covenant relationship.

What is Covenant

The Bible is an Ancient Near Eastern document authored by Holy Spirit inspired people; dictated into sixty-six books or letters across thousands of years. It is God choosing people whose real-life experiences are used to teach or reveal the truth. Sometimes these historical events foreshadow future larger scale prophetic events. Sometimes they are demonstrations or patterns of social, psychological, and spiritual laws, principles or national trends. Knowing the right context (proper political, religious, economic, and cultural setting) of scripture is key to understanding what God is saying to us in our time.

A covenant is a Biblical term for a binding agreement. Whether it's a last will and testament, insurance contract, or mortgage contract a binding and enforceable agreement is entered into. The terms of any contract determine the potential or promised benefits, and potential or sure penalties, for following or breaking the agreement. As a citizen of the United States, our government has a relationship to us which other governments before us did not. We can be drafted for war, arrested for a crime, or protected by a right ensuring free speech or the right to sue the government, as outlined in the covenant or agreement which Americans live under; the U.S. Constitution. A Constitution is another word or term for covenant. Another example is a service member committing a crime in another country may be turned over to U.S. authorities or stay in the custody of the host nation. What happens to the service member depends upon the terms of the status of forces agreement (a covenant) between the U.S. and the host nation. Another example is if a U.S. citizen commits a crime and runs to another country for refuge. If the U.S. has an extradition agreement (another type of covenant) with that nation, if caught, the criminal is returned. If the criminal finds a sanctuary nation, then he or she is not returned, willingly. We cannot publicly or openly regain custody of them.

Covenant is the structure or guidelines God put in place for us to relate to Him. Covenant is one of the ways God reveals Himself to us. Covenant is a basis for expressing lawful authority. When Lucifer rebelled, he broke covenant with God, permanently altering the terms of his existence and role he was created to fulfill. Lucifer is the first covenant breaker. Anyone living outside of covenant with God, or living as if they don't have a covenant, is vulnerable to the influence of the powers of darkness. Non-covenant personnel can legally be taken captive, killed, afflicted, or affected by the forces of evil without their permission, and often without their knowledge.

God is not three Gods, but three persons in One God. It is not an idea of a man so, not entirely understandable, or knowable this side of Heaven. It is important to understand Jesus though, for He is our source and example of the Trinity. Jesus represents our Heavenly Fathers love for and power towards us. The Lord Jesus, the Holy Spirit, and our Father cannot be trusted until they are known. Not because they aren't trustworthy, of course, they are. The problem is us. We are a suspicious bunch because people lie. We must be cautious who and what we believe. We are the ones with trust and deception issues, not the Lord. It is hard to trust a person until you know them, so, get to know the Holy Spirit. As you read the Scriptures, ask God the Holy Spirit to help you understand, and apply the word He inspired/wrote through prophets to you.

Trust at all its levels is based on the development of a relationship. Trust is based on our knowledge and experience with a person. Are they reliable or dependable? The covenant relationship is the most secure. God knows us, but we must learn of Him. Of all the possible covenants, the blood covenant is the strongest. Violation of a blood covenant carries the sentence of death, carried out by the offended partner. There are punishments or consequences if you lie in court under oath. This is important to know when learning to trust God and build your faith in His word. God cannot break the Covenant in Jesus blood, or He would cease to be... God binds Himself by His own word, and when He promises something, makes His word 100% dependable, 100% of the time. God cannot and would not go back on His word.

Job Lessons Learned

In many Bibles, the lord is also spelled, Lord, or LORD. You also see God and the LORD GOD. There are many names of God in Hebrew reveal things about the character of, power from, and our relationship to God. The different spellings denote some of these various Hebrew names of God. For this book, one is essential to know, capital LORD. This spelling occurs representing when the Hebrew name YAH-WEH, or in English JE-HO-VAH is used. It is the covenant name of God. It means ever existent one. Existing in our past, present, and future, all at the same time, even before time.

Time itself is a created thing. That time is created is a verifiable scientific fact, too have a creation you logically need a creator. Not matter how hard secular scientists want something other than a Creator to explain existence, it futile. As intelligent as many non-Christian scientists, and Christian scientists are, a theory is still just that, only a theory. A theory is not an empirical (proven) fact such as the Big Bang; caused by God. And if there is nothing (no physical substance), then that would include no gravity, so the theory of nothing suddenly creating something is illogical and contrary to the laws of physics.

God is a living dimension of sorts all unto Himself, existing outside of, within, and throughout all creation. God is all-powerful [omnipotent] and all-knowing [omnipresent] or aware of everything while ever-present always (on the moon, while flying, swimming, in a submarine, knowing your thoughts). Nevertheless, the Lord is not a bully. God did not make us zombie creations without a free will. Angels, humans, and demons all have a free will.

All relationships are covenant based. You are either in agreement or not in agreement with whoever, about whatever. One example is the institution of marriage. Marriage is a sacred example of a covenant, an intimate dedication, and commitment to a relationship inclusive of God. Covenants are conditional, unconditional, event-driven, short-term, and or last forever. There are many combinations of agreements between people and between God and people. God conveys His temporary and everlasting goals, His end game vision in His word, to us through the Holy Spirit and the loyal angels of the Lord.

Work on not thinking like an American, European, Asian, African, or South American...so to speak. Think like an Israeli, a Middle Eastern who knows his or her Hebrew roots. Biblical context: the times and customs of the people through whom the Holy Spirit inspired His word are of the Ancient Near East (ANE). To understand what God says about war, you must see and read with ANE and Jewish cultural eyes. Everything in the Bible is truly recorded, as it truly happened and was said. This doesn't mean that everything said or done in the Bible is right and true. A familiar Bible story is a good example.

Most people are not taught or do not read, the details of the Satan's attack on Job, nor how it played out unto the end. Most people are familiar with Job's cry unto the Lord, as it is often quoted in movies. "And Job said, Naked came I out of my mother's womb, and naked shall I return thither: the LORD gave, and the LORD hath taken away; blessed be the name of the LORD" (Job 1:21-22). It *is true* Job said this, but what Job said *is not true*. By the way, Job's name and title of his book mean persecuted one. So, Job may not be his true name, but his nickname or a type of title he is known by after all his troubles.

It is true the Lord did not correct Job on who took from him. It is true Job did not speak evil of God but submitted respectfully in his statement. This was all Job knew. Job only understood the Lord as he was taught and later by the Lord revealing Himself to Job personally. It is important to note God did not correct Job's theology. God never took from Job. It was Satan who stole from Job. A misunderstanding still prevalent today. Notice also only the reader, and inspired writer of Job have the information about the spiritual activity taking place behind the scenes. God's primary concern is Jobs personal meeting with God. Job spoke according to his understanding of reality, but his perception didn't include the activity in the spiritual realm.

Job shows the Lord teaches us about Him through negative and positive statements. God uses examples of what is right and wrong to teach us the difference and give us confidence and boldness when doing the right things. It reminds us just because people say, "God is this or that," or "God said, such and such," does not mean it's true unless it passes the Biblical test. The Biblical test is one that it comes to pass, and two that it lines up with already revealed scripture. The book of Job also introduces a spiritual chain of command, limits of spiritual authority, and cause and effect interaction between the spiritual and physical dimensions or realities also called heavens in the Bible.

Jobs story takes place during the time of Abraham, or as many scholars think shortly before Abraham lived, but is the same culture. The story starts by introducing and defining the roles and relationship between powerful supernatural beings. And lightning used to kill Job's flocks and children. Even human free will is swayed by evil entities directing the marauding bands of thieves and murderers stealing Job's assets and killing his employees. Sickness is caused by evil spirits as seen with Job's boils from head to toe. And the in swaying or magnifying of emotions; as with Job's wife, lost in understandable grief, tells Job to curse God and die, but he refuses. The enemies areas of influence and relationships between the supernatural and the natural are revealed. The battle zone is not just physical; it is interdimensional.

We live in a three-dimensional world- length, width, height, and a fourth - time. Spiritual planes of existence, such as the first through third Heavens as the Bible calls them. We live in and experience the plane of the First Heaven which is all the planets, Earth, the atmosphere, outer space, the stars visible to us or through a telescope, etc. Science is catching up with the Bible in predicting through string theory (not getting into all that in this book) around ten dimensions or coexistent planes of existence, beyond our immediate senses of sight, touch, smell, hearing, and taste. The spiritual realms are the other dimensions co-existing and intersecting with our dimension and experiences.

Covenant further Explained

Why is this mini-lesson in Bible interpretation relevant to the soldier on the field of battle? Basic first aid and combat lifesavers refresher classes can be boring. Until the day you must stop a sucking chest wound, put on a tourniquet, or find a vein. Then all the repetition is worth it- your muscle memory and training automatically kick in, if you paid attention you'd do it right. It takes an extra effort to retrain what is learned the first time incorrectly. This is the process we are in now, retraining our mind on how we think about covenant and spirit. The idea is to develop a new 'first response' or 'second nature' and develop a broader more accurate perception of what is really going on around you, and what is the right response to it.

In Greek, the word for Covenant is diatheke. This means last will or testament. Diatheke is the Greek translation of the Hebrew word expressing covenant concept- berith- to cut or make a treaty, promise, compact, or agreement. The book of the Old Testament (OT) could be called the books of the Original or first covenants, instead of outdated or 'Old.' This New Covenant (New Testament) is the best of all prior covenants and the manifestation of foreshadowed concepts from the Old Testament, plus many added benefits of its own. The New Covenant is foretold in Jeremiah 31:31-34.

This book is not about the creation debate, though a creation statement must be made. It is foundational to covenant and structure. Why? Because, if God is not Creator and Sovereign, then how can we depend on Him. Plenty of other books, whether in agreement or not, are available for you to study and decide for yourself. This belief is the reference point used in the interpretation of God's Word, for my commentary in this book. Each of us is responsible for the reference point we choose. God imagined the universe, then spoke it into existence causing the Big Bang! Now a universe in all its dimensions comes into existence, not in six twenty-four-hour days, but in six ages of time or time periods. This is Biblical, scientific, and true. We appear on the scene after about 12 or 13 plus billion years of activity, and after the fall of Lucifer, the angels being in existence before us.

Don't make it say, what it doesn't

God reveals Himself within a cultural context, past and present. Job worshiped God with offerings and obedience the best he was taught. His life and view of God transformed after his personal encounter with God. It is written Judas went and hanged himself. Does this mean we should commit suicide? Of course not, but people, cults, and some churches twist things to manipulate individuals and leaders. They want to rationalize their actions and try to make God appear to say what He has not said, mischaracterizing Him.

Some examples of the Bible being misapplied are the Spanish Inquisition and expulsion of the Jews, Nazi Concentration Camps (yes Hitler used the Bible against the Jews), and in Uganda Jim Jones followers drinking poisoned Kool-Aid just to name a few. Why are there thousands of years of persecution of the Jews and/or Christians? They are persecuted because they are the only people group assembled by the Father. All the Word of God came from Jews. Jesus is a Jew. Christians follow a Jewish Rabbi who is the Son of God, their Savior. Satan hates the Jew.

White supremacists may say they are Christian, but show they are not in many ways, one of which is their hatred of the Jews. Additionally, their hatred and violence in general also betray they work for the Devil knowingly, or are deceived by Satan into thinking they work for God in all their hatred. This goes for all hate-based and divisive racist groups. Satan loves division and conflict. In God's word, it says nation shall be against the nation. In the Greek, the word for nation is ethnos. It is where we get the words ethnic or ethnicity; racism is a demonic spirit from the pit of Hell. God's word says ethnic conflicts or racial tension are expected, but that He is not behind them. Peaceful and necessary demonstrations like those led by Dr. Martin Luther King are from God. Don't get the good movements confused with those masquerading as good, but have violence and hatred in their words and actions.

Don't get sidetracked, start thinking in a different context. This is good practice because, to contend with your enemy efficiently, you must know how they think. The culture of Heaven is able to merge itself into all technological, scientific, philosophical, political, ethnic, moral, and cultural circumstances across all space and time. A merger or collision which separates good from evil. You have to perceive God's word through ANE, and Holy Spirit focused lenses. Then apply eternal truths to the current situation. To merge here is to superimpose and integrate without compromise. Any needful changes take place in the human culture, not the Heavenly culture.

You can only receive for yourself what you believe for in faith. You have wisdom just for yourself. For example, if you are taught healing is passed, then you possibly will miss God's present available healing for you. The irony is many unbelievers receive God's healing and miracles, prayed for by believers on their behalf (intercessors) before believers receive from Him. When an unbeliever is healed, they usually convert afterward. Healings and miracles soften the human heart opening them to the gospel. Your speech is what controls your life. Foundational principles for receiving from God, besides Mark 11:22, is also Ephesians 2:8-9.

> "BY grace you have been saved [*healed, protected, etc.*] THROUGH faith, not of yourselves [<u>our own will or power</u>] it is the GIFT of God [<u>not anything we are entitled to because of our righteousness</u>], not of works [<u>our own efforts or good deeds</u>] lest any man should boast" (Eph 2:8-9, my emphasis added: hereafter annotated as <u>em ad</u>)

I quote a lot of scriptures for two reasons. One to validate my commentary and guidance, and two because the word of God says faith come be hearing and hearing by the word of God. My commentary is good, but doesn't produce faith. Love gives. Grace supplies. Faith is a substance and force used to take or obtain what is provided or given, to bring it from the true spiritual reality of Heaven into the physical reality of Earth; changing the physical reality by superimposing the supernatural reality upon it. Covenant lets you know why, how, when, and what you can ask God for and boldly expect it. There is no room for doubt in the middle of a fight. Sometimes there is no time to think. Calling upon, or saying or screaming out one name, Jesus, can be enough.

When you study the Bible, it should be to see what it says. It should not be to find a way to justify your own actions. You can twist God's words for your own ends, to look good in the eyes of others. Nevertheless, you cannot bend or change the truth and willfully mishandle it, and escape the consequences. This book reveals what the Bible says about various aspects of war to build a foundation for a Biblical Doctrine of Violence.

Hebrew Thinking and the Oath of Enlistment

Covenants were treaties, lands pacts, weddings, and cover every relationship in society, including war. The covenant custom or concept 'All which is mine is now all yours,' and vice versa is in effect. In a covenant with God, He is the senior partner. Whatever the senior partner demands of the lesser, the senior partner must also perform or reciprocate. A senior partner may do something on behalf of the junior partner, which the junior partner cannot duplicate, reciprocate, or repay. If this is done, the junior partner is not expected to do anything in return. This is important because in the covenant cut with Jesus blood on the cross all that is His becomes ours and vice versa. We cannot add to that or duplicate that for the Lord Jesus. Moreover, God as Senior Partner in redeeming us knows that gift cannot be repaid, only received.

Before a swearing-in ceremony in the presence of the American flag, a potential service member took the ASVAB, met other qualifications, looked over job options, and time in service obligations. They decided on a combination of authorized options then signed a contract. This contract states what you expect in return for your oath to perform duties as required. This included submitting to the rigors of basic training. One expectation is VA access if a vet and a pension if a retiree. If you signed the covenant agreement and refused to swear in with an oath of binding: stronger than, and in addition to your signature, your contract is voided.

The contract states the terms. Speaking your loyalty and willingness to submit to military authority is the priority. It is what solidifies the covenant. Without an oath or swearing in, you cannot be trusted, regardless of the signed contract agreement; no trust means no deal. Your word is your bond. Are there Biblical parallels or lessons we can draw from a sample oath? Yes.

Oath of enlistment example unpacked

"I, (your name), do solemnly swear (or affirm) that I will support and defend the Constitution of the United States against all enemies, foreign and domestic; that I will bear true faith and allegiance to the same; and that I will obey the orders of the President of the United States and the orders of the officers appointed over me, according to regulations and the Uniform Code of Military Justice. So help me God." (Title 10, US Code; Act of 5 May 1960 replacing the wording first adopted in 1789, with amendment effective 5 October 1962).

Officers have a similar oath. These words are uttered by hundreds each day of the week at enlistment, commissioning, and reenlistment ceremonies. These words are not spoken for show. They bind a person to servitude in the military culture. This is a covenant relationship. What are we really saying when we take this vow?

1 Support and defend the Constitution of the United States against all enemies, foreign and domestic -uphold and protect from destruction the governmental structure of the American way of life as outlined in our founding covenant documents: The Declaration of Independence, U.S. Constitution, Bill of Rights, and Amendments.
2 bear true faith and allegiance to the same- to uncompromisingly live a patriotic lifestyle upholding the ideals and principals of our founding documents.
3 obey the orders of-of the proper legal authority, submitting to those in lawful authority over you as designated by the rank or structure in effect.
4 according to regulations and the Uniform Code of Military Justice -in agreement with established terms of covenant/oath/affirmation- current regulations and UCMJ, along with any changes made to these during the time of service. Also, a term of service may be extended or cut short to meet the needs of the military as they see fit.
5 So help me God -Binding in the sight of God, committing an act of treason (breaking covenant) against your country, also treason against God. Both will hold you accountable. To call upon Him

> (saying So help me God), is asking the Lord for help in the issuing and fulfillment of all orders, duties, and accomplishment of assigned missions. This last line is often spoken out of tradition and without any real conviction. This line of the oath is often spoken with little thought for what is really being said. You cannot call upon a covenant for help from God if you do not know what it says God will do for you. You cannot call upon someone you do not believe exist. You can call upon God, asking that if He lives, to reveal Himself to you. He will reveal Himself because Jesus loves you. Without respect for and belief in God, the real strength of the oath and accountability is undermined or lost.

This oath and others like it are solemn, carrying an expectation of unwavering loyalty. No one asked us to draw blood from ourselves or an animal in taking man-made oaths, which come with expectations. With this oath all the resources of the military are expected by you, to be used on your behalf. Also, your efforts to keep physically fit, follow orders, accomplish the mission, be weapons proficient, tactically and technically proficient, etc., are expected of you by the military.

Is it so surprising God expects a reasonable service (Romans12:1) for saving you? Is it surprising that He has divine laws which govern actions and situations? Unlike the rules of the nation or UCMJ, Jesus promises, and truths are unchanging. He committed Himself to us, enduring death on the cross. Then He rose from the dead to demonstrate His ability, authority, and desire to make good on all promises.

When you read the Old Testament or OT, you find rankings such as captain of tens, captain of hundreds...and a particular captain of the three. The captain of three in this reference is listed among mighty heroes of war in the scriptures, valiant men. They would be today's special operations persons. The Lord is the Captain of the Host of Heaven, all the armies in the Heavens, and armies of Heaven on Earth. Most people are familiar with the saying turn the other cheek. There is a time and place for cheek turning, and for cheek busting. Joshua, General of the Hebrew Army, and successor to Moses for national leadership had a meeting with the pre-incarnate Jesus (before His official birth into this dimension through Mary) as Commander. Yes, Jesus is a Commander of armies.

> "And it happened when Joshua was by Jericho, that he lifted up his eyes and looked and, behold, there stood a Man opposite him with His sword drawn in His hand. And Joshua went to Him and said to Him, Are you for us, or for our adversaries? And He said, No, but I have come as Captain of the Army of the LORD. And Joshua fell on his face to the earth **and worshipped** and said to Him. What does my Lord say to His servant? And the Captain of the LORD's army said to Joshua. "Loose your shoe from off your foot, for the place where you are standing is holy. And Joshua did so." (Jos 5:13-15, ONM em ad).

Where the Lord walks, the ground is holy, His presence makes all the difference. The Lord spoke to Moses at the burning bush the same way, "loose your sandals..."

I hope this analogy of our oath helps you to begin to take God's word at face value, understand covenant, and begin to believe and receive. We believe the words and contracts of men, even coupons in a newspaper. Shouldn't we trust the word or covenant of the living God? As a believer in Jesus as Savior, the Holy Spirit dwells in you. You are the vessel (body of Christ on Earth) of the Holy Spirit. Where you walk: the field of battle, undercover, analyzing intelligence, or a traffic stop; is holy ground.

Uncle Sam Wants You!

Over 100 years ago a famous WW I recruiting poster you might remember; the iconic picture of Uncle Sam is pointing at you saying "I Want You- U.S. Army,"(Poster History, 2017) was posted across the country. It's still found in antique stores or military museums. This American poster depicted a patriotic sentiment along with a call to arms. It evoked a response to aggression and injustice. Millions answered that posters call in WW I against the Central Powers, and in WW II against the Axis threat of National Socialism (Nazi Germany), Fascism (Italy) and Imperial Japan.

Since before the creation of humanity and its fall, our Father in Heaven, His Son, Holy Spirit, and loyal angels have known war- why it is, how it's fought and how it's won. Since before Moses was spoken to by the great, I AM (the eternal God existing yesterday, today and tomorrow) from a burning bush, God has a poster which read, and still reads -

I AM

Wants You

Army of the LORD

> "The tree of liberty must be refreshed from time to time with the blood of patriots and tyrants. It is its natural manure."
>
> Thomas Jefferson
>
> Signer of the Declaration of Independence

CHAPTER 2

War and Religion

War is inescapable as recorded throughout human history. What do the primary or most enduring religions say about it? What is acceptable violence? Given the need throughout civilization to defend persons, property, tribes, or nations from enslavement or destruction, or other various reasons; what does the divine say about the use of force? There is violent activity going on 24/7 in the spiritual and physical realms: in the dark corners of society, on its mean streets, and alleyways. These are not the places average people want to go, nor care to acknowledge. To quote the movie A Few Good Men "You want me on that wall." Many don't want to be on or think about the wall and why it's there.

Many people don't want to know what really is going on. Many try to downplay the dangers in our society and make excuses for criminals, terrorists, and renegade nations. Some say war is not necessary and is always evil. Others say war is necessary but, if not actually evil, it is at least morally compromising. War is not a necessary evil; war is necessary because of evil. If we do not understand what we do, and how what we do is good, and that we have the moral high ground, even when it's ugly. It is no wonder that suffering PTSD and walking away from the Lord became common among modern warriors.

Before jumping into God's supernatural fighting assistance, and ways to partner with Him before, during, and after time spent downrange, we'll compare some of what other faiths say about war. Not all those who read these pages are Christians; some are seekers, some researchers. Does only the Jewish, Judeo-Christian, and Islamic religions condone violence?

Are so-called peaceful religions devoid of dealing with the realities of armed conflict?

There are too many variations of beliefs, some new religions such as Jehovah's Witnesses, Mormonism, or Scientology, and ancient ones like Zoroastrianism, or Voodoo to cover them all. The dominant or foundational worldviews have extensive comments on war. These are the ones we will take a look at. Many other religions or variations of the dominant worldviews are less structured, such as Wicca, Voodoo, Yoruba, and Santeria. Views on warfare in these belief systems often are left up to individual practitioners.

Evolution and War

The theory of evolution is unproven, and in many scientific respects disproven. It is a religious belief and pseudo-science taught as truth among some teachers and some scientists. Charles Darwin's writings are racist, leaning toward white supremacy. If you are Jewish or non-Caucasian, believing in evolution is counter to the truth that all men are created equal and made of one blood. Evolution is a false religious belief against God, the evidence of intelligent design, and is saturated with racism. Research and see for yourself.

Therefore, all is permissible in evolution if you are the higher or dominant species. An example of this is the Nazis concentration camps and torturous medical research. Atheist evolutionists and spiritual evolutionists (those who believe God created evolution) are the religions of socialist, communist, and fascist nations. Atheism is their state religion. Make no mistake Atheism is a belief there is no God; it is a religious system. It is the religion of believing in self and not in a higher power. All forms of evolution permit war, and that without laws or restraint, for only the strong deserve to survive, it is their right.

Hinduism and War

Hinduism is approximately 4000 years old. It is a caste system religion with a multitude of gods and goddesses, all incarnations of the all, or Atman. You are born into whatever level of the caste system your parents occupy unless you are born outside the system as an 'untouchable.' This religion began, in the region now known as India and Pakistan.

You have three divisions within Hinduism which all commonly follow Karma (reincarnation principles). The desire is to reincarnate more favorably, in the caste system, to eventually accomplish enlightenment-being one with the Brahman or Soul of the universe. Upon attainment of enlightenment, an event called the Moksha occurs. This is when the person is no longer part of the life death and rebirth cycle called Samsara. What conduct if any, in war, produces good Karma versus bad Karma in the Hindu worldview? One of their oldest books contains an account of Krishna advising a prince on battle.

> *"May your weapons be strong to drive away the attackers, may your arms be powerful enough to check the foes let your army be glorious, not the evil-doer"* (Rig Veda 1-39:2).

Interestingly considering the reincarnation aspect of Hindi thought, another set of writings talks of Heaven for death in battle, which is contradictory to reincarnation unless it is interpreted (which it is not) for the sake of conversation as a free pass straight to Moksha. Dying in combat as a means to earn instant access to Heaven is a mindset taught in more than one religion.

> *"Kaunteya, if you are killed (in battle) you will ascend to heaven, On the contrary, if you win the war, you will enjoy the comforts of earthly kingdom. Therefore, get up and fight with the determination. With eqnaumity towards happiness, and sorrow, gain, and loss, victory, and defeat, fight. This way you will not incur any sin."* Bhagavad Gita 2.37-38.

So, self-defense is condoned, and war is embraced. There are even verses for rules of war with warnings of going to a Hindu version of Hell. In the Hindu belief you are sent to Hindi Hell for using poison or attack on the old or women, and attack from behind is also a sin. So, Hinduism makes no provision for assaults by stealth or collateral damage; things, which are unavoidable in combat, if one desires to win. Moreover, the principles of Ahimsa (Non-injury) add to the apparent conflict of doctrine. Violence creates bad Karma, yet violence is unavoidable. Ahimsa is the way Gandhi followed in his resistance to British rule. It is the avoidance of seeking to harm any living thing for any reason. Harm is defined can be physical, mental and emotional.

Hinduism accepts the necessity of war, self-defense and even has a code of conduct for fighting. It is at odds with its very tenants of doing good deeds, according to some vague estimation, enough to tilt Karma in your favor, unless you die in battle without sinning. Good works which may not have carried over from the last life- especially if you are a soldier. You may find yourself in Hell for doing a sanctioned work or doomed to repeat soldiering, over and over again, never achieving Moksha or release from Samsara. Do not be deceived by the demonic doctrines or ways of Karma.

What help or guidance does this provide the warrior, yesterday, today and tomorrow? What solace is offered concerning if a sin by Hindu standards is committed, standards not entirely covering the full spectrum of operations, then and now? The answer is none. If Hinduism is correct you have to make up for past lives sins (unknowable) while not committing more sins. While making up for sins, you don't know about you must also do more good than the present evils (which are relative and even entirely unknowable in Hinduism) to get promoted in the next life. This is an unrealistic worldview of fatalism and depression. What it asks is impossible to do. There are unverifiable claims some have accomplished this very action, though how you achieve this and return to tell about it is unknown. The truth is you cannot truly know or go back to a past life because a past life does not exist. Reincarnation does not exist. It is a deception of the Devil designed to keep you in bondage, as are all religious deceptions.

Jainism strictly follows the principle of Ahimsa. It lacks the conflict of Hinduism relating to violence and nonviolence. For the utter pacifism of Jainism, is the only way to break out of the Samsara via Moksha, according to that worldview. Jainism is a pacifist Hindu sect which implicitly condemns warriors to Hell or eternal struggle to ascend above out of the Samsara. Neither Jainism or Hinduism are able to reconcile war and peace among humanity.

Imagine no police, soldiers, judges, juries, correctional officers, or executioners; all part of a penal system which by Jainism standards causes injury to people who have been deemed unfit to roam society freely. Anarchy would reign, eventually evolving politically into an oppressive form of government. The principles seem good- even witchcraft has its mantra 'an it harm none it will be done.' Of course subject to whose definitions of what counts as a harm; by whose authority are these rules or guidelines given? The idea of Ahimsa is nice, but unrealistic. What is needed is a doctrine or worldview which realistically addresses the real issues faced in the real world of human nature.

Taoism and War

Taoism is the believed by some to be the path on the journey of life experiencing reality and the origin of the universe. Lao Tzu wrote on life about 2600 years ago in the Tao Te Ching. Lao says Tao is the being or substance of all creation. He says it is the natural order of things. Chi or energy is represented in the Yin and Yan. Lao's comments on violence and attitudes one should have about war are few.

> *The superior man ordinarily considers the left hand the most honorable place, but in time of war the right hand. Those sharp weapons are instruments of evil omen, and not the instruments of the superior man;--he uses them only on the compulsion of necessity. Calm and repose are what he prizes; victory (by force of arms) is to him undesirable. To consider this desirable would be to delight in the slaughter of men; and he who delights in the slaughter of men cannot get his will in the kingdom.* (Tao 31:2).

> *"When the Tao prevails in the world, they send back their swift horses to (draw) the dung-carts. When the Tao is disregarded in the world, the war-horses breed in the border lands"* (Tao 46. 1).

> *"There is no calamity greater than lightly engaging in war. To do that is near losing (the gentleness) which is so precious. Thus*

> *it is that when opposing weapons are (actually) crossed, he who deplores (the situation) conquers."* 69:2.

What Lao is saying is war is to be avoided, but if it cannot be, fighting with the right attitude is essential. This concept is correct.

Confucius and War

Confucius (Kong Tzu) wrote on civics in China between 557-479 B.C. His writings are in a compilation now called the Analects. Confucian thought dominates China to this day. Chinese education and government draw heavily from Confucian thought. Kong makes three references to war.

> *The master (Tzu) also exercised great caution concerning -- fasting, war, and sickness. 1:12*

> *The Master said, "When a good man has taught the common people for seven years, they should be ready to be employed in war." The Master said, "To lead the people to war without having taught them is to throw them away."* 13:29-30

In three sentences on war Kong accepts war as reality, training is mandatory, and people are expected to serve the ruler and participate in war. As for whether to wage war aggressively or only defensively, or other subjects of a warrior's concern, Kong is silent. He just teaches that war is considered significant and to be approached cautiously. This is not much help to the warrior in the realm of conscience having no teaching on the moral high ground. War is the duty of people at the whim of a ruler. Means, justification, and rules of conflict or violence are not considered. The only directive is an implied- win at any cost in any way possible. The end justifies the means, which is very dangerous.

Buddhism and War

When I talk to people who speak of Buddhism, the Four Noble Truths and the Eight-Fold Path they often refer to the peaceful, don't hurt anything concept of Buddhism. Most are shocked to find war is condoned by a noted Zen master's interpretation of the principle of Ahimsa as well as the Fifth Dalai Lama. Even though it apparently is forbidden, even in self-defense.

> *"Even if thieves carve you limb from limb with a double-handed saw, if you make your mind hostile you are not following my teaching." Kamcupamsutta, Majjhima-Nikkaya I 38-39.*

Ahimsa is also rigorously followed in Buddhism. Granted there have been some wars that Buddhists engaged in combat against the Mongol. In Japan Samurai were trained by Zen Buddhists. Of course, Buddhist Japan has been involved in a war. Also in the Sri Lanka civil war. Zen master of Japan, Sawaki Kodo was quoted on the war in 1942. His interpretation of the precept of the hostility of the mind, allows for violence, just with a right attitude.

> *"It is just to punish those who disturb the public order. Whether one kills or does not kill, the precept forbidding killing is preserved. It is the precept forbidding killing that wields the sword. It is the precept that throws the bomb."*

Traditionally Buddhism, along with Jainism prohibited violence to the point of being problematic in the area of law enforcement. If all violence and use of force are wrong, how do you handle criminals? Shaolin monks are reputed to have trained for self-defense and defense of others. The use of their skills being limited, meeting force with equal force, never to the point of death of the opponent. A balanced force response lethal or not is still violence. The monks in their noble attitude still violate their beliefs unless Kodo's interpretation was invoked centuries earlier by an unnamed source. Dr. Derek F. Maher, a professor of Tibetan Buddhism, analyzed actions of the Fifth Dalai Lama concerning war.

> This assessment of the Fifth Dalai Lama's understanding of violence sheds light on the two initial examples we examined from his *Song of the Queen of Spring*. Although

> the motives differed in those cases, Lha lung dPal gyi rdo rje's assassination of the anti-Buddhist King gLang dar ma and sPyan snga Rin po che's yogic execution of Dor rta nag po, the situations are alike in that a realized Buddhist teacher carried out an act of violence. It would seem that the Dalai Lama told those two stories in an effort to lay the groundwork for justifying Gushri Khan's broader violence. Finally, this theme sheds light on the Dalai Lama's sense of a just war. A war is just or not just by virtue of whether it is undertaken by a sufficiently advanced spiritual practitioner. In such a case, the just cause criteria familiar in standard just war traditions is of less concern than the identity of the instigator.(Maher, 2008)

Notwithstanding commentary, but several wars in Sri Lanka and other parts of the world have been conducted by Buddhists besides twentieth century Imperial Japan. Buddhist resistance fighters led the uprising expelling the Mongols from China. In ancient Japan, Buddhist monks trained Samurai warriors in meditation they believed made them better fighters. One of Japan's most famous Buddhist samurai, Miyamoto Musashi, wrote Go Rin No Sho, the Book of Five Rings. It is recomnded reading for warriors studying strategy.

Abrahamic worldviews and War

The Abrahamic faiths are those who claim Abraham whose sons are Ishmael and Isaac (Arabs from Ishmael and Jews from Isaac) as a father of their respective faiths. In this comparison I consider Catholics, and the various Protestant faiths as people of the Judeo-Christian faith, not Islam. There are many differences among the doctrines of these denominations or systems, but on the subject of war, they are the same. In keeping with human nature, there are individuals who through design or ignorance hide or withhold the truth about the God of Abraham, Isaac, and Jacob as a God of war, not only of mercy, grace, and peace. I am analyzing the actions of leadership within a system, and some system doctrine about violence and war.

The people belonging to these systems may agree, disagree, or perhaps be angry at this oversimplification, that is not my intention. I apologize for any offense to individuals, but I do not apologize for revealing a false religious system, especially of hate, no matter whose name is painted on the sign out front. We all have a free will, and I think no less of any member of any faith group, Christian or pagan, all people deserve respect, but not all belief systems, only each person's God-given right to choose. However, if they take up arms against family and country, a confrontation on a physical, instead of just a spiritual, an academic, or debate level, is unavoidable.

For example, I started out on the Southern Baptist side of the Christian faith. There is one Baptist group, which twists the Word of God. They recruit people to picket the funerals of patriotic warriors deserving of the honor. They have God on their signs, but Jesus is not with those who dishonor heroes sacrifices and speak hatred against others claiming it's in his name. Criticizing them is not to criticize all Baptists, only challenge followers of that particular false church; calling them out as liars against God, false prophets. If we warriors cannot honestly self-examine our faith, whatever the type, how are we ever to make peace with what we do, have done, or will do? None of us should ever blindly follow any teaching, but pray and research it thoroughly. The truth will always withstand the test of being applied in real-world situations.

The Catholic Church has sanctioned many wars as suited their rise to power in the Papal States. The Vatican was silent about Hitler, with the just-retired Pope Benedict XIII attending and participating in religious activities apart from Christianity, in several religiously ecumenical events. Even during the Civil War in the United States, the Vatican sided against the North being sympathetic to the slave retaining Rebellious South. This is seen in Vatican letters to Jefferson Davis addressing him as President of the Confederate States of America (CSA). These letters from the Vatican internationally acknowledged the South as its own nation, apart from the already established United States.

For the record, according to accepted laws of war. If the CSA had won, it would have established legitimacy. It is suggested in some circles the Vatican blames the American Revolution for igniting late Europe revolutions, ending their rule of the Papal States. Of note is the historical fact the Vatican wants control of Jerusalem or at least part of it. The willingness and use of influence to divide Israel, Jerusalem in particular, is explicitly against God's will in the Bible (any version). Israel was reinstated as a legitimate nation once recognized by the United States in 1948, fulfilling the prophecy of Isaiah around 1500 B.C. Israel had always been the home of the Jews since its conquest around four thousand years ago. It has been occupied many times since then, but the Jews return if driven out, and some Jews have always lived there. It is not an occupied territory as the Palestinian story would have you believe.

The Old Testament and New Testament of the Bible at first glance seem at odds with their instructions. If you are strictly Jewish, the Old Testament instructs 'Thou shalt not kill,' yet Abraham, General Joshua, Samson, and King David did a fair amount of killing. In the New Testament Jesus calls people to 'love their neighbor as themselves' and 'turn the other cheek.' And when Peter draws his sword to cut off the head of an arresting officer, who came to take Jesus into custody, Jesus reprimands Peter "Those who take up the sword die by the sword." Mat 26:52. Shortly before this incident, Jesus says to buy a sword: Luke 22:36. The reason the ear was cut off in the Scriptures is the officer was attempting to evade the sword strike aimed at his neck.

In the Old Testament, you have Daniel peacefully defying a civil law against prayer and submitting to arrest. Then you have Shadrach, Meshach, and Abednego similarly peacefully defy the public law and submit to arrest even when threatened with being burned in a fiery furnace. Moreover, the Apostle Paul says in Romans 13 to obey the laws of the governing authority. In Acts, Paul escapes arrest by being let down a wall with a rope. In Ecclesiastes, it is written there is a time to kill and make war. Are these Biblical examples of scripture contradicting one another? At a glance, it appears they do contradict each other. As we unpack this puzzle, we will learn they do not conflict but are situationally dependent. First, an important distinction must be made concerning the Abrahamic faiths, only Judaism and Christianity are Abrahamic religions. Muslims do not worship the same God, although by blood relation Ishmael, father of the Arabs, is Abrahams son, worship of the God of Abraham did not continue in successive generations.

Christianity is a Jewish religion. It is the fulfillment of the Jewish prophecy, through a Jewish Rabbi (teacher), Jesus of Nazareth. It is a lie from the Kingdom of Darkness that they are separate. Jesus is the Jewish Messiah for all humanity, prophesied in the Law and the Prophets. The difference is being Jewish and in covenant with God was a physical birthright, until the prophesied crucifixion and resurrection took place. Now to be in covenant with God you only have to believe in Jesus, for salvation is of the Jews.

Believing is also now needful for those born Jews of the flesh, by physical birth. All must repent. All the first Christians or followers of the Christ were and remained faithful Jews. Sadly, most churches and seminary's don't even teach the roots of the faith. Somewhere along the way they became separated and as a result sometimes leaders thinking they served the Lord, persecuted the Jews. God is not finished with Israel, nor will He ever be. Christians look forward to the new Heaven and new Earth (rejuvenated after the last battle between good and evil, not a new planet), with our future home the New Jerusalem (Revelation chapter 21).

If you hate Jews, then you hate Jesus. The rulers of the Jews, the Roman Governor, a wicked King Herod, and the sins of all humanity, yours and mine included - caused Jesus to suffer and need to die on the cross. No man killed the Lord Jesus; He laid down His life of His own free will. We killed Him, but only because He allowed it. He allowed it because it was the only way to save the creation He loves, you and I.

> "No man taketh it from me, but I lay it down of myself. I have power to lay it down, and I have power to take it again. This commandment have I received of my Father" (John 10:18).
>
> Into Your hand I commit my spirit: You have redeemed me, O Lord God of truth" Psalm 35:5 – one of over 300 fulfilled prophecies).

The Hebrew word translated redeemed in this verse, is Padah (paw-daw). Padah denotes a specific type of redemption: a ransom, to pay a price of redemption or to redeem through a substitutionary act.

> "And when Jesus had cried out with a loud voice, He said, 'Father, into Your hands I commend My spirit.' And having said this, he breathed His last"(Luke 23:46, MJKV).

Islam

Islam arrived on the panorama of history around 622 A.D. I am old school and not politically correct. Being politically correct does not mean a person is right, in many cases, is blatantly wrong. My preference is the dating of A.D. (Anno Domini- Latin for Year of our Lord) and B.C. (Before Christ) used for almost two thousand years. The recent substitutions B.C.E. (Before Common Era) and C.E. (Common Era) are ignored. Islamic tradition says Abraham built the Kaaba and founded Mecca in Arabia, a couple of thousand years before Christ. No historical or archeological evidence supports this. Pre-Islamic regional history indicates the Kaaba was built around the late 300's (4th Century A.D.); over two hundred years before Mohamed and roughly eighteen hundred years after Abraham.

Approximately 360 other gods were worshiped at the Kaaba in Mecca. During Mohammed's encounters, over the span of about ten years, and under duress, with a supernatural being, he thought at first was a Jinn (demon), Islam was born. The supernatural being ordered him to receive and recite spiritual insights, and in the process, Mohammed acted to remove and destroy the worship of other gods and clear their idols out of the Kaaba. He then declared it now the House of Allah. The supernatural being claimed to be Gabriel, an Archangel messenger of God.

Eventually Mecca became the central focus of Islam, with the Kabba, the Black House a focal point for the worship of Allah since around 630 A.D. Islam has several critical points or core beliefs, and of course, the Five Pillars. Islam's assertion Allah is the God of Abraham is through the bloodline of the Arabs. Arabs (Ishmaelite's) are descendants of Abraham and Hagar's (Abrahams Egyptian slave) son Ishmael.

Islam has over 100 verses of peace, but what does Islam consider as peace? Self-defense initially appears the rule of warfare for Mohammed. There are several verses which are controversial. These are the verses of the sword. They were later 'revelation' from the being called Gabriel, received within a year or so of Mohammed's death. Here is the problem.

In the Quran, there is a doctrine of abrogation. Abrogation means to rescind, repeal, supersede, or annul a previous verse. One of the most infamous, of many examples, is Surah 9:5.

> *"But when the forbidden months are past, then fight and slay the Pagans wherever ye find them, and seize them, beleaguer them, and lie in wait for them in every stratagem (of war); but if they repent, and establish regular prayers and practice regular charity, then open the way for them: for Allah is Oft-forgiving, Most Merciful".*

This verse, one of the last received by Mohammed, supersedes over 100 prior verses. Acclaimed teacher Dr. Joel Hayward (Dean of the Royal Air Force College, Co-Director of the Royal Air Force Centre for Air Power Studies, appointed as 'Strategic Policy Adviser to Dr. Muhammad Tahir-ul-Qadri'), promotes a contextual error. An error negating the sweeping scope of abrogation attributed to the verse. Of course, Dr. Hayward is employed by an Islamic leader. Dr. Hayward, from his work "The Qur'an and War: Observations on Islamic Just War" responds to the allegation made by another scholar saying-

> Therefore, that the verse of the sword was a context-specific verse relating to the cleansing and purification of Mecca and its environs of all Arab polytheism and idolatry so that the sanctuary in particular, with the Ka'aba at its centre, would never again be rendered unclean...It was proclaimed publicly as a warning, followed by a period of grace which allowed the wrong-doers to desist or leave the region, and qualified by humane caveats that allowed for forgiveness, mercy and protection. It is thus not as bloodthirsty as Robert Spencer and his colleagues portray it. Indeed, it is so context-specific that, even if it WERE still in force — and I share the assessment that it *has not abrogated* the scriptures encouraging peace, tolerance and reconciliation — it would only nowadays have any relevance and applicability if polytheists and idolaters

> ever tried to undertake and re-establish pagan practices in the Saudi Arabian cities devoted only to Allāh: Mecca and Medina. In other words, in today's world it is not relevant or applicable... (Hayward, 2010, my emphasis added)

Dr. Hayward is reaching for some type of reconciliation between what is said and what is done, which does not hold up for two reasons. One he is looking at the Quran through western eyes and possibly reiterating what his employer believes. Writing criticism on your employer's religion is not good job security. Secondly, his conclusions disregard the common knowledge that a significant number of Muslims worldwide follow the abrogation principle. The radical Muslims do not share his infidel interpretation, but strictly observe the verses of the sword doctrine, unto the death of themselves and or others.

For the fundamentalist Muslim, Islamic just war theory and authority for war is about what they believe Allah wants and is telling them to do, and how to treat non-Muslims or infidels. Islamic war theory justifies an attack upon any non-believer unless they accept Islam. This is not merciful, or forgiving; it is coercion. Islam not only recognizes war as a reality, it demands it as a type of evangelism. In fact, unlike Judaism and Christianity, Islam is a military, political and religious system all in one. Islam is the State sponsored religion which follows Mohammad's spiritually militant and political goal of world domination by Islam. The Mosque (place of worship) and State are one, and all other faiths are forbidden. The military and law enforcement are there to enforce the Islamic faith-based State governments rule called Sharia Law.

Though considered an Abrahamic religion in truth it is not. The Arabs were worshiping many gods long before Mohammed. The Quran does not reflect the words of God in the Old and New Testaments but recurrently contradicts the Bible. The Quran is itself an attempt to abrogate (replace and rescind) the Bible. What I mean by this is God did not suddenly change his mind about almost everything, send Gabriel to Mohamed, contradict what He said for the past few thousand years, only to replace it with the Quran. The deceptive replacement includes denying Jesus is His Son, or that He was crucified and raised from the dead (a historical fact). It is not possible that God is Allah. The God of Abraham, Isaac, Jacob, and Jesus the Christ does not make mistakes and contradict Himself. An Imposter casts doubt.

Creator of all things, Yahweh (Jehovah in English) the Trinitarian Godhead (Father, Son: Jesus or Yeshua, and Holy Spirit), is all-powerful and all-knowing operating outside of and across all time and space which He created. If you already know everything how are you contradicting yourself? The Lord does not ever say what He does not mean. Apparent contradictions in the Bible are the result of out of context interpretations. Versus in one book of the Bible to not abrogate other verses. The Moon god Allah should never be confused with the Judeo-Christian God. There are no errors in the word of the Living God. It is important to understand this, which is why I gave it so much space up front. Confusing Islam and Judeo Christianity is to mix oil and water. Anyone who says they are the same God did not do their homework. Even a basic reading of these two religions show they cannot be the same god. These belief systems are contrary to each other. Again, I say two, and not three, because I tie Christianity to Judaism since Christianity is the New Jewish Covenant from Yahweh (God) to all humanity. (Heb 8:11-13)

Throughout history, many Christians neglected, misunderstood, or rejected the truth that their faith is a Jewish religion. Christianity says the Jews are the people of God and that God created the nation of Israel. Islam says all Jews must be killed and are sub-human (like evolution). Among Jews, Christians, and liberal or moderate Muslims, who agree to disagree on core values, we are not enemies. The enemies are the radical Muslims who will not agree or rest until all the Earth is converted to Islam. Incidentally, the Quran says Israel and Jerusalem belong to the Jews, but this is ignored by radical Jihadist and Pro Palestinian Authorities.

> "And [mention, O Muhammad], when Moses said to his people, "O my people, remember the favor of Allah [God] upon you when He appointed among you prophets and made you possessors and gave you that which He had not given anyone among the worlds. O my people, enter the Holy Land which Allah has assigned to you and do not turn back and [thus] become losers" (Surah Al-Ma'idah 5:20-21).

Much research is devoted to the examination of historical, scientific, and theological errors, as well as actual roots, and identity of Allah worship (modern Islam). It is beyond this book to explain and or summarize them all. It is enough to know. Jesus is the Son of God, and that Islam does not worship Yahweh (God), but the moon god Allah.

Non-Christian Warriors

At this point, it must be stated that the majority of military, intelligence community and law enforcement members are not Christians. Christians are in the minority or almost nonexistent in some areas of operations. I think this is true partly because of so many misrepresentations of Jesus and what the Bible really says about what must be done. One reason for writing this book is to change that. Others are to help, heal, and empower fellow warriors.

They (the unbelieving in Jesus as Lord) are excellent ministers of God's as agents, sailors, police, etc. They took the same oath to protect and defend the U.S. Constitution and swore the same allegiance or loyalty to the United States of America (or other nation for international readers), and to serve and protect local communities as we did and do. Being a Christian doesn't give you some arbitrary moral high ground or make you a better spy, soldier, or police officer automatically. They have the anointing and calling same as you, or else they wouldn't be there. Whether they believe or not they serve the Lord same as you. God called a pagan king His servant because he was doing/fulfilling what God had said would happen.

The difference is they don't have access to all you do, but carry the same responsibility, integrity, and walk in the same noble character as you do- or should. They are patriots and willing to sacrifice all that you are ready to sacrifice. If you think you're better than those, who don't share your faith- "If they believe that their comrades who don't share their religious beliefs aren't as good a those who do, then they should leave the military and seek another career. Equating the morality of all to the religion of some is incompatible with ensuring effective armed forces for the United States of America" (Parco, 2010, One True Religion). I couldn't agree more. It is neither a godly attitude nor a good attitude to have. A

Christian who knows the Lord, but doesn't know, or is unable to do a job, needs to find a job they can do.

For example, a Christian can be just as susceptible to becoming a traitor, or becoming corrupt, if they first turn their back on the Lord and break their own hedge. For a Christian, to become a traitor to your nation means you abandoned your God first, then your country. If you truly are a Christian and not just someone who calls themselves one and checks the church block each week. God will forgive you, but prison and or a scarlet letter to wear forever is still a consequence. Of course, God will forgive anyone who repents.

To help prevent our fellow ministers of vengeance from feeling as though we may think less of them, for we do not, I quote from Parco's book "Attitudes Aren't Free, Thinking Deeply about Diversity in the US Armed Forces." Parco and Fagan, co-authors of the One True Religion chapter of the book, proposed an Oath of Equal Character. You can insert your faith into it as easily as any others. Though not part of the example of the oath, if you are a police officer, or other agent feel free to insert your occupation in place of the soldier.

> "I am a <Christian>. I will not use my position to influence individual or the chain of command to adopt <Christianity>, because I believe that soldiers, who are not <Christians> are just as trustworthy, honorable, and good as those who are. The standards of those who are not <Christian> are as high as mine. Their integrity is beyond reproach. They will not lie, cheat, or steal, and they will not fail when called upon to serve. I trust them completely and without reservation. They can trust me in exactly the same way." (Parco, 2010)

As Covenant Warriors, we should always strive to be the best in the Lord at our assigned missions and tasks. Being and striving to be the best does not make you a better person. We are all equal before the Lord in needing Him. The oath does not violate your conscious or your commission to evangelize and make disciples. Being your best in the Lord will generate personal opportunity to witness and lead co-workers, superiors, and subordinates to the Lord. This does not give them special favor, it then demands they do better.

This is not using your position or influence to convert people. They will privately come to you, ask you questions, and ask to be saved. A true friend, and or believer should never try to compromise a fellow believer or non-believer in the course of their sworn duties. If you try to compromise anyone to protect yourself, you have become the problem, not the solution. They have no obligation to you. I'm not talking about helping each other out ethically, but 'helping' unethically. They have a duty to God and Country to handle you as if they didn't know you.

CHAPTER 3

Morality, Relatively Speaking

This short chapter is the foundation of explaining the existence and reason for evil in the next chapter. Many who read this may already have a good grasp on the subject of absolute morality. However, as previously stated I want to ensure all readers have similar exposure and understanding before moving into viewing and relating to God, as the God of armies, spies, and law enforcement.Is morality universal? Biblically, yes, there is an absolute objective standard of morality. The worldly answer is a sense of morality is universal, but particular morals are not. Instead, individual moral systems are associated with specific social groups of various sizes.

There are many respected voices throughout the ages with complimentary and contradictory opinions about moral absolutes, or absolute truths. Dr. Ray Jacknedoff, professor of philosophy emeritus at Tufts University, says a person should resist the impulse to arrive at an objective morality. He expresses the belief that left and right both want to integrate laws and morality. The question then becomes which version of morality dominates the integration, and what is the nature of the combining of law and morality? Who has a right, or authority, or the objectivity to decide what is moral and ethical? He answers the question indirectly, concluding with the realization whatever system is decided upon it will serve a special interest. Moreover, he sees that all special interest is subjective. In being subjective, it cannot be objective according to his rationale. If not objective then it is relative, and if relative, becomes invalid as morality.

> "Nevertheless, there is a strong impulse, even among moral philosophers and psychologists of morality to want morals to be objective, universal, and timeless: "If morality is relative, then there is no morality." "If morality is relative, then why couldn't Hitler be considered moral in his own terms?" (And we can equally imagine the Nazis saying, 'Only we recognize the true objective morality')" (Jacknedoff, 2009).

Jacknedoff makes a compelling argument but, he is only half correct. There is Earthly special interest party, whose subjective interpretation of morality outlines an objective morality, impartial to cultural or social changes or differences. No person is objective, trustworthy, and knowledgeable enough of all things spiritual and physical, to construct a perfect moral code for all to follow. In our case, the special interest party is God. Who is objective, knowledgeable, and trustworthy. His system subjectively serves His purposes as all systems do their facilitators, but with God, all is just. This exception is because of God's uniqueness. He has our eternal, and temporal good in mind. His alone is objective as it relates to humanity, no other system of morality designed by men accomplishes this. For example, from a human subjective perspective, many moral codes or systems have emerged promoting: honor killings, genocide, unlimited slavery, and female circumcision, just to mention a few immoral things. The groups practicing in suicide martyrdom (suicide bombings and shootings) believe it's not only acceptable but, encourage and expect it as a societal norm. Even among early Christians exist contradictory commentary on war and soldiering.

Why is all this important to the Warrior? A warrior's sanity, morale, and ability to do his/her job and still enjoy the benefits of the way of life they helped preserve is tied to knowing they have the moral high ground. A clear understanding the why of the horrors of war and crime they are exposed to is critical to the root of spiritual, mental, emotional, and physical health, having a clear conscience. A conscience not seared by the selfish rationale for wanton acts of violence against whomever, for little or no reason. A guilt-free conscience, not crippled by lying or misrepresenting, and the self-justifying of violence. A conscience washed in God's word and Jesus blood, so you can hold your head high before God, Country, and family.

You deserve a peaceful conscience because you do the dirty work which must be done. Working to stem the tide of wickedness, preserving a semblance of peace and justice. To know you are not alone in this calling as military, intelligence, or law enforcement operatives. The Lord, who has called you, also empowers and assists you in that calling- if you'll let Him.

> "Spiritual well-being is important since soldier's function more effectively when they have a support system or framework of meaning to sustain them...Spiritual fitness is the development of those personal qualities needed to sustain a person in times of stress, hardship, and tragedy. These qualities come from religious, philosophical, or human values and form the basis for character, disposition, decision-making, and integrity." (DA PAM 600-63-12)

As we build the foundation of thought and perspective, setting you up to receive the spiritual gifts and resources from Heaven. You will learn about what Jesus died and rose for. His provisions for fighting crime and defeating enemies in the streets, and on the field of battle. The right mindset, a covenant mindset, confident of your place, purpose, and calling is imperative to have. The ability to maintain the moral high ground, stay safe, and be victorious is linked to the right mindset.

> "[War] takes its moral character from who uses it, from the reasons used to justify it, and from the intention with which it is used. . . To be sure, force is evil when it is employed to attack the justice and peace of a political order oriented toward these goods, but it is precisely to defend against such evil that the use of force may be good. Just war tradition has to do with defining the possible good use of force, not finding exceptional cases when it is possible to use something inherently evil (force) for the purpose of good. (1999: 36) O' Driscoll

A Tree and its Fruits

Jesus said you shall know a tree by its fruit. The use of force is not evil in and of itself, though force is used by many to commit evil. Influence as a minister, political figure, military leader, a religious speaker, a judge, or musician can inspire patriotism and godly living, or be subversive. The power they possess to influence is not inherently evil. The content, intent, and meaning of their messages, laws, decisions, communications, judgments, or lyrics and the actions produced by them determine goodness or wickedness. The effect created by the content is the fruit of their influence.

Money is another example. Money is not evil, but the love or greed for money is. Wealth, force, and influence are not evil. The question is its use, what is the fruit of yours, or their labor? If it is prostitution, drug-related, pornographically related, treasonous, or in other ways criminally related. Then the case can be made your utilization of the force, wealth, and influence available to you is evil. When you give to a godly charity, the money goes to helping others, the fruit of your labor, you are funding goodness. If you choose to frequent strip clubs giving them the fruit of your work, your money, you are supporting darkness. How you use the fruits of your labor is your choice.

God is explicit in some things and implicit with others. War and commerce both have explicit and implicit principles which are to direct, and guide decision makers along similar moral lines. This makes sense that certain moral lines are clearly drawn, their principles or laws made known as a guide to what you should be consenting and non-consenting too. Just as we impose judgment upon those who break our laws and codes, and even if the judgment is altered in some way (a plea bargain for immunity for example) there are still consequences which are experienced. People follow the rules for beneficial consequences (a favorable judgment) leading to rewards, benefits, and praise. For these same reasons, evil people don't do evil for fear of getting caught, and or work hard not to get caught, for fear of judgment. It is no different with judgment from God, except ultimately no one who has not repented, escapes condemning judgment. God offers pardons and forgiveness, but not everyone accepts them.

Therefore, philosophically and religiously the questions surrounding war and use of force need exploration. An exploration pouring religion and philosophy into the refinery of reality, and see what remains. The purpose of this refining process is forging a pure and tempered worldview or doctrine of violence in keeping with the word of God. The refinery of reality encompasses humanity's free will, perceptions of good and evil, degrees of desire, and or willingness to commit acts of violence against, or on behalf of one another, with mixed motives. You must know for yourself that you have the moral high ground. None can answer for you to God and your own conscience. You must answer your own conscience. But is your conscience clear and free, or seared into thinking good is evil, and evil is good?

Defining Morals and Ethics

Morals and ethics, these two words are often misunderstood and misused, though intertwined one with another. Webster's Dictionary defines morality as upholding the standards of good conduct and behavior and conforming to the rules of proper conduct. Being moral is being able to differentiate between right and wrong. Ethics is defined as "...a system or philosophy of conduct or principles practiced by a group...The principles of morality, or the field of study of morals or right conduct." Ethics are defined by the group.

Sexuality and theft are some examples. Sexual promiscuity is immoral, though not unethical. Theft is both immoral and unethical. In analogy, war may be moral to conduct (justified) though waged unethically (criminally or immorally). War may also be immoral to conduct or start though carried out ethically. Jacknedoff is right to say the moral code is subjective, but remember God's moral law is subjective (His decree) and objective (equal to all, and for the benefit of all). Just because something seems right or feels good at the time does not mean there are no hidden negative consequences to doing it. Sin is a sin, and immorality immoral. Sin has pleasure for a season, but ultimately these things are self-destructive and counterproductive to a safe, prosperous, and healthy life for yourself and others. You don't feel a poisonous effect at first.

Thoughts on the Morality of War across Time

Apostles and Disciples, as well as multitudes of other people knew or met Jesus personally. Apostolic Fathers are those who knew the apostles and disciples of Jesus personally. Church Fathers are the first generation of believers after the apostles, those who sat under them and their teachings. Most were of the hundreds of eyewitnesses to Jesus resurrection, or who personally knew those who were eyewitnesses. Both groups are historically foundational to the development and understanding of the faith we practice today. Others we will briefly look at are better-known world leaders. All their thoughts and insights are helping us find our path of morality down which to travel.

Not all opinions, Christian and secular (non-religious) agree on the Christians or anyone's role in warfare. But, to develop a sound moral and ethical line, we review comments against and for, what is debated about as right and proper. Christian and non-Christian commentators use of Biblical verses out of context are the source of much confusion or controversy for warriors, philosophers and ministers alike. Seneca, a respected Roman historian, said two interesting things about war. "Dying is more honorable than killing" and

> "We check manslaughter and isolated murders; but what of war and the much-vaunted crime of slaughtering whole peoples? ...Deeds which would be punished by loss of life when committed in secret, are praised by us because uniformed generals have carried them out". (Epistuloe)

Seneca's anti-war cry in ancient Rome (fascinating since Rome was a militaristic world class conquering power) stands in sharp contrast to some modern comments. President Woodrow Wilson's in his World War I address to Congress April 2, 1917, said: "The world must be made safe for democracy." Then Winston Churchill in his speech to Britain against the Nazi war machine May 13, 1940, said "Victory at all costs, victory in spite of all terror, victory however long and hard the road may be, for without victory there is no survival." This may lead some to believe pro-war is a current sentiment and anti-war an ancient one. Not true. There have and always will be anti-war voices and pro-war voices.

Our Judeo-Christian heritage is no different among Apostolic and Church Fathers. Some were committed to no violence at all; some supported soldiering. But what does God say? At times to be a soldier or citizen, such as in ancient Rome, a person had to worship the Emperor (Caesar), which of course Christians and devout Jews cannot and would not do. This led to them being viewed as disloyal and anti-patriotic. Such sentiments are some of the reasons why several Emperors killed Christians for public sport and as violators of the law saying they must worship Caesar as a god. It is during these times many church and apostolic fathers like Clement, who is pro-soldier, wrote.

> "Let us therefore enlist ourselves, brethren, with all earnestness in His faultless ordinances. Let us mark the soldiers that are enlisted under our rulers, how exactly, how readily, how submissively, they execute the orders given them. All are not prefects, nor rulers of thousands, nor rulers of hundreds, nor rulers of fifties, and so forth; but each man in his own rank executeth the orders given by the king and the governors." -First Letter of Clement 37.1-4

Other respected early church writers, like Justin Martyr, became committed to complete non-violence. Not everything they say is Biblical, or correct, in the context of the verses they base their commentary on. This is a classic error on the part of Christians of yesteryear and today; looking to Scriptures to affirm their belief, instead of letting their belief be defined by the Scriptures.

> "We who were filled with war, and mutual slaughter, and every wickedness, have each through the whole earth changed our warlike weapons,--our swords into ploughshares, and our spears into implements of tillage." Justin Martyr15

> "We have learned, not only not to return blow for blow, nor to go to law with those who plunder and rob us, but to those who smite us on one side of the face to offer the other side also" –Athenagoras

> "But how will a Christian man war, nay, how will he serve even in peace, without a sword, which the Lord has taken away?_For albeit soldiers had come unto John, and had received the formula of their rule; albeit, likewise, a centurion had believed; still the Lord afterward, in disarming Peter, disarmed every soldier. No dress is lawful among us if assigned to any unlawful action." – Tertullian 20

Like Clement, others embraced the role and honor of military service. Besides Clement, there is Emperor Augustine (a Christian and some call a father of just war theory), Aquinas, and Grotius (commonly credited with development and defense of just war theory). These men spoke well of and about the profession of arms. It's encouraging to know the discussion about support for the military, intelligence, and law enforcement is not a new issue.

> "Laying hold of what is intimately and peculiarly his own as distinct from other living things, we advise him to outfit himself with godliness as an adequate preparation for his eternal journey. If you are a <u>farmer</u>, we say till the earth, but acknowledge the God of farmers; if you love <u>seafaring</u>, sail on, but remember to call upon the celestial Helmsman. If you were in the <u>army</u> when you were seized by the knowledge of God, obey the Commander who gives just commands." – Clement: Exhortation to the Greeks X.100.2 em ad

> "For it is the injustice of the opposing side that lays on the wise man the <u>duty of waging wars</u>; and this injustice is assuredly to be deplored by a human being, since it is the

> injustice of human beings, even though no necessity for war should arise from it" - Augustine, Contra Faustum, Book XIX:9862

> "Thus it belongs properly and directly to the object of fortitude, to face the dangers of death, and to charge at the foe with danger to oneself, for the sake of the common good: yet that, in a just war, a man be armed, or strike another with his sword, and so forth, is reduced to the object of fortitude, but indirectly." - St. Thomas Aquinas Suma Theologica

Quoting or referencing the loose and vicious just war theories of ancient Assyria (modern Turkey), Babylon, Medio Persian (current Iran/ Iraq), or other ancient people groups and cultures, would be redundant. Suffice to say these, and some ancient Asian cultures, known to be violent. They threatened or engaged in war for various reasons. They are judged today as just or unjust in retrospect. War is in their history and seemingly in their blood. Looking back a little further there is well-known Plato and not as well-known Thucydides.

> "Plato advocated a close relationship between ethics (or virtue, to use his preferred idiom) and military training in the Republic. The main point was that a just city can never be realized without the proper education of soldiers." -Platonic roots

> "You may be sure that we are as well aware as you of the difficulty of contending against your power and fortune unless the terms are equal. But we trust that the gods may grant us a fortune as good as yours since we are just men fighting against unjust." – Thucydides, The History Peloponnesian War

Not all moral violations are criminal violations, nor should they be. Neither are all criminal violations moral violations. Peaceful civil disobedience marches for example, or decriminalization versus legalization. Legalization is an endorsement of immoral or dangerous activity by those in authority. Decriminalization does not endorse immoral action but downgrades it to non-criminal status. It is then a moral transgression presenting no criminal danger to another. It is not victimless. A person's bad choices damage themselves, and at times indirectly damage others.

The grief of a family at a funeral of an overdose victim is the indirect or collateral emotional damage inflicted by the actions of the deceased. Not a crime, but incredibly sad and traumatic. A crime is committed when there are direct victims. Decriminalizing an act does not make it socially acceptable. It frees up law enforcement resources to focus on those who are a danger to their neighbor. Decriminalization does not compete with or undermine parents and church's teaching their children and congregation's values and a moral code.

Saying the means justify the end is a moral absolute in that how something is done determines the righteousness of the outcome. The end justifying the means, allows anything to be done in pursuit of a supposedly virtuous result. This is often used as a false justification for evil. The means, the ends, and the circumstances, decisions and outcomes, <u>all matter</u> in moral absolutes. Freedom has boundaries, or else freedom is not freedom but anarchy. Means versus end, and vice versa is at times a thin line or tightrope to walk, but walk it we do.

The Voices in Your Head

Facts change when new evidence is presented, truth never changes. Truth is absolute. Our perception of truth is vulnerable to manipulation. Our view of truth governs our reality and judgment. Cults indoctrinate to control beliefs and perception. Actions are determined by feelings, or by a decision to act differently than how you feel, such as acting by faith. Emotions felt in a situation, come from your perception of the truth about the situation, which is shaped by your beliefs, then determine your actions. Beliefs define our identity; they influence how you will act. Change a person's beliefs you change their actions.

All communication is indoctrination or attempts to influence us to do or not do something. Communication seeks to deprogram, reprogram, reinforce programming, or trigger our programming. Following an order from a superior officer, or following what the preacher is saying is right, is submitting to types of programming. Programming we submitted to when we enlisted or attended. Some programming we don't even filter like commercials or sales pitches.

I'm not saying commercial, or sales pitches are wrong, on the contrary, they prove my point. All communication is indoctrination or influencing us to take some action. Gossip fuels our need to know what others do not, or think we're better than someone or something else among other things. Usually, the point of an article is either to impart information, inspire you to take action, or at the very least entice you to keep buying the magazine, again, and again, and again. Not always a bad thing, but it is a thing.

Who is altering our perceptions of ourselves, situations, life, and death, or the world? Whom do you allow to shape your understanding: Satan, ungodly people, family, a minister, the Word of God, bankers, the news (fake news?) salesmen, White House spokeswoman, the weather channel...? Whose voice(s) dominate your values system? Your sovereign God-given free will is the power to decide, to choose for yourself who, what, and when to listen or filter out.

It is permissible too sometimes recreationally kill babies.

This is an absurd statement, with an obvious answer, to a reasonable person. It is never permissible. Yet this then becomes proof of a moral absolute. Our perceptions of what is true shapes our morality. An individual who believes in situational ethics or moral relativity cannot agree that the above statement is always untrue. If they do, they have conceded there is an absolute truth. Where there is one absolute truth, there are others. Our understanding of truth frames the accuracy of our perception of the facts.

It is crazy to believe cannibalism is relatively moral, good, and acceptable for one society while not in all societies. If we believe this, then each people group determines their morality. Then it is not our business to interfere with others morality or ethics just because we say such acts are evil, even use of chemical warfare by a nation on its own citizens. Of course, we should interfere! But in intervening, we acknowledge a moral absolute has been violated. It is no different from saying female circumcision, rape or honor killing is relatively moral, and acceptable, being ethical to one society, though not in all societies.

How a person is programmed or reprogrammed dictates their relative or absolute morality. What we say and do is commonly based on how we feel. How we feel is governed by what we think. How we think is rooted in what we believe. Our belief is developed and shaped by what we hear and see. We decide, for various reasons, whether to reject or accept what we see and hear. So, what do we think about evils existence in light of God being a good God?

CHAPTER 4

The Problem of Evil

The problem of evil, also called theodicy, is with good reason the longest chapter of this book. Most people avoid evil, while warriors face evil as an occupation. To have a good understanding of why things are the way they are we must know in our hearts (spirit) and minds (soul) what God's relationship to evil is. Without a working knowledge of the truth behind wickedness, disasters, and death, it may be hard to develop your faith in God's word and put it into action in real-world situations. It's easy to fake it at home or in church about your trust in God. We so quickly say "Hallelujah in the sweet bye and bye" and "Praise the Lord" or " It's the Lords will,"or "Well, you know everything has a purpose" or "God works in mysterious ways." These are faithless statements covering up not knowing what is going on, or doubts about God. Then the pressure comes from the Enemy, due to ungodly preaching from some pulpits, attacks with doubts, confusion, and unbelief. Demons lay siege to your soul, attacking your mind like soldiers attacking a bunker, attempting to influence your free will, faith, and the outcome or fruit of any given situation.

Lack of understanding how things operate renders the rest of this book nothing more than engaging reading. You will still be fighting the good fight, but with one hand tied behind your back, as it was before you read this book. The difference is you will have more frustration as you will have more wisdom and knowledge which you will not be efficiently applying. The Enemy will attack you with lying feelings of inadequacy, self-condemnation, or some type of guilt; none of which would be true, but will emotionally feel true. Pay attention to this chapter to avoid this spiritual minefield.

You can't have faith when there is no trust. You can't have confidence when you are not sure the other person isn't working against you or that they are not doing as much as you think they should be; pulling their weight. It is no different with God. The problem of trustworthiness and such is not coming from the Lord Jesus, but from us toward him. You can't have doubt in God's good toward you or dependability to keep His word. Misunderstanding breeds doubt leads to misapplication of God's word and undermines your faith. When this happens to negate God's provisions and protections. When this happens, the Enemy gets the upper hand. Satan's vast psychological and supernatural warfare machine generates propaganda which causes doubt, unbelief, and fear. Satan deceives us into believing lies about God, ourselves, and the world around us. It is beyond the term fake news; it's very deadly news.

Covenant Warriors are not dumb, blunt instruments of violence, destruction, or death. You are free thinkers, leaders of all ranks choosing to follow one another for the greater good. You are philosophers, scholars, and statesmen who know right from wrong, can sift through the swamp of anti-war and anti-police rhetoric, and stand above it. The voices of Anarchy, Socialism, Jihad, Communism, and others do not shake you. No, you the patriot of freedom shake them. Yet to be the soldier, officer, scholar, and statesman one essential subject must be understood. Why is there evil if God is good and all-powerful?

To many, the presence of evil is why they do not believe in a God at all. As a covenant warrior you are, will, or already have been faced with great evil and horror, which can cause the questioning of your faith, or of God's motives, character or power. God is omniscient (all-knowing). The LORD is also omnipotent (all-powerful), and omnipresent(all-knowing): awareness of and or presence in, though not always detected by us, among all thoughts and actions of everything, everyone, everywhere, including Satan and his minions, in all places, dimensions, and times simultaneously. The Creator is the uncreated uncaused cause, whose essence is self-existent. The Lord Jesus is the Godhead (Trinitarian essence or being of God) in spirit, flesh, and blood. The prophet Amos said "How can two walks together except they are agreed?

It is hard to be in a relationship of trust when you are not sure what or why the other person is doing or not doing something. God promised to have your six (watching your back). But if you don't know His promises and trust Him, you won't be able to have faith that God has got your six. We trust officers arriving on a scene for back up, that a safe house is safe, and that a service member to our left or right is protecting your life as you are defending theirs. We trust them because we trained with them and developed trust in them. We took the same oath of service. We expect, not hope or wish, but expect specific behavior under various circumstances. This same expectation is needed of God, trusting in Him, and what He will do in different situations.

We have been let down sometimes by the behavior or expectation of our fellow warriors from time to time, but we keep on trusting and expecting from the others. However, with God, who cannot lie and who can be depended upon to do the same thing every time, we often don't even give Him the benefit of the doubt. When we think God did not, or would not, come through for us, according to our will and perception, or some church member, or supposed Christian does something stupid, mean or crazy, we throw in the towel and kick the Holy Spirit to the curb. Wow! You extended to your fellow warriors the same trust, respect, and assurance that you still had their back despite what others did who betrayed their oath, shield or uniform. You have even let some fellow warriors earn back or regain your trust. I challenge you to give the same courtesy to the God of Abraham, Isaac, and Jacob, the Lord Jesus of Nazareth; God of all warriors, who already laid down His life for yours.

Everyone encounters rough times and tragedy in life, some common to all and some not so common. Many people are faced with dangerous situations, and a few (relatively speaking since there are 7 billion plus people on the Earth) are confronted with uncommon, or rare and overwhelming circumstances whether in an instant or cumulative over time. The accumulation of bad things happening is usually manageable to a point with a good support system, which many do not have, or until their support system fails them.

If or when your support system breaks, you may become hardened toward or disillusioned with God, life in general, people, maybe even yourself. These feelings often stem from unrealistic and misperceived roles and expectations. Whatever the reason, when a person breaks inside they become dysfunctional, unable to live life, have healthy relationships, or experience what used to be normal. You may keep doing the job because it's all you know to do, but with less passion, or sense of accomplishment. You may even leave the field of battle forsaking your calling to find help and relief. You may have lost belief that what you did mattered, or matters since the madness never seems to end.

There is a difference between hearing the statistics on murder or rape on the news, and seeing all the people, the victims themselves, time and time again. Hearing and seeing the lament of people's souls, broken, crushed in trauma by the death of a loved one. There is a difference between seeing a funeral for a victim, or not having any closure for murder, overdose or suicide, and being a first responder to scene after scene, after scene... Those who do an analysis of data, collect information, investigate, apprehend, testify, do the forensics in the coroner's office and labs, see evidence of evil, and meet the enemy in battle in court, or in the shadowed corners of society over, and over, and over.

Many are seeing day in and day out humanity at its best and worst. These examples could go on, but the point is made. Though there are differences, all can experience times of doubt, suffering, anger and sometimes depression or frustration. Trauma and disaster are experienced in many ways by people. No person or family is untouched. Tragedy does not discriminate between social, ethnic, or economic status.

The illusion or feeling of safety and security most people have, at least in the United States, is because you stand toe to toe, and face to face against evil - for months, years, and sometimes decades- a lifetime. You have the greatest need for heavenly, divine, and angelic assistance personally and professionally, since confronting evil is your job. Unless you battle harden your soul, you are at high risk of becoming hardened of heart, disillusioned or disappointed in God. From being exposed to so much evil and violence you are at risk of hating, not believing in, or ignoring God.

Recall Abraham's nephew, righteous Lot, he and his family lived in Sodom. Surrounded by wickedness continually, like living in a mental, spiritual, and emotional minefield, it confused his soul terribly. We must battle harden our spirit and soul to stay out of or get out of the minefield.

You might be in the minefield at this moment. If so keep reading- it's time to heal, strengthen and re-enter the fray with new purpose, energy, and power.

Logic, God, and Evil

How then can Jesus of Nazareth, the Christ (Greek for Messiah), His Father, and the Holy Spirit- the loving Triune God tolerate or allow the existence of evil? Why create Lucifer knowing he is going to rebel and become Satan? Why let Adam and Eve fall in the Garden? Many blame God for the evils of the world asking why? Why do good things happen to bad people and bad things happen to good people? Where are you Lord, during these rapes, accidents, tragedy's, wars, murders, thefts, broken hearts, absentee or abusive family members? The questions go on and on. Why did we or should we ever need soldiers, police, morticians, or doctors? Why are we fighting crime and enemies? Is it because God made a mistake or is not involved? Why is there evil, what is its purpose if any, and will it ever end? I don't have all the answers, but what answers I have, I am giving to you in this book.

We start with an assumption that God is smarter, more powerful, and sees things very differently than us. Imagine an aquarium full of fish. Your perception of them as you watch them, or feed them, or clean the tank for them is vastly different from their experience as a fish in the tank itself. This analogy is admittedly not a perfect parallel to our relationship with God but serves to explain in part the drastic differences of insight of the same circumstances. God's perception is truth without any confusion or misunderstanding, taking into account every possible variable you can imagine, and the ones beyond our limited human imagination. Laws govern the universe He created, and Jesus is bound by His word, which created those rules. If these assumptions, any one of them, are not correct, then nothing God or anyone says or does can be trusted, and Evil indeed runs amok in the universe forever. God's character and motives are not questioned, but it is natural to ask for an explanation of why things are the way they are and expect some answer. The laws of the universe are spiritual, multidimensional, and interdependent with our immediate reality, as experienced by us through our five senses.

God cannot do anything illogical as this is against His nature or personality. All evil is illogical. God remains all-powerful, perfect, and dependable while at the same time unable to do, speak or think evil. His complete understanding of all sides of good and evil does not taint God's character or being. Only God is qualified to determine what is acceptable and what is not. Current cultural trends do not define truth but often twist it. We take advice from professionals in the fields of money, love, law, and business, often paying high fees for their advice. We take advice from people we love since we trust them to have our best interest at heart and to tell us the truth even if it hurts. This is not a bad thing to do since the Bible says in the multitude of counselors is safety.

Therefore it only makes sense to trust God, the expert in everything, for counsel on how to live and how to fight. We say we trust or love the Lord, and if we do, are we showing it by listening to His advice, even if it's not always what we want to hear? Nothing evil is in our best interest to do. However, we cannot always see clearly the line between right and wrong without the Lord's help. Seek God first and filter all advice given through the Bible.

The reason Jesus cannot do evil is that being God the Son, anything he says will come to pass. This also means he cannot lie because it would happen or become real once he said it. God knows evil is wrong, unethical, immoral and not in anyone or any things best interest. Not being able to do evil does not mean God is not all powerful, quite the opposite. God would never do evil or anything absurd, or crazy because being almighty also means you are not a bully. The question "Can God create a rock so heavy He cannot lift it" is irrational, it's a stupid task, nonproductive, illogical, and foolish. Therefore, not only can God not do it, He would not do it even if He could because it's idiotic. Those who think either answer of no or yes means God is not all powerful are foolish; not realizing being all powerful is the reason He can't or wouldn't.

Doing something stupid or ludicrous is not part of God's character. If it were He would not be trustworthy. It is easy to say you trust God. However, at first, it is often tough to demonstrate trust with action. Experience with God shows us and helps us to believe in Him. Remember the trust issues come from our backgrounds and experiences. God knows whom to trust and always gives us a chance to become trustworthy. He is faithful when we are faithless.

The Beginning of Evil

Evil is not an equal opposite of Good. Evil is the absence of Good. There could be no evil without good to oppose. Good on the other hand can exist without the presence of evil, for good does not need opposition. Goodness is not the aggressor, but love is the intervening, overcoming, delivering, and final judging authority over evil. Evil serves the Good. Sounds crazy, doesn't it? Goodness must temporarily allow for Evil while remaining entirely good. Evil doesn't allow good; it fights against it always.

The sufferings of today being agonizing and horrific are unavoidable and thankfully temporary. "Woe unto the world because of offenses! For it must needs be that offences come; but woe to that man by whom the offence cometh!" (Matt 18:6). It is already established misuse or abuse of free will is the primary cause of evils being committed. Yet we all have the God-given right to choose. A right with the responsibility to use it well.

> See, I have set before thee this day life and good, and death and evil; ...But if thine heart turn away, so that thou wilt not hear, but shalt be drawn away, and worship other gods, and serve them...ye shall surely perish, and that ye shall not prolong your days upon the land... I call heaven and earth to record this day against you, that I have set before you life and death, blessing and cursing: therefore choose life, that both thou and thy seed may live: (Deut 30:15-19)

The phrase other gods are not limited to false religions and doctrines of demons. One example of a god is being selfish, being your own god and making prideful, stubborn, and foolish decisions. The choice given us is not a threat but reveals the consequences of a wrong choice. This is the same choice given to Adam and Eve at the Tree of the Knowledge of Good and Evil and to you and me today.

Now that we've mentioned Adam and Eve, why would God let them sin? Why create the Archangel Lucifer (son of the morning star or the moon) if you know he'll turn into the Devil (the Accuser) and Satan (the Adversary)? Why not unmake him, not make him, or even better, prevent him from rebelling? Seems like we have more questions and fewer answers. Let's get some answers so we as warriors can know our fight is not in vain, is unavoidable, not forever, and that we are on God's side which means He is on our side.

Through the prophet Isaiah, the Lord makes what at a glance is a stunning statement while dealing with a King of Persia (modern Iraq). Isaiah speaking God's word is addressing King Cyrus of Persia. "...I have even called you by your name. I have surnamed you, though you have not known Me. I AM the LORD, and there is no one else, there is no God besides Me..."(ONM Isaiah 45:4-5). In the middle of explaining why King Cyrus is chosen the LORD reveals something else about His sovereignty (power over all things). God makes the stunning statement while taking responsibility for evil's existence. "...I AM the LORD, and there is no other. I form the light and create darkness. I make peace and create chaos (chaos is Ra in Hebrew, also translated as evil: the opposite of Shalom wholeness and peace). I AM the LORD Who does all these things" (ONM Isaiah 45:6-7 note added).

Wow! God created evil? Not exactly. God is taking responsibility for evils existence and asserting His sovereignty over it. In the Beginning, God created everything and all was good. When God created humanity, He said it was very good. When God created Lucifer and all the angels of the Heavens they were good, although God knew some of them, and all of humanity would rebel against Him becoming evil. God created evil indirectly, through the good creations which He fore-knew would become evil by their own choice.

A Christian philosopher named Alvin Plantinga developed an explanation for understanding the creation of evil, or rather the creation of beings which would become evil. It is Transdimensional Depravity or TD (Sennett, 1998). Every creation, unlike the Creator, inherently has limited knowledge, power, and expression. The Archangels Lucifer, Michael, and Gabriel along with all the multitudes of other spiritual beings created by God have a free will. They lived in a utopia, a paradise, or perfect society and environment. No evil, death, sickness, or poverty. They are created of pure spirit essence which I call hyper-substance, who cannot die or cease to exist. They are immortal creations which are very powerful, who witnessed God creating the physical universe and us. They walked in Jesus presence and understood Him in a way we do not. Then one of them, the first of them, the praise and worship leader of all Heaven, became full of pride at his own beauty and wisdom. He wanted to be worshiped and praised like the Most High (Jesus). He chose poorly.

Without choice and something to choose between, we would be nothing more than zombies or rats in a cage of perfection, creatures of instinct following a program of behavior, like a spider spinning a web to catch a fly. No one teaches the spider how, when, why and where to do this. It has no imagination, and any decision the spider makes is restricted by inherent parameters. Any feeling of free will a spider possesses is genuine, but unknown to the spider is its limitations. The spider is programmed a certain way at its creation. It is its instinct.

It is still a living thing with purpose, but not with any higher significance beyond its intent. Spiders mate, but do not dream or create. They do not exchange web design or share location ideas at a spider self-help seminar, such as Strategies for Bug Catching. Unlike spiders or any other animals, angels and people were created with the high capacity for understanding, creativity, and action. Unlike the angels, people are designed with an imagination and creative ability. We are uniquely made in God's image, with much-unrealized potential.

Theory of the Unavoidable

The rebellion of Lucifer was inevitable, as was the fall of Adam and Eve. Alvin Plantinga theory of Trans-dimensional depravity states every created being no matter how intelligent has limitations in their wisdom, knowledge, and understanding. Having a limited understanding and knowledge, along with free will (also called free moral agency), means eventually you will make the wrong decision even in a perfect environment. Only God knows all the variables and consequences in every situation and exercises perfect self-control so never makes a bad choice. This explains the human side of the equation and rebellion of the fallen angels. Only an external experience can prevent or fix TD.

Fellowship in a relationship cannot be forced or it is no longer love, but tyranny and abuse. Creations must develop trust with their Creator.

According to Trans-dimensional depravity given enough time and opportunity to choose, without artificially introduced external influences (bullying or dictator like actions by God), eventually, a moment will occur when the wrong choice is made. This is true no matter how many times you make a universe(s) or what triggers or factors you emplace. The law of trans-dimensional depravity remains unchanged.

You might ask are the 2/3 loyal angels who have never sinned doomed to sin eventually? No. They witnessed firsthand the immediate results, effects, consequences, and judgment upon Satan and his angels and that it was their own doing. The loyal holy angels see more precise than you or I the evils of this world and why they are committed. Evil is a separation from God or an absence of good. Angels experience the goodness of God and witness His works, and help bring His will to pass among humanity minute by minute. New knowledge generated from new experiences from an external influence which is not artificial or forced, changes the dynamic. Because of what the loyal angels saw and see they will never even want to rebel, they will remain loyal forever. In fact, they are more excited or motivated toward loyalty and love of God after witnessing the fall, and wickedness caused by their fellow angels. They are very eager to fight against them on our behalf.

Experiential knowledge expands understanding and naturally alters the effect of trans-dimensional depravity. The law doesn't change, but naturally occurring external influences reverses the effect. The altering effect is different on angels than humans since we are two separate species of spirit. We are human spirits (a different hyper-substance from angels) who have souls (a meta hyper-substance creation) and operate in, and through physical bodies, angels are not constructed as we are. They may temporarily take on physical form (a benefit of being made of pure hyper-substance), but they are not created in the image of God as we are. About the soul, what I mean by meta hyper-substance is that the soul is the bridge between our physical body and spiritual body. Only God is unaffected by the law of trans-dimensional depravity.

The opposing forces used to be loyal but used their free will to defect. When they decided to rebel with Lucifer, it caused them to be disconnected from God who is the source of life and goodness. Sin changed the nature of their essence permanently. Satan and his treacherous kind, being made of pure hyper-substance, cannot be redeemed and cannot be recreated. With all their intelligence, understanding of God, and greater knowledge of the workings of the universe (technology, elements, the human mind, etc.), they are degenerated by their disconnection from God. They do not even want to be redeemed. The forces of Darkness are sociopathic in their delight in and the pursuit of evil. Even knowing their end in fire, they are so driven and enslaved by evil, they wouldn't even ask for forgiveness.

The war is not between God and Satan anymore. That's been over since he was cast out of Heaven, before the fall of Adam and Eve. The war now is for supremacy of Earth and the corruption of humans. So, Satan as our enemy and Jesus is our champion and resource through whom, and by whom, we defeat the Old Serpent and his minions. But, did Adam and Eve have to fall? Could, or should, it have been prevented?

Thank God for the Devil

We, humans, know less about aspects of God, the universe, Heaven and creation than the fallen angels did. It goes without saying our susceptibility to trans-dimensional depravity is greater than theirs. It stands to reason also that since we are made in the image of God the fallout from our inevitable rebellion would be different than theirs was. What would it be like if Adam and Eve had not rebelled, or if Satan didn't exist, or is not permitted to tempt them?

Only 1/3 of the angels rebelled while the other 2/3 we have already shown will never rebel. The damage and fallout are contained so to speak. If there were no fallen angels, and or no Serpent allowed access to humanity to tempt them, what might that look like? We cannot speculate on any other sin being committed except eating from the Tree, because that was the only and first law of God's in the Garden until after the fall. It could be hundreds or thousands of years until someone eats from the Tree of the Knowledge of Good and Evil. It was billions of years after the initial creation of the universe until Satans fall.

After a long time, untold numbers of people would be born and living. Remember there is no death, sickness, or aging until sin enters the scene. Once sin enters, humanity is immediately disconnected spiritually from God the source of life and health. Only after sin came in did aging begin.

People were created to live forever connected to God, on Earth, and freely eating from the Tree of Life. That tree sustains and rejuvenates life. Can you imagine the impact on humanity when the first fallen human is judged by a righteous and holy God? When God justly judges, rejects and sentences them. It could mean a full-scale rebellion of epic proportions. Most likely all of humanity would be lost to Hell.

Imagine if your son, daughter, husband, or wife ate from the tree and is condemned, how would you feel? What would you do? Can you imagine a ripple effect of emotions and loyalties causing more and more to rebel in anger against God, not understanding the evil which will come of their choice? Not seeing the far-reaching effects, effects we see reported on the daily news. Unlike the angels, the results upon the fallen human spirit, including beginning to age, and being subject to disease, is not seen or experienced immediately, only over time. It would be catastrophic. God would lose the whole human race, each person made in His image, each individual whom He genuinely loves. He likely would lose them all, under those circumstances, they most likely would become like the fallen angels, and not want forgiveness. Moreover, there would never be an opportunity for a messiah, crucifixion, or resurrection. There would be no hope of saving any of humanity. Sin would enter in and legally begin to kill all rebels, Satan or no Satan.

Families would be divided, or take sides, etc. The potential destruction, death, and wickedness, apart from Satan and his demons, assuming they didn't exist in this scenario, are still conceivable. Imagine the world much worse than it is now, but with no hope or guidance from a loving Creator. Another alternative is even worse. If Satan and his demons could enter into the Earth as they have with the real fall. It is more likely that all would be lost. God would be forced to cleanse the world of evil in some cataclysmic global judgment. An event like what happened after the fall of Lucifer (Genesis opens up with all mountain's flattened and the Earth covered in water), as the flood of Noah or the destruction by fire of Sodom and Gomorrah also depict and foreshadow. Unlike those two incidents, in this scenario, there would be no survivors.

Thank God this is not how it went. As crazy as it now is, we could have had it much worse and that without hope. Therefore, God, foreknowing mankind, and Lucifer would unavoidably and inevitably sin because of trans-dimensional depravity. The Lord sovereignly organized everything to maximize the good and minimize the unavoidable, temporary, presence, and influence of evil. If there were a better way to handle TD or do this God would have done it.

Allowing Satan to tempt Adam and Eve to sin, and knowing they would, is God controlling the inevitable. In so doing we all become sinful rebels, with interference from the Devil. Demonic intervention is not an excuse for our sin but is a legal situation justifying God's grace to provide Jesus to suffer once for all humanity across time and space, to provide redemption for all the human race. It also allows God to enter into time and space as a human (at the birth of Jesus) obtaining the right to rule, judge Satan, and save all humanity.

Jesus, the Word made flesh did not cheat and use his divinity to overcome the effects of the Fall (Satan becoming the god of the world instead of Adam and Eve). Jesus changed the circumstances of relationship with God the Father empowering us to reconnect, become adopted sons and daughters of God, and become a force for good on this Earth, in this world. God is everyone's Creator, but not everyone's Father. Accepting Jesus as savior, believing God raised him from the dead- Gospel of John 3:16 and Romans 10: 8-13, is the only way to Heaven. This is also when you are adopted back into the family of God, who then becomes your Father, now that Jesus nature is in you, your new spirit. It is also the single starting point for truly fixing the problem of evil.

Being born-again is when God re-creates a new pure, sinless, human spirit replacing your former fallen human spirit. This is part of the uniqueness of the human spirit that God can destroy and create a new (born again) spirit in the same instant. This new spirit is sealed by the Holy Spirit and cannot sin. It's stupid human proof. Until you are born-again God is your Creator, but your father is Satan since it is his fallen nature dominating your fallen spirit.

A little more on Lucifer's Fall and Evils End

Lucifer wanted the position of the Son in the Trinity. (Job 38:6-7; Isaiah 14:12-14; Ezekiel 28). Worship and loyalty are worthless if not voluntary. God is not a bully and had he prevented Lucifer from rebelling, or Adam and Eve from rebelling He would be a tyrant. All creation would serve God in terror instead of love or 'The fear of the Lord' which is respect and reverence, not actually being afraid. Had Satan and his followers been snuffed out or de-existed by God, again terror would follow. God proved His case against Satan before the witnesses of angels and humans through overpowering the Devil within the confines of already established Divine laws, through Jesus incarnation (virgin birth), life, crucifixion, resurrection, and ascension. God beat Satan at His own game through the power of love.

Therefore, in the future when Satan and the rest of the wicked spirits and unredeemed humanity are judged, sentenced, and imprisoned to eternal burning in the Lake of Fire, none will dispute the goodness, justice, and love of the Lord Jesus (the judge) in any matter. No one will be afraid of the Lord, but love Him and live forever. There will never be another rebellion ever again forever; no more crying, wars, prison, death, trauma, loss, or pain.

Brothers and sisters in arms, killing people (or Satan if it were possible), or anyone evil, even incarcerating them in jail for short or long periods of time, does not solve the problem of crime or evil. But our solutions though temporary are vital consequences. The final destination of evil spirits human and angelic is the Lake of Fire, but this doesn't settle or prevent evil. It is the final consequence or permanent containment of evil. Laws do not prevent crimes if the criminal mind thinks it won't get caught or doesn't care.

Laws define what the crimes are, and the punishment for breaking them. A person decides not to be a criminal or terrorist is because their personal moral compass or internal values system says it is not right, and not in their best interest. A person whose moral compass is set different than other peoples may be deterred from committing a crime if they either believe they will get caught or the risk-reward is not worth the chance of being caught. Some are not deterred at all but have a solid criminal or sociopathic ideological mindset. Many do not regret getting caught, because the reward of street credit, revenge, instant access to heaven, or they feel justified. Sometimes people are coerced, or deceived into committing criminal acts or doing acts of terror.

There are 613 commandments under the Old Testament, including the Big Ten. They defined or directed the arrow of the moral compass, but never completely prevented violations. Jesus made it harder to not keep the Divine law when he added the standard of not thinking evil in your heart: lusting, coveting, and unrighteous anger equaling murder are all violations. No person except Jesus ever perfectly fulfilled all of God the Father's commands, including the higher standard of not thinking it in his heart. God is perfect, and His standard of conduct is one hundred percent perfection. Ninety-nine-point-nine percent is point zero one percent evil, and unacceptable.

Heaven has a zero tolerance for sin. The blood alcohol limit for driving drunk is .08% with no margin for error. If you have .01% sin, then you are completely unrighteous, not 99% righteous. When you're born-again, you are credited with Jesus perfection, his righteousness nature.

The overview of events of how it all ends is that the Lord Jesus will appear at the rapture or catching up/gathering together of the Church. This is the resurrection of the Saints. It is our physical leaving from Earth to Heaven in a moment, a global scale event. Even godless news networks will cover it, and people alive at the time will witness it. This is not Jesus Second Coming, or second physical return to Earth to make war against the armies of the Anti-Christ (Mahdi), at the battle of Armageddon.

At the end of the seven years Tribulation (the deceptive seven-year peace treaty between Israel and an Islamic Caliphate). A time of terrible wars and Christian persecution worldwide, under the direction of the Anti-Christ (false substitute messiah) and his False Prophet (Some evidence leads to him being a renegade Pope of the future). All believers will return to Earth with the Lord Jesus. We will be in new bodies (younger appearances of ourselves) very and designed differently from the angels. A body which will never grow old or decay feels no pain, and cannot be damaged. After a person is born-again in spirit (in an instant) their soul; mind, will, and emotions change over time and experience in the Word, an opportunity for the continuous renewing of the mind while alive on Earth. The new body is given at the resurrection.

Our return is with Jesus for the Battle of Armageddon, at the valley of Megiddo, in Israel is the total defeat of enemy armies. The Anti- Christ, also called the Assyrian, and the False Prophet is cast alive into the Lake of Fire. Michael the Archangel and the holy angels arrest Satan and all his fallen angels and demons. Then they are thrown into lockdown in the bottomless pit (a wormhole). This starts the one thousand years of peace with Jesus ruling on Earth through us (no more war or need for soldiers then). After the thousand years are up Satan is released from the bottomless pit and allowed to deceive the nations. After a thousand years of peace, seeing Jesus in the flesh, ruling over that nations. With Biblical end time prophecy fullied before their very eyes, amazingly, almost all the people of Earth join Satan and attempt another rebellion. People still use their free will and choose against the LORD.

This offensive is met with seismic (earthquakes) and volcanic activity the world over. All rebels are destroyed in front of the faithful, who are all gathered in Israel. This is the final battle between good and evil. Then, the fallen angels are judged and sentenced to an eternity in the Lake of Fire. The Lord Jesus Christ will judge humanity. If your name is written in the Lambs Book of Life, it is because you are redeemed or born-again. Your judgment is being rewarded for what you did for the Lord while living on Earth the first time, whatever survives the test of fire. Any evil works you did will be burned in the fire testing your works, but because of Jesus sacrifice on the cross, you do not burn. You do not burn because after Jesus paid for all sin on the cross, but before his resurrection, He was also tormented in Hellfire in your place.

There are books in Heaven where your every thought, intent, word and deed of every life is recorded. Those whose names are not written in the Book of Life will be judged according to their works and words alone, apart from Jesus. They will be justified or condemned on their merits alone. Only Jesus life is acceptable to God. Therefore all works apart from Jesus are worthless and evil. Since this group is not redeemed, after their works stand the test of fire, they're sentenced to the Lake of Fire for eternity.

Because of our naturally occurring experience with being evil, and then the experience of becoming saved. Our experiences with God now, as with those who do not rebel in the final attack, will render us as the loyal angels of Heaven. We will love the Lord with all our hearts, without any fear, and our loyalty will never fade. There will never again be a time of evil or rebellion forever after this time period we are in now. The law of trans-dimensional depravities impact will be nullified. We will live in paradise, Heaven on Earth, with no evil, no death, no sickness, no poverty, etc., until then… we have work to do.

Trouble is still Coming

The rapture hasn't happened, nor the battle of Armageddon, neither is the day of final judgment upon us, not yet. It's no rush either because every day Jesus does not appear and start the clock ticking down, is another day a person can be saved and avoid the trauma of the Tribulation period or even Hell itself. Your efforts each day in the muck and mire of society has a significant influence now and in the future more than you realize.

Today we are still fighting against the Devil and those under his influence. Today things are still unjust until the day final justice is served. The Lord Jesus said "…In the world ye shall have **tribulation**: but be of good cheer; I have overcome the world" (John 16:33 em ad). Tribulation, translated from the Greek means pressure, anguish, and trouble. There are several Greek words translated into the English word- world. Here twice the word is translated from the Greek word cosmos. Cosmos is the entirety of the structure and order of the universe. It involves activity and influences on and beyond the Earth.

The Lord did not promise a life without trouble or pressure, just the opposite. He warned life would include problems and evil. Then God encourages us not be dismayed, but joyful because He has overcome these troubles. Jesus provides the solutions to avoiding, preparing for, overcoming, and minimizing the impact of a crisis. James, the half-brother of the Lord Jesus, says war comes from unlawful desires. That people are envious and jealous, fight, and war to obtain things, even asking God for ungodly things, and wondering why they didn't receive them. They do not receive because they ask with the wrong heart, or motive, and for the wrong or harmful things. Here the Greek word for world is cosmos refers to the righteous and fallen order of things, the competing influences for the hearts and wills of humanity.

> "From where do wars and fighting's among you come? Is it not from this, from your…You desire, and do not have. You murder, and are jealous, and cannot obtain.

> You fight and war, yet you have not <u>because you ask not</u>. <u>You ask and receive not,</u> because you ask amiss, that you may spend it upon your lusts (ungodly desires)...Do you not know that the friendship of the **world** is enmity with God? Therefore whoever desires to be a friend of the **world** is the enemy of God" (James 4:1-4 MKJV em ad).

Good things and bad people

Why do bad things happen to good people? Wrong question. Well, first let's get it straight. All people are evil having sinned in one fashion or another, all of us. We all started out disconnected from the Lord. Apart from being in covenant with Jesus, the Father is under no obligation to help the evil and rebellious. Thank God for His grace, because of His love for us, even while we were His enemies. Therefore, the real question is why don't more bad things happen to more people, since all start out with Satans nature? Even once we are born-again, we still make mistakes and commit sins in body and soul.

And what about earthquakes, mudslides, forest fires, hurricanes, etc., what about them? Aren't those acts of God? This is a good question for the warrior since often we are the first responders and aftermath support. If it's God's will then why are we helping people in trouble? Could it be their own fault, even the death of children? Could it be by chance in a hostile world? How can you faithfully, morally and ethically execute the duty of warriorhood, serving a God who sends calamity upon humanity killing woman, children, and destroying families without rhyme or reason? To have the moral high ground, the source of your authority must be moral. These events don't look morally justified.

Yes, there is an incident in the Bible where God judged a group of cities; Sodom and Gomorrah and three others in their area. It is a particular case used as the foreshadowing of the end time judgment on the Earth when the last human rebellion takes place. These cities were populated by people whose judges allowed rape in the streets; they had a reprobate mind (seared conscience and hardened heart) against God, unredeemable, for they would never repent. And there is the sentence of death upon all the men, women and children in parts of the Promised

Land whom the Israelites were ordered to kill during the conquest. What is left unsaid about this incident is that these nations had already attacked the Hebrews in the wilderness, habitually sacrificed their children to demon gods, and were involved in all manner of wickedness, they also were reprobate or unredeemable in their hardened heart state.

Furthermore, children of Nephilim, giants of which Goliath who was killed by David was born, lived and ruled the land of ancient Israel. After this, the Lord never ordered Israel to take out a people group, and all God directed combat after this is defensive. Many ministers or critiques of the Bible do not read or research extra-Biblical text or archeological findings. The children killed in these battles were all under the law of innocent blood and went to Heaven. The wicked and depraved culture did not spread to neighboring nations. If they had grown up, they would have made war with Israel and followed the evil ways of their parents, maybe also corrupt Israel, then end up in Hell.

After God answered the prophet Elijah by fire, showing Himself to be the one true God and not Baal or Ashtaroth, all the prophets of Baal and Ashtaroth were executed - about 750 total. Then in chapter 19 of First Kings Elijah is told to go to Mount Horeb and wait for the Lord. While in a cave on Mt. Horeb Elijah experienced a tornado, an earthquake, and wilderness fire, and saw the Lord was not in them. The Lord was in a still small voice.

The spiritual virus of sin infected all the elements down unto the molecular or sub-atomic level, not just the heavenly dimension, but the whole Earth. As we learned from Job and Genesis angels of the Lord, or angels of the Devil can manipulate volcanos, tornados, tidal waves, hurricanes, etc., and then there are natural disturbances in the fallen physical realm of the elements. When God four times used, not was in, but used, seismic activity (volcanic or earthquake), twice no one was injured. A jail was broken open by an earthquake to free Paul. A third was a judgment on a group of rebel Hebrews in the wilderness. Then, there was Sodom and Gomorrah matching the archeological evidence.

As for Sodom and Gomorrah even then God debated with Abraham about sparing those five cities for ten righteous people. Ten which could not be found, but for ten He would have spared five wicked cities (Genesis 18). God is looking for ways to save and delay judgment, not reasons to judge and destroy. Satan is the destroyer and deceiver who shifts blame to God. Don't confuse judgment with naturally, or demonically occurring circumstances. Judgments are another topic unto itself linked to the problem of evil, but outside the scope of this book to fully explore.

What about people killed or hurt by accidents in general?

In Ecclesiastes, you find observations on how life is lived and death viewed. Not everything is an attack of the Devil or the will of God, sometimes in this fallen, broken, crazy world- stuff happens.

> "I returned, and saw under the sun, that the race is not to the swift, nor the battle to the strong, neither yet bread to the wise, nor yet riches to men of understanding, nor yet favour to men of skill; <u>but time and chance happeneth to them all</u>. For man also knoweth not his time; as the fishes that are taken in an evil net, and as the birds that are caught in the snare, even so, are the sons of men snared in an evil time, when it falleth suddenly upon them" (Ecclesiastes 9:11-12 em ad).

Except for the Lord's protection through covenant; by design of the Enemy, chance or our own foolish actions, accidents or death are the nets trying to catch us the fish. In combat, during a routine traffic stop, while taking a shower, or driving a car. The difference lies in our perception that some places and situations are more hostile than others are. Our knowledge does not always take into account the reality of slipping in the shower, being hit by a drunk driver, or getting on a plane about to be hijacked, or malfunction and crash. Exercising our covenant is what tips the scales from chance toward safety under the wings of His angels.

We are not to walk in fear of things, but in faith, the Lord according to covenant promises forewarns us to avoid, protect, and guide us away from or through the evils of this world. Are we listening though? Walking by faith (making choices which are not logical or reasonable to the natural mindset) by following the leading of the Lord, can prevent and overcome any accidents or attacks of the Enemy. We can escape the net, which the fish does not see, then in a moment, without warning is caught, killed, and eaten. Often by our own words and or other distractions we miss the still small voice of the Holy Spirit trying to guide us and are injured or die before we should. When should we die then? As Job who died old and full of days (over 100 years and healthy) seeing his great-great-grandchildren, or Moses who lived healthy and vigorous until age 120. There are many scriptures on long life, health, as well as on sickness, weakness and premature death. Teaching on communion talks about this.

Good deeds and bad

People think their goodness (belief in false Karma concepts) helps them out and deflects evil. Our best is still evil in God's sight. The Lord does not deal in degrees of evil; evil is evil. Accidents in combat, or during training do not mean a curse is upon anyone. It also does not mean that one person is good or better than another. It is an accident or tragedy brought about by someone not following safety procedures for example, but not always.

Questions about peoples goodness and deserving of death or unfortunate circumstances are ancient. Jesus was asked about this. Once was about when the Roman Governor Pontius Pilate mingled Jewish blood with their pagan sacrifices in Galilee. The question is did the sinfulness of those Jews allow or cause them to be sacrificed. Jesus is also asked about a construction accident which killed some workers and possibly bystanders.

> "And Jesus answering said unto them, Suppose ye that these Galileans were sinners above all the Galileans because they suffered such things? I tell you, Nay: **but, except ye repent, ye shall all likewise perish**. Or those eighteen, upon whom the tower in Siloam fell, and slew them, think ye that they were sinners above all men that dwelt in Jerusalem? I tell you, Nay: **but, except ye repent, ye shall all likewise perish**"(Luke 13:1-5 em ad).

All have sinned and fallen short of God's glory. There is none of us who is wholly good except God. Our standard is not His standard. Except you repent (change your mind), get saved, and walk by faith you risk death as those sacrificed or by accident. Without God, we're a breath or heartbeat away from being six feet under by the end of the week. Our good deeds do not balance out or compensate for our wickedness. This is the lie of Karma and another false religious doctrine, which talk about balance, and good vs. evil. Sowing and reaping is God's system, and though they seem similar, they are not.

All the Earth is a spiritual combat zone with our Enemy always looking for a time or place to strike. It is no more dangerous to be in physical combat than walking out our daily lives from a certain viewpoint. In one situation you're wary because of known or suspected threats, while in other you take your safety for granted per se. Not a bad thing, of course, you don't need to be paranoid, just simply understand apart from the Lord you are vulnerable on many fronts.

Get me out of this mess

Peter is told by Jesus that Satan desires to sift him like wheat. We would hope or expect Jesus to petition the Father not to let this happen. Most would think letting Peter go through a trial or tribulation would be evil. Jesus however, says He is praying Peter's faith does not fail. Peter is informed Satan has been given permission to move against him. Jesus has stated He is praying Peter's faith does not fail. Satan moves, Peter denies the Lord. Satan moves, and Judas Iscariot that same night betrayed Jesus.

After the resurrection, Peter is restored by Jesus. After the coming of the Holy Spirit on the day of Pentecost, Peter who was a coward a month or so ago stands up publicly and speaks boldly. Judas Iscariot in tremendous grief for betraying Jesus commits suicide before Jesus raises from the dead. Judas missed his opportunity at restoration. Peter did not; his faith did not fail.

Had Peter not sunk so low he would not have risen so high, and we benefit from his experiences to this day. Let me be clear, however. God does NOT, and never has never PLACED disease or tragedy upon any person except in some very rare documented occasions. Even then God does not issue the curse, but in the Hebrew grammar, God must permit it, as a consequence for some action directly against the covenant: justice.

God either delivers us, or the Holy Spirit goes through it with and next to us, encouraging us not to quit (run and grow not weary). Or, He lets us walk through it not changing the circumstances as in the first two options, but develops us, builds our faith, and strengthens our character in a situation, to then rise above it at the end (walk and not grow faint).

He did not 'need that child in Heaven,' or 'call them home' at age forty with a heart attack (forget that they drank and smoked too much, etc). Nor did God decide today this drug addict dies, or some other such nonsense. Straight up my friends, accidents death, disease, mental and physical ailments are not from a good God. God did not hurt you and is not teaching you a lesson. These are products of genetic and spiritual generational curses, the taint of a supernatural virus called sin, speaking against yourself, general effects of living in a fallen world, an unhealthy lifestyle, and demonic attacks. Jesus life, death, and resurrection defeated and provided grace and faith to overcome all challenges.

Stop blaming God because your friend died in a car accident while speeding and not wearing a seatbelt or died of an overdose. I've lost family to drugs, and it wasn't Gods fault. At least by His grace, that person was saved before they were overcome by addiction. Why some recover from their addictions and other, do not- I don't have all those answers, but it is not God's fault. If you have to lay blame, blame the Devil, no one cares about him. Losing friends, family, and fellow warriors are not the fault of God. We live in a broken world until it is remade, after the New Millennium. Expect trouble, but let's work to keep the trouble in our lives to a minimum.

Prayers Answered-but not how you would think

I heard the true account of a 9/11 story as an answer to prayer while watching a sermon on tv by a noted and reputable preacher. One part of the family had a flat tire which caused them to miss one of the flights which ended in disaster on 9/11 that fateful September. As one family in New York heard the news of their loved ones being saved by God through a flat tire, another family was experiencing tragedy. Their dad was a retired fireman, and not saved. He left to help on his own at the World Trade Center. He died there, a family not knowing if he ever made a confession of faith or not, was in Hell or not. His son had prayed for him to no apparent end.

Then came a knock at the door a year or so later. It was a couple with a baby, named after the man who had saved her life but lost his own going back in once the pregnant woman was safely out of the building. It took a while to get her out, and she was a Christian. While helping her, she had witnessed to him, and once on the ground he prayed and accepted Jesus, then went back in, for the last time. Tears came to my eyes as I heard the sermon, and as I tell you the story also, one story among many heard in churches around the country of God's providence during a national attack and disaster.

The reason for telling you the story is to help you stay focused. Pray and trust the Lord. He will not always, and often doesn't reveal until the last moment or after the fact **how** He will do or did something, or **how** it must be done to answer the prayer and fit into His plan for us all. The **how,** is not what's important. Trusting the Lord to handle what you cannot is essential.

Bottom Line Up Front

When I don't understand, I give my Lord Jesus, who sacrificed his life tortuously on every level, the benefit of the doubt, to trust Him who has proven trustworthy to say the least. We will not always be told the why. We may not want to know why, if it can be used against us by the Enemy to cause us unnecessary guilt or more trauma. We will not always have the capacity to understand the why it happened the way it did. There are more variable influences at work than we can fully comprehend this side of Heaven.

Job didn't understand all of what was going on but made a comment based on knowing God's character and trusting Him, when all the answers are not immediately available. Trusting God when it looks like He is either not helping, or maybe even against you, but God is for you and is helping. Job did not know and is never told what all the forces were at work behind the scenes. He thought God was doing things He was not. And in the midst of this Job (13:15) makes a declaration I am impressed with and follow to this day.

"Though He slay me, yet will I trust Him."

I love that statement. It shows Job's trust in God's ultimate justice, redemption, and judgment in the face of the total loss of health, family, and wealth. God did not slay Job, but Job did not know that. Job spoke what was in his heart that what he feared came upon him. In Psalm 103 we learn the angels listen to the words of God to be spoken by us in faith. This then authorizes them to operate in our lives and enforce God's word without violating free will. In the course of tragedy, Job said he knows his Redeemer lives, trusting in the Lord to work it out. In the end, Job was given seven more children (add the seven in Heaven, and that is double the children), and double back all his losses and even health. He lived to see great, great, great-grandchildren. Jobs unswerving loyalty paid off.

Sovereignty or godship over the earth is given to humanity. The authority of death and life are in the power of humanities tongue. God is all-powerful but delegated the authority of life and death to mankind to exercise over itself, under his guidance. God no longer has the authority of death, and neither does Satan. Satan and his angels are waiting for you to speak his words and thoughts of fear, doubt, unbelief, and cursing. Then we are authorizing the demons to operate in our lives without violating our free will, against ourselves.

The godship of humanity is in authorizing either Satan's worldly system of doing things or the Lord Jesus system of doing things on this earth. By our actions and speech, we bow to one or the other and authorize one or the other to operate. There is no in between. Satan is the god of the worldly system, and mid heavens or dimensions between Earth and Heaven of Heavens (God's throne), but not the Earth or Heaven of Heavens. God is not killing babies, taking people home to be with Him early, etc. God is getting a bad rap from the propaganda machine of the enemy. That avalanche, fire, flood, tornado, or accident was not sent by God to judge people and kill children! Cancer in adults or children is not from God!

When Jesus raised a little girl from the dead, or Lazarus from the dead, he would have been going against His Fathers will if his Father had killed them, to begin with? Healing a person who you think is struck by God would then be going against God's will. It makes no sense God is a healer and killer, in the general sense outside of a military or law enforcement context. Of course, God has killed or sent an angel, or person(s) in judgment against wicked humans. But don't forget Jesus stopped the storm from sinking a ship, the three Hebrews were saved from the furnace of fire, and Daniel saved from hungry lions. Examples abound in the word of God. Our problem is we speak Satan's words instead of Jesus' according to the Mark 11 law of faith, and believe it, then receive it, then it happens (the bad), then we blame God; that's crazy! But I've done it in the past too, just being honest. Our own words save or sink us.

Lingering Thoughts

Now that you know, it's time to learn and work God's system the way He intended it to work through us. Death and life are in your tongue, your authority, not God's or the Devils. It was/is worth mentioning more than once. Jesus said you must repent or you will perish. Repent in this context is not about salvation, but mindset and speech. If you are not praying and speaking against, tornados, earthquakes, flood, accidents, hurricanes, etc. according to a promise from God. A promise such as from Psalm 91- a thousand may fall at my side and ten thousand at my right hand, but it will not come near me- you are leaving your life up to chance and the demons.

A hedge is a wall protecting something from harm or threat. Job was hedged in by God in three layers; his individual self, all his family, his business or possessions. Fear of losing these things fear someone in his family may curse God, not knowing God's goodness. Fear (contaminated force or substance of faith) broke the hedges of protection <u>from within</u> allowing the Devil in through those holes. Notice as you read the beginning of Job that God had to call attention to the Devil that there is a breach. Satan had become so accustomed to not being able to touch Job, his family or business that he quit looking or trying- concerning Job. Better hedges around ourselves, our family and business are available for us today, in the New Covenant in Christ. God's timing is perfect, and in the end, Job is vindicated and compensated, and a better relationship develops between them, devoid of any fear.

Job lived long before Moses, operating under grace, not the Law; the

Ten Commandments and additional 600 plus rules. Job lived around the time of Abraham, possibly before him. In Job's defense, he did not have a personal relationship with God until the end of the book of Job. We have the Holy Spirit indwelling us, the name above every name to speak for and under, and permanent right standing with God, with no fear because of the blood of Jesus. We can boldly cultivate a personal relationship with God as Dad with a capital D. Not some distant creator, off somewhere… We have no excuses for blaming God for untimely, unjust, unfair, and tragic deaths or accidents of people. It is Satan's worldly system and many times our own recklessness, or ignorance of how things work, which brings these things about.

God's will is not always done in the short term. Therefore, you the warrior, are charged with defending against, defeating, and punishing the wickedness of those who do evil; honorably. Evil is a necessary part of the plan, not to bow down to, but overcome. There is no plan B.

COVENANT WARRIOR

CHAPTER 5
Lethal Force Authority

You should punish in the same manner those who commit crimes with those who accuse falsely." – Thucydides

Thou shalt not kill

Straightforward and to the point, but is there more behind it. Are there exceptions and or explanations for covering various types of killing? Both civil and ceremonial Jewish law changes took effect after the crucifixion and resurrection of the Lord Jesus. The sentence of capital punishment is no longer in effect for the sexual deviances of homosexuality, or the practice of witchcraft are two examples of criminal code changes. Moral violations each carry natural consequences for practicing them which continue to this day. Remember not all moral violations are criminal violations, nor should they be. A criminal statute can be added or stricken from the law. The Lord does not change concerning criteria for moral violation. More on this when we discuss undercover operations.

The most straightforward understanding of these changes is Jesus not only became sin and a curse for us but also took upon Himself God's just wrath and punishment for our sin. Jesus provided the vaccine for the virus, his precious blood. Before the divine blood is spilled there was only one cure for being infected with advanced stages of the spiritual sin virus, and ensuring it did not spread; kill the carrier of the disease. I use the analogy of disease and contagious because spiritually sin can become contagious.

Witchcraft and sorcery in the Old and New Testaments both deal not only with spell casting but drug and poison manufacturing and use on other people for various reasons. The Greek word is Pharmakeia where we get out word Pharmacy from. There is illegal drug manufacture and uses as well as legal drug manufacture and uses from thousands of years ago. Though spell casting and such are no longer on the kill list, drug dealers (a subcategory of witch and sorcerer) still are worthy of death. They manufacture and sell addictive poisons to people, advertising them as recreation and relief, but really are peddling slow death and a form of human slavery.

The Hebrew word used in Exodus 20:13 "Thou shalt not kill" is Ratsach (raw-tsakh). It means specifically to murder. Killing in combat, in self-defense, or a criminal shootout is not, and never will be Ratsach, when the shot is fired under righteous authority within the laws of war and conflict. To further verify this when Jesus referred back to this scripture the Greek word used is Phoneuo (fon-you-o) meaning specifically to murder. Again; killing in combat, in self-defense, or in a criminal shootout, including military and S.W.A.T. snipers are not, never were, and never will be guilty of Phoneuo. You are not a murderer for taking the authorized shot, defending your life, and that of your family.

We know governments authorize the taking of life, but governments are not God. For covenant warriors the question is not **can I**? Of course, you can. You are able to do X or Y the same as anyone. Asking **can I** is the wrong question Biblically. The question is, **should I, or may I** do X, or do Y. Under what circumstances, if any, does God authorize X or Y and to what extent? We now know kill in Thou Shalt Not Kill refers to murder, so murder is not authorized. What then is our authority to take life and it not be murder?

Institutional Structure

There are three basic institutions of society: the congregation of worshipers (consisting of believers, priests, etc.), the family, and government. The first institution is worship, which is fellowshipping with and obeying God. The second institution is a marriage between a man and woman. The family is inclusive of God, a picture of the Godhead. The family is the basic building block of society and worship.

Worship included Cain and Abel worshiping in their offerings to God. The first recorded crime since The Fall is when Cain murdered Abel. There were no judges or government officials sanctioned by the Lord at this time. God judged and sentenced directly. During this period, people used their free will, influenced by Satan, the god of the worldly ways to rebel. Thier rebellion and relationships with fallen angels justified the Flood Judgement.

Adam and Eve, along with the rest of humanity, were the gods of the Earth, under regents with delegated authority from God. Using the term gods for humanity ruffles a lot of feathers, but look it up yourself you will be surprised. The word says we are gods, small g, emphasizing in the image of our Creator God. Our free will, soul, spirit, and physical body are His image of Himself in us. Being a god; having free will, imagination, and creative ability carries a lot of responsibility and opportunity. Creative not in the sense of God bringing something from nothing, but able to invent and manipulate the elements of this world naturally. For example; air conditioning, flight, the light bulb, etc.

Jesus was confronted by Jewish religious leadership concerning whether or not he was the Messiah. He told them "I already told you," and that the miracles or works he is doing prove it, but they refuse to believe. Then picking up rocks to stone him, charged him with blasphemy, because he said he is God's Son, making himself equal with God. Jesus response is from Psalm 82.

> "Jesus answered them, "Is it not written in your law, 'I said, "You are gods"'? "If He called them gods, to whom the word of God came (and the Scripture cannot be broken), do you say of Him whom the Father sanctified and sent into the world, 'You are blaspheming,' because I said, 'I am the Son of God'? "If I do not do the works of My Father, do not believe me; but if I do, though you do not believe Me, believe the works, that you may know and believe that the Father is in Me, and I in Him." (John 10:34-38, NJKV)

Being a god/human, in the image of God; it is more than you think, but not exactly what you would think. Jesus is God the Son, and human;

the Godman. This is proven by his works and resurrection which demonstrate all He claimed to be he is. Being a god is not as mystical, elusive, or arrogant as it might appear. It is not new age mumbo jumbo, or some deception involving ascending masters. The only physical transformation is at the resurrection, the spiritual has already taken place, and our soul (mind, will, and emotions) is current work in progress.

Historical Background on Government

In due time humanity began to have relations with powerful Fallen Angels. This corrupted the DNA of humanity with the cross-species breeding. Intercourse with human females created the Nephilim an ungodly hybrid. These demi-gods; half angel and half human increased over hundreds of years. They can be called demigods because the angels are also called the sons of God as he created them also, but not in His image as with us. God forbids cross-species breeding and mixing of DNA (a criminal and moral violation). By the time Noah had finished building the Ark, these wicked angels and their offspring had tainted humanities blood, all except for Noah's family. Hybrid blood cannot be used to produce Jesus human incarnation in the future, only pure human blood.

Satan was not only trying to wipe out humanity because he hates them. His strategy was to taint all human blood so Jesus could not come to Earth as a human. The Savior of humanity is also the Judge to sentence Lucifer to the Lake of Fire. After this failed attempt, Satan continued to try to prevent the Son of God's first physical appearance by tampering with specific bloodlines more than once; all his efforts failed of course. This is one reason why there are two genealogies in the gospels which are not identical.

Joseph's bloodline is tainted not by Nephilim but is cursed because of King Jeconiah actions a long time before him. Josephs birthright to rule as King, as a descendant of David, is still intact but not honored in that day. Mary's human blood still has original sin in it; her bloodline is not cursed. Joseph, Jesus stepfather, is of the Tribe of Judah (the Tribe prophesied from whom the Messiah would come), whose family traces back through a different son of David. Jesus lineage through both Joseph and his mother give him the right to rule Israel. He is born of Mary as a pure human without taint from fallen angels, or original sin. The Holy Spirit spiritually provided the seed which is not tainted by sin, like all humans having a human father are. God works through lawful or legal chains of authority or command. Jesus has authority in Heaven and on Earth being fully human and fully God.

So, the right to rule as a human king is from Joseph, and to rule in Heaven from His Father, God. Becoming, incarnating into, or being born a human is from Mary. Modern medical science discovered the mother's blood never mixes with the child's – Meaning Jesus blood never mixed with sinful blood. The blood, spirit, and soul are provided by God, which makes Jesus both God and god (human), the Godman. This provides the legal way to redemption before the Court of Heaven: in the name above all names; Jesus.

Now, after the flood God re-commissions Noah, his three sons and their wives to repopulate the Earth. God adds additional instructions for social conduct and accountability ordaining the institution of government authority. The government has the purpose of governing the people on God's behalf, with His guidance. Government officials have delegated authority to make laws and enforce them. Officials in an administration are accountable to God for how well they treat citizens. People in power were never supposed to govern apart or independent of God but collaborate with the Holy Spirit. The reason for oppression of people is because of godless use and abuse of authority. Just because a person or institution says, they represent God does not mean it's true. After instituting government, God delegates lethal, (and implicitly non-lethal) force authority and as well as the commission to make and enforce laws.

> "Only the flesh with the life thereof, which is the blood thereof, shall ye not eat. And surely your blood of your lives will I require; at the hand of every beast will I require it; and at the hand of man, even at the hand of every man's brother, will I require the life of man. Whoso sheddeth man's blood, by man, shall his blood be shed; for in the image of God made He man"(Gen 9:4-6 JPS em ad).

We, as gods, now are to be self-accountable. This is the original source for all lethal force authority. Government is not to take on the responsibilities of the other two institutions (family and church) and vice versa. The three are complementary and interdependent as societal checks and balances. Verses in the book of Romans chapters 12 and 13 reinforce those of Genesis 9:4-6. These foundational bookended scriptures are a basis for a Doctrine of Violence.

Abuses of authority are no surprise but expected when leaders (parents, clergy, supervisors, CEO's, or other officials) do not integrate God in their daily lives both the personal and the professional. Such a renegade country becomes a danger to its neighboring countries. Renegade civilizations today suffer under the penalty of the curses of the Law having separated themselves from God's providence. In the civil arena, usually, governments deteriorate then recover if they listen to Gods warnings or harbingers. Remember disobedience creates a spiritual vulnerability to the forces of darkness or incurs judgment. God desires to have mercy on nations until there is no option left due to non-repentance; Jonah and the city of Nineveh (present day Mosul in Iraq) or Abram and the cities of Sodom and Gomorrah are prime examples.

God always provides for repentance, but if it does not come, and their sin become full. Then as with the Amorites the cycle happens again, Four hundred years after Nineveh (who wasn't Jewish or in covenant and whom Jonah hated) repented at the word of Jonah, they rebelled again four hundred years later and were destroyed. God loves all people, but there comes a time when evil must be dealt with harshly and no more probation time exists.

Where does America stand you might ask

All gentile nations (Israel is exempt being the only people group ordained by God Himself and under special Covenants and always returns to God-all Israel will be saved) have undergone one or more permanent regime, cultural, Constitutional replacements, and or political structural changes. America is as this is being written been through some harsh times, but things are looking up as we have a President, not perfect of course, but is patriotic unlike some in the past. Some say our spiritual founding is 1620, the Mayflower Compact. Rabbi Jonathan Cahn has published sound research books and videos on God's Harbingers or warnings to the United States; all worth reading and seeing for a good understanding of the subject and modern events. I am in agreement with the Mayflower Compact being a seed of our spiritual birth view.

I believe our spiritual and political conception is at the signing of the Declaration of Independence. I would say our spiritual and political birth in 1789 at the signing of the U.S. Constitution. Our cultural birth (which could include spiritual and political at this time) is the signing of the Bill of Rights in 1791. These milestones in American history and subsequent Amendments are shining examples of the great experiment of a Representative Republic in operation; American exceptionalism.

I believe the four hundred years general cycle started in 1791. We are a bit away from our four hundred years, but it does not mean we cannot be judged before this, or after. It also does not mean we don't need national repentance or a change of cultural forces returning to God. After all, we are the only nation created by man based the Bible, contrary to the propaganda of Satan in our educational system and revisionist history books since around 1929.

Our Profession

The Office of Arms or Profession of Arms is under the ordained institution of government. Our purpose is to be the actionable arm of God's vengeance. When the Almighty Judge decrees a thing, it is officers of the Court, the loyal angels of God and or the human Ministers of Vengeance who execute it.

> "If I whet My glittering sword, and My hand take hold on judgment; **I will render vengeance to Mine adversaries**, and will **recompense** them that hate Me" (Deuteronomy 32:41 em ad).

> "O LORD God, to whom **vengeance** belongeth; O God, to whom **vengeance** belongeth, shew thyself" (Psalm 94:1 em ad).

> "Dearly beloved, **avenge not yourselves**, but rather give place unto **wrath**: for it is written, **Vengeance is mine; I will repay, saith the Lord**" (Romans 12:19 em ad).

Execution of Vengeance

Faith comes by hearing the word of God on a subject. Time to build the faith. The covenant warrior should be knowledgeable in the scripture concerning what, how, when and why you do what must be done. No room for errors...authority to deal death is no business to skim over. Keywords are Require, Image, Power, Beareth, Terror/Afraid, Minister, Revenger, Wrath, and Sword. The context of the Old and New Testaments together -

> "And surely your blood of your lives will I **require**; at the hand of every beast will I **require** it, and at the hand of man; at the hand of every man's brother will I **require** the life of man. *Whoso sheddeth man's blood, by man shall his blood be shed*; for in the **image** of God made He man" (Genesis 9:4 -6em ad).

> "For rulers are not a **terror** to good works, but to the evil. Wilt thou then not be afraid of the <u>**power**</u>? Do that which is good, and thou shalt have praise of the same: <u>For he is the **minister** of God to thee for good</u>. But if thou do that which is evil, **be afraid**; for he **beareth** not the **sword** in vain: for he is the **minister** of God, a **revenger** to execute **wrath** upon him that doeth evil" (Rom 13:3-4 em ad).

Require

The word daw-rawsh means two things at once in this context. The first is to demand an accounting or inquire as to the reason for something. The second is in how the demand is met, being searched out, followed or pursued to reach the truth and exact payment. The terms of the payment are expressed in the following verse; it is the life of the criminal.

Who is to do the pursuing, searching for the truth and extraction of the payment? Humans have delegated authority to investigate, judge and execute sentences, under God's counsel and along with His Spirit. This is ideal, but most of the time the Holy Spirit is shut out from assisting in the execution of the duties delegated to humanity. The Lord will not force Himself into a situation out of covenant. The Lord does not act like the Enemy. Even sovereign or overriding acts of power by God are within a covenant context.

Praying allows/invites/demands God's influence in a situation without violating the gift of free will covenant. It is not a paradox God nullifying or manipulating some of the 'free will' choices of the enemy, (human or other) for they have no covenant. But they may be in conflict with a person who is in the covenant. God's responsibility is to those in covenant before those outside of the covenant; this is His favor.

Image

In Hebrew Tseh'lem – meaning: a resemblance or representative figure

We are created holy, creative beings, on a level with our Creator. He Created us gods (little g) for His good pleasure, fellowship with and a means to reveal Himself through: a unique creation of body, soul, and spirit. This is a creation able to create through its words by faith. Only the Creator can create from nothing. His creation in His image can create from provided materials. Materials include mental, emotional, spiritual, and physical things. This shaping, changing, forming, and manipulating within an order of things is accomplished through the spoken word. The word coupled with the real primal material, the **substance** of faith, see Hebrews 11:1.

Our uniqueness means should one of us harm another to one extreme or the other unlawfully, a reckoning or accounting must take place among ourselves. "Whoso sheddeth man's blood, by man, shall his blood be shed; for in the image of God made He man" (Genesis 9:6). When Satan fell, he remained an archangel and all that goes with being an archangel, except he is no longer under righteous authority. God was no longer his father but became only his Creator. The same goes for we humans. Redeemed means God is our Father- again and we have all that goes with that covenant relationship. If unredeemed we are still in His image and all which goes with that uniqueness, only as stated earlier, God is not Father, but only Creator.

Power

Here the passage from Romans is the Greek word exousia meaning authority. In Luke 10:19 there are two words (in most Bibles) both translated as power. In Greek, the two words are dunamis and exousia. Dunamis means miraculous energy or raw power. This is where we get the English words dynamo and dynamite. Exousia means authority. Exousia used in Romans 13: 3 refers to the soldier whom Jesus said had great faith. He understood why Jesus dunamis to perform miracles flowed through him to raise the dead and heal the maimed. This power flowed because of the exousia Jesus is under. Under the authority of the Father, the power of the Holy Spirit flows through the Son to alter the circumstances supernaturally.

Rulers have authority, the right make rules or to give a directive to do something. Power is the enforcement of a rule and or the action of doing or making happen what was ordered. Rulers have the authority to commission people to carry out or enforce their laws or directives. All authority is delegated or comes from God. Each person is responsible for how they obtain and use their authority, as well as respond to authority. If you hate the police, God's ministers of vengeance in law enforcement, you hate Jesus from whom their authority comes. You cannot say I love Jesus, but hate the way he enforces the law, or hate the law also. Those people are hypocrites of the first order deceiving themselves. Whatever the position: public service, law enforcement, military, or intelligence community, whether you are a believer or not. You are a ruler, judge, or minister of vengeance commissioned by God to do good to the people, and bring justice to the evil.

Bear

This Greek word is pronounced For-eh-o, meaning- to have a burden; wear as clothing or constant companion. It is the picture of being a lawfully commissioned or appointed person for a task. What is worn, or the burden of responsibility placed upon, or given to an individual? Bear means to have authority in verse 3 bestowed upon or assigned to qualified individuals by a righteous authority, the government. This is typically done through some type of official ceremony. Jesus told Peter in the Garden of Gethsemane "whoever **takes up** the sword dies by the sword." This was after Peter attempted to cut the head off a lawful authority. You cannot take up authority; it must be given.

Jesus did not resist arrest, even though the charges against him were unfounded. He submitted to the arresting authority, which had a right to arrest him with their warrant. The issuers of the warrant were in the wrong, but the arresting officials did not know that. Peter is not a soldier/ officer of the High Priest or Rome. Interfering with this arrest is taking the sword, not bearing it. Peter is not justified in resisting the authorities in this instance.

Peter took up the sword (lethal force) against righteous authority, and attacked an officer of the law, a capital offense. Jesus warned all who use force without legal justification. In Mathew 26 Jesus told Peter to put up his sword for all who take up the sword will die by the sword. Taking up the sword is using lethal force wickedly, without authority, which then means vengeance or wrath is marked out against them. These people may die in combat, be punished under lawful authority, maybe die in conflict with police, die at the hands of other wicked people, or be imprisoned. We will not get everyone in this life. But rest assured there is no escaping the wrath of God in the next. None of the wicked escape.

Terror (fob-os) and Afraid (fob-eh-o)

Verse 4 warns 'but if you do evil be **afraid**...' These Greek words are the root words for our word phobia. These words are what the effect of being a minister of vengeance should have on criminals. They should be terrified to resist righteous authority. They have no fear of the Lord. However, when covenant ministers of vengeance are executing their duties with the Lord, this will begin to happen. Your name or unit will become known and feared in the criminal, corrupt political, and evil military realms. The Lord and His angels will be with you in all situations, call upon Him and expect Him to answer for it is God's will to answer. You won't have to feel alone ever again at any traffic stop, domestic dispute, regular duty or special task. Even when you have back up or fellow soldiers are near, He is always nearer. He is around the corner warning you of the trap, so you do not fall into it. Listen to your gut feelings. Who do you think is giving you these spiritual 'gut' feelings? It is a good, calming, and secure feeling.

They should always '**be afraid**' or be exceedingly **terrified**. Those who do evil should always be looking over their shoulder experiencing a healthy dose of stress and paranoia. Their minds wondering if they will be brought to justice, killed in a double cross of betrayal, or fall on the field of battle fighting on the wrong side. Fear of retribution should strike the hearts of the wicked; they should not even sleep well in their wickedness. Many say they are not scared of the police but still, run like cockroaches when the lights come on. Say what they may, no reasonable person wants to get caught. A reasonable person or a criminal element works hard not to get caught.

Minister

In the Greek it is Diakonos meaning- run errands, an attendant, teacher, pastor or servant- male or female, also called deacons. These individuals are bound or loyal to the conferring authority, whether government, religious or family institutions. All spheres of society have authority assigned to them, but only government wields lethal force, the sword. Whenever the church has taken it upon them to wield the sword...it's always bad, and not from God.

The servant or minister has a purpose, a specific area of expertise in the body of Christ. Different areas of the Bible list different gifts whether of governments, or wisdom. In 1st Corinthians 12, the people of God or Body of Christ are arranged in areas or callings of special anointing. A warrior serves the state in which the people have granted the authority too officially conduct statecraft. When we take our oaths of service, we become ministers or servants under the authority of our respective branches.

During the revolutionary war, many commanders were pastors.

They closed their churches and went with their parishioners to service in the military. They left one institutional function to serve under another.

Revenger

The Greek is ek-dik-os meaning- to carrying justice out. One who is a punisher an avenger, or revenger. Personal vengeance is revenge. Individuals have no authority to take revenge themselves, that is, taking the matter into your own hands. Taking personal revenge is motivated by selfishness, is often emotionally driven or random, and without checks and balances.

Vengeance belongs to God. One of the ways He executes justice is through government, righteous 'objective' authority. As objective as possible with God-fearing and non-God-fearing people in the administration. Under the Torah (Teaching), a person accused of murder is brought before the judge. Upon investigation, if found guilty are sentenced to death. The closest family member of the victim is appointed as the avenger of blood. They, once a conviction is reached, execute the sentence of death.

If in a fight one person broke an arm or took out an eyeball of another. The matter would go to court. If found guilty a court-appointed person would break the arm, or take out an eye of the offender. Jesus in the Gospels addresses this. He admonishes the rulers for twisting His word and making it ineffectual. Jesus brought up the eye for an eye and life for life scenario from the Teaching. The Teaching is not to be confused with the Law-, which is the Ten Commandments. However, He corrects their 'revenging themselves,' instructing them to personally turn the other cheek.

Turning the other cheek from Matthew 5 and Luke 6 is covered by two Greek words having three meanings. The meanings are sometimes in effect at the same time and in context of culture some time not at the same time. One is being struck by a palm or fist. The other is being struck by a stick or bastinado. The third meaning is being struck with the offense, insulted or lied about. In each instance, Jesus is speaking in the context of personal response to action without authority, an abuse of authority, and to personal retaliation to insults.

The point is not to wrongly react, but too rightly respond. Let the proper authority handle it. If the proper authority is the abuser, then take it to a higher authority, and ultimately possibly God Himself. However, while going up the chain of command authority, you should be praying and taking it to God first. Vengeance is His; He will repay. When we exact personal revenge, this is not justice, but taking His authority upon ourselves. All authority originates with God. When leaders, ministers of His delegated authority abuse it, judgment comes upon the abuser sooner or later. Taking judgment into our own hands, takes it out of God's hand, leaving us on our own. And in our own hand's justice is all to often not served or prevented from being served in this life.

At this point, someone might cry self-defense even though I already included it with the lawful use of lethal force. Biblically this is not taking the sword. When each person's life or family is threatened, they have the authority to defend it with lethal force. The same goes for protecting another who cannot protect themselves. Murder and abuses are unlawful uses of force. It would not make sense to authorize national and local government use of force to intervene in criminal activity and not allow a person to do the same on a personal level.

God's word is not always explicit, but also implicit. You can learn much from an absence of scripture as well as from an abundance. God does expect us to use the brain He gave us. For example, if the word specifically said self-defense on a personal level is authorized. You could conclude since self-defense is authorized at the personal level, it stands to reason defense by law enforcement, or military force is nothing more than self-defense of persons conducted by more than one person on behalf of others. Ultimately you are still defending, protecting, or enforcing someone's right to life, liberty and the pursuit of happiness.

You do have the option too not defend yourself, or an innocent person, some exercise this option. I defend their right to exercise that option. I would not ridicule or cause a person to violate their conscience. There was a Christian warrior, who was a conscientious objector and is a Congressional Medal of Honor awardee. He was a WWII Medic in the Pacific. He swore never to take a life as a Christian, nor carry a weapon even to protect his own life, and never did. His name is Desmond T. Doss. Thou shalt not kill, and honor the Sabbath was unshakable for Doss. His story is on documentary DVD with interviews from those who insulted him, but later saved their lives is amazing. Desmond never put down others for taking up arms; he just felt he couldn't do it himself. The movie Hacksaw Ridge told a small part of the story.

Another Christian was convinced he must take life to serve his nation and protect it. Jesus said to render unto Caesar what is Caesar's and to God what is Gods. This speaks of the civil and religious duty of Christians. He took this to heart as being duty bound to fight. He was a crack shot and courageous. During WW II his exploits in Germany earned him the Medal of Honor also. His name is SGT Alvin C. York. Both men followed their conscience before the Lord, and the Lord honored both men's consciences (1 COR 14:6-8).

Note the individual and family [self-defense only] and governmental institutions have inherent authority to use lethal force. The Church does not have the power to bear the sword. Samuel killed king Agak, only because God ordered King Saul to do it, but he didn't. Elijah ordered the killing of the false prophets according to the Law of Moses although the sentence is not carried out by him. The Vatican and many other religious organizations, congregations and faith groups should remember this. One of the reasons for the founding of America was to escape and prevent abuses of the religious authority abusing its power, monarchs unduly influenced by the Vatican (Papal States), and Anglican Church. Interesting fact. The Founding Fathers choice of Bible is the Geneva Bible with commentary, not King James.

The word for Church in the New Covenant is Ecclesia. Ecclesia means to summon people from their homes (called out ones). They are summoned for a gathering in a public place for specific reasons. In the case of believers, this was to worship. Houses often were the gathering place of believers in the early centuries. Churches as we know they are not bad but did not arrive on the scene until the 4th century A.D. As a Revenger in the Ministry of Vengeance, a function of the Office of Arms you are the called-out ones into this ministry. Have you ever felt like you were born to do what you do? You probably are. As with the preaching ministry, you can also volunteer or be recruited into the ministry, good Ministers of Vengeance are always needed.

Wrath

This in the Greek is or-gay: having a violent passion, a justifiable passionate abhorrence, revulsion, or disgust. Also included are righteous anger or indignation. When you see or hear of an injustice, criminal activity, wickedness, or perversity. When this happens and as the saying goes, your blood boils crying out for retribution and judgement; this is righteous anger. The English words are not exactly interchangeable with vengeance. Acting on your righteous anger,under proper authority, is an act of vengeance.

> "Recompense (reward) to no man evil for evil. Provide things honest in the sight of all men. **If it be possible, as much as lieth in you, live peaceably** with all men. Dearly beloved, **avenge not yourselves**, but rather give place unto **wrath**: for it is written, **Vengeance is mine; I will repay,** saith the Lord. Therefore, if thine enemy hunger, feed him; if he thirst, give him drink: for **in so doing thou shalt heap coals of fire on his head**. Be not overcome of evil, but overcome evil with good" (Rom 12:17-21 em ad).

'Avenging not yourselves' means you are not conducting your own retribution or retaliation against an evil act. Wrath is the hot displeasure, desire for justice, punishment, and retribution against the evil activity. Having wrath at evil is normal. Vengeance is the actual enacting, enforcing, or meting out of punishment for the crime. Satan is ultimately Jesus' responsibility to punish not ours. We are not his Jailer or Punisher. He will get his in due time once he and all his horde of evil spirits are sentenced to the Lake of Fire. Hell was created for the Devil and his angels, not humans; humans are sentenced there because of non-repentance. From the Lake, there is no pardon or escape. Mercy is not giving you what you deserve. Grace is providing you what you do not deserve. Mercy rejoices over judgment. Jimmy Evans, a well-known counselor, puts it like this. "Truth without mercy is mean. Mercy without truth is meaningless." As Ministers of Vengeance mercy is essential for you to exercise when possible.

The Sword

The sword is the symbolic instrument of violence, just or unjust. Judges issue warrants, which officers enforce using the sword. Some say the pen is mightier than the sword. I say the sword is directed by the pen. Without a sword to enforce it, the written word means nothing. Judges do not possess the sword but can direct it. The job is collaborating with the Holy Spirit in a hostile world doing chaos control and cleanup. It is a dirty, violent, horrifying assault on a person's body, soul, and spirit. It is a calling that is necessary and righteous, but ugly and sad. Thank Jesus for His assistance, protections, provisions, and guidance for our body, soul, and spirits.

The first we see the sword mentioned is in the Garden in Eden. The angel's sword is guarding the way to the Tree of Life. It is a dual function. It warns Adam, Eve and all the inhabitants of earth not to attempt to access the Tree of Life. It is off limits as a protective measure, not punitive. The sword is passive. Use of force is only when necessary. The second function is to kill or injure in preventing any attempted access the tree and violate the decree. The first show of lethal force is passive. Clear warnings and understood consequences as the angel stands his post. The second is during an attempted violation, or a violation when lethal action must be taken. There are no exceptions, no hesitation, and no remorse; the law is unbendable.

Ever since Genesis 9:6 and again Romans 12:17-13:4 the authority to wield lethal and non-lethal force, the Sword is in effect. You bear and are commissioned with authority to wield the Sword. The right to keep and bear arms is from the authority of the Sword. Every person has the right to defend themselves against criminals or a corrupt government. No weapons mean no possible resistance to tyranny. No personal weapons would have meant no Revolutionary War and no United States of America.

CHAPTER 6
Battlespace of the Soul

"Let the word of my mouth and the meditation of my heart be acceptable in Your sight, O Lord, my strength, and my Redeemer"(MLB Psalm 19:4).

The Frontline of Asymmetric Warfare

Unlike other chapters where I quote some verses, paraphrase others, and of course, make comments and write information based on Bible verses and outside sources, this chapter is scripture intense. Without faith, it is impossible to please God and get anything done. I want you to know that you know. We're used to calling 'the war on terror' the war without borders, or definitive frontlines, uncommon, irregular, or by the popular term asymmetric. Unlike this is the spiritual war which has a frontline.

All violence for good or evil is a spiritual force at work, prompting or manipulating from the good or the evil. There is a standard frontline in all conflict, the battlespace of the mind. Satan, his fallen angels, and demons want to control or keep your mind busy with thoughts, beliefs, emotions, they want you to express in words and actions which prevent you from being dangerous to them and ineffective for the Lord Jesus; this equates to faithlessness on our part. The opposite is true of the loyal angels.

> "...that he would grant you, according to the riches of His glory, to be strengthened with might through His Spirit in the **inner man**. That Christ may dwell in your hearts grounded in love, may be able to **comprehend** with all the saints what is the **width** and **length** and **depth** and **height**- to know the love of Christ which pass knowledge; that you may be filled with all the fullness of God. (Eph 3: 16-18 NJKV em ad)

In the scripture above the inner man is your spirit, and the Lord wants you to comprehend in your mind, the battle zone, and heart His power. Now think about it, we operate in a four-dimensional space of length, width, height, and time. Time is a dimension which overlaps multiple dimensions. Time is experienced differently in some of these dimensions than how we experience it here. Time is fluid and can be extended or compressed.

So, what is the depth Paul is talking about? It is the unseen dimensions also called heavens connected to what we see and feel in the world. The spiritual realms. Satan operates in the first and second set of heavens. We operate in the first, but also from where Jesus is in the third. Jesus is above all this positionally seated next to the Father who is on His Throne, above in presence and authority all other powers, names, and positions.

> "For we do not **wrestle** against flesh and blood, but against principalities, against powers, against the rulers of the darkness of this age, against **spiritual hosts of wickedness** in the **heavenly places**" (Eph 6:12, NJKV em ad).

The Greek for wrestle is not a scripted fight in a ring for entertainment, whose wrestlers will live to fight another day, in another town. Its root word and meaning refer to fighting to the death for entertainment, or until one of them are maimed and disabled in the fight. The Rulers of the darkness swaying the worldly ways are hell-bent on destroying us with our own ignorance of the higher spiritual rules of engagement. This ends now. No longer does the prophet Hosea's word ring true for readers of this book. "My people are destroyed for lack of knowledge" (Hosea 4:6 NJKV).

Renew, Renew, Renew

We have all fallen prey to the Devil's schemes and brainwashing, the never-ending onslaught of ungodly information. When we went to police training institute (PTI), or basic military training or an agent academy we all had to learn to think and see things differently. This is the way we were trained to do our jobs well and be in tune with our comrades. We had to be deprogrammed from thinking about things, prioritizing situations, and making split decisions as civilians. We had to be reprogrammed from the initial way we were taught about many things; like what we thought leadership was, or what to do when a flare goes off at night. You close your firing eye to protect night vision, seek cover in the shadow, or drop/freeze if in the light so as not to attract attention through movement and watch with your non-firing eye. This is counter to the normal reaction of staring at the flare once it goes off with both eyes. We all learned to think and act in new ways needed to accomplish the mission or jobs we do.

> "I beseech you, therefore, brethren, by the mercies of God, that you present your bodies a living sacrifice, holy, acceptable to God, which is your reasonable service. And to not be conformed to this world, but **be transformed by the renewing of your mind**, that you may prove what is that good and acceptable and perfect will of God." (Rom 12:1-4 NJKV em ad)

Remember renewing the mind is from the Greek word for repentance; metanoia (meta-an-oy-ah). It means to change your mind after the fact, or as an afterthought, once you've reconsidered what you said or did, or are saying or doing. Renewing your mind is about seeing things the Lord's way and handling situations as the word of God teaches you to. Not as a zombie, but carefully, purposefully, and after examining what is good or not before doing or not doing something. God expects you to use the brain he gave you and to work with the Holy Spirit concerning all things.

"Prove (or test) all things; hold fast to that which is good. Abstain from every form of evil" (1 Thess 5:21-22).

You did not learn profanity, gossip, and anger towards anyone, or anything overnight. It will not always go away overnight, though God can do such a thing, He operates typically through a process. Do not get discouraged when you make mistakes; it's a process. Forgive yourself since God forgave you, why or how dare we hold anything against ourselves, Christ on the cross is sufficient. Do not believe the lies of the enemy in your mind saying you are a hypocrite. Hypocrisy is when you pretend to be something you are not. You are being who you are in Christ; you are no hypocrite, you are strengthening your faith, and clearing the muck out of your mind through the process.

Farming for Warriors

Jesus has just spoken the parable of the sower and the seeds to the public. This parable is the cornerstone of them all. In private, the disciples ask Jesus to explain it. The same story has different information spoken in private and public in Matthew. Remember Jesus spoke the same parables and sermons over and over for three years with different audiences. The apostles heard all the versions. These versions included different though not contradictory information. Surely the disciples asked Jesus more than once about this or others when it was heard a little differently. Here is Marks version.

> "And he said unto them, Know ye not this parable? And how then will ye know all parables? The sower soweth the word. And these are they by **the way side**, where the word is sown; but when they have heard, **Satan** cometh immediately, and **taketh away** the word that was **sown in their hearts**" (Mark 4:13-15).

> "And these are they likewise which are **sown on stony ground**; who, when they have heard the word, immediately receive it with gladness; And have no root in themselves, and so endure but for a time: afterward,

> when affliction or persecution ariseth for the word's sake, immediately they are offended" (Mark 4:16-17 em ad).
>
> "And these are they which are **sown among thorns**; such as hear the word, and the cares of this world, and the deceitfulness of riches, and the lusts of other things entering in, choke the word, and it becometh unfruitful." "And these are they which are **sown on good ground**; such as hear the word, and receive it, and bring forth fruit, some thirtyfold, some sixty, and some a hundred" (Mark 4:18-20 em ad).

Matthew chapter 13 and Luke chapter 8 are the other accounts, all with slightly different information.

> "When **any one** heareth the word of the kingdom, and **understandeth it not**, then cometh the **wicked one**, and **catcheth away** that which was sown in his heart. This is he which received seed by the wayside" (Mat 13:19).
>
> "A sower went out to sow his seed: and as he sowed, some fell by the way side; and it **was trodden down**, and the **fowls of the air devoured it**"(Luke 8:5).

The hundredfold return on investment is not a number meaning a hundred times. It is a metaphor for something having the maximum effect possible. Keep in mind as we grow in faith (or fear) the results come faster and stronger for good or evil. The term good ground does not mean good is put into the ground. It symbolizes a heart and soul receptive to one thing or another. Once a person understands, has meditated on, or thought about something over and over it takes root as a mindset, then it begins to produce fruit in the physical world. Fruit is tied to the seed. Whatever you plant will grow and blossom, for good or evil.

How does this work

Everything you hear plants, or attempts to plant a thought, perspective, desire, image, emotion, character building, or self-image destroying mindset. The purpose of these implantations is simple. Get you to buy the product, whether it is soap, sin, or sanctification. The messenger or sower is whoever is sending words, images, thoughts, or philosophies through media, education, sermons, music, and so on. The message being sown may be good; reconcile with your husband, or evil; your alcohol addiction doesn't hurt anyone.' We are easily influenced if we're not paying attention.

> "When modes of music change, the fundamental laws of the state always change with them." - Aristotle

> "I can explain everything better through music. You hypnotize people, and when you get people at their weakest point, you can preach into their subconscious what we want to say." - Jimmy Hendrix

> "Consensus Programming is dangerous to your health; the brainwashed do not know they are being brainwashed." - Wendy O and the Plasmatics, Coup d' Etat album, 1982.

The last quote was purposefully humanly electronically back-masked onto the album. It was not demonically placed or back-masked, and the irony of the truth of what she said being purposefully recorded in a subliminally understood way is not lost. "The brainwashed do not know they are brainwashed" even backmasked and though heard garbled electronically, registers clearly in our unconscious. The forces of Darkness are attempting to brainwash you, numbing your spiritual and natural senses so what is evil is seen as harmless. In many cases, we then begin to see what is good as radical and dangerous, even oppressive and to see evil as good and true. This is a cultural and personal attack on humanity

When your natural and supernatural senses become numb or clouded, the consequences are not visible or detected until its sometimes too late. This is not Karma; there is no Karma or reincarnation. Karma and its' sister systems of belief, are the demonic rip-off of sowing and reaping. The Law of Sowing and reaping can be intentional and is as dependable as the Law of gravity. Just like the law of gravity it is in effect all the time. You may do something stupid or sinful, or experience some strange problems, feel like you're having a run of bad luck, or maybe even seem to never get out of a rut. Nothing is a coincidence. What you say, said about it, and or over something determines the outcome as you believe it in your heart. There is a reason for everything. I don't know them all, but they're there.

Actions stem from emotions (whether you have control of them or your emotions have control over you), which are guided by your thoughts toward the situation. Realize your feelings are God-given, are good, and important, but are also deceptive and easily manipulated. How you feel is often not how things really are. Your feelings or emotional response often lead you to do the wrong thing. On the other hand, our deep passion for our nation and way of life and care for our fellow man, our patriotism, and sense of duty, inspire us to do extraordinary feats and daring in battle, or in a rescue situation.

Your thoughts are controlled by your worldview about the situation. Beliefs are your point of reference in coping or relating to circumstances. Words are the container and clarifiers of our beliefs. Our beliefs dictate our circumstances and responses. Control someone's beliefs, and you control them or free them, depending on what is believed to be true-lies or truth. You will speak what you believe, correct or incorrect as it may be. What humans speak, and fully believe and have faith that what they speak will happen, whether believer or unbeliever it will happen; unless trumped by covenant faith in action. Doubt affects believer and unbeliever equally in destroying what is being believed for.

Why is this so important

Remember death and life are not in the authority of God or the Devil but under our authority. "A man's belly shall be filled with the fruit of his mouth; with the increase of his lips shall he be satisfied. Death and life are in the power of the tongue; and they that indulge it shall eat the fruit thereof" (Pro 18:20-21). And since faith is contained in our words, we must learn to speak the right words and avoid the wrong ones. We must retrain our spirits to receive the good word into the good ground and stop planting or harden our hearts to evil concepts trying to be planted in our spirits.

Faith is a force, and all have a starting supply of it. "For I say, through the grace given unto me, to every man that is among you, not to think of himself more highly than he ought to think; but to think soberly, according to as God hath dealt with every man the measure of faith" (Rom 12:3). Demons will seek to deceive you into using your faith and gifting from God for them. Hebrews chapter eleven is the role call people and their faith in action. Here's an excerpt, my emphasis added.

> "Now faith is the substance of things hoped for (expected not wished), the evidence (proof, physical reality) of things not seen (not seen yet in our reality, but seen spiritually)." (Heb 11:1, NJKV em ad)

"By faith, we understand that the worlds were framed by the word of God so that the things which are seen were not made of the things which are visible." (11:3) This is often misunderstood to mean faith is how we understand. This is not true. We understand God used faith (primal spiritual substance and force) to frame or create the universe.

The process of being led astray and for following the right path is the same. We are dealing with spiritual laws. Laws which apply to every believer and unbeliever alike. These laws operate as dependable as the law of gravity or the law which causes your water to freeze into ice in your freezer. Spiritual laws are higher or supersede physical laws. They co-exist and are naturally occurring. Not knowing a law doesn't exempt you from its effects. Through trial and error, we learned about electricity- how to generate it, protect ourselves from it, and utilize it. The laws of electricity when violated still killed or wounded many people during this trial and error, and even today.

Steps of the Process

Our minds are biological supercomputers which are connected to our spirits. Words, any words, are spiritual for good, or neutral or evil. Neutral appearing words or phrases, are not truly neutral but are detrimental in a different way. The firewall protecting our minds and spirits is our free will, which can block or accept information. What is blocked or not, is based on your knowledge and application of the word of the Lord.

The process of what requests entrance into your heart (spirit) through our mind (soul) and what happens when something (a thought, idea, emotional response...) that is evil, gains access through your firewall is in the book of James. James, the half-brother of Jesus the Lord, the book is nicknamed The How-To Manual of Christianity. The sister scripture to this is the parable of the sower and the seed. The parable of the sower and the seed is the same process with a different description and view of what is going on behind the visible scenes.

James 1:12-15 says- Blessed is the man that endureth temptation: for when he is tried, he shall receive the crown of life, which the Lord hath promised to them that love him. Let no man say when he is tempted, I am tempted of God: for God cannot be tempted with evil, neither tempteth he any man-

1. *But every man is tempted*, -this we know. Jesus underwent every temptation we are faced with, only He remained sinless.
2. *when he is drawn away of his own lust*, -the mind and eyes look/ lust or long after, wants, imagines, is presented with or offered, pressured to partake of or try, or take a specific action. Always it looks to your advantage at first. This is where renewing the mind comes in - you cannot be tempted by what you don't desire. Godly desires are obviously different than ungodly, though without renewal of the mind we often can't tell the difference.
3. *and enticed.* – This is the trap or lure when you bite the hook, are deceived, charmed, or beguiled, and believe the lie. What you meditate on you now are speaking on. Instead of taking captive the thoughts, feelings, cravings, etc., they are taking you captive... you surrender to it.

4. *Then when lust hath conceived,* - it takes root in you, is happening in your mind, becomes a Stronghold or mindset, and eventually a habit, addiction, or natural reaction- only negative and undisciplined. Your spirit like soil wants all seeds planted in it to grow and come to pass, or be put into action.
5. *it bringeth forth sin:* - ready for watering the crops to grow; a plan is in place you are seeking to do or say, follow through with the longing, satisfy the developed hunger. You and the demons are working to make it happen.
6. *and sin, when it is finished,* - completed, fully grown, harvested, allowed to run its full course. Finished means when it is finished with you, not when you want to be finished with it.
7. *bringeth forth death.* – In one form or another, or a combination thereof: socially, spiritually, mentally, physically, and emotionally. There is no place untouched: relationships, at work, some or many aspects of your life can be ended, wounded, severely damaged, become sickly or diseased, and cause pain to others. The fruit is ripe for harvest, and the effect of the process of causes. Death comes in many fashions, not just physical. You can cut your own life short naturally and supernaturally. The opposite is also true.

There are several keys for the warrior in James. You have not committed sin being enticed or presented with the images, thoughts, of a sinful nature and action. Sin does not have to run its entire course, it can be cut off with repentance and pleading the Blood of Jesus over it, applying pertinent scriptures, and of course, changing what you are doing. However, what you say, or do not say, has an effect on everything. Look closer at the process shown above. It is the blueprint for bringing to pass good or evil. The illustration just uses an evil outcome to warn about and show how to avoid evil. It all depends on what you are sowing, or allowing to be sowed in your life.

> "Have faith in God. For assuredly, I say to you, whoever says to this mountain, 'Be removed and be cast into the sea,' and does not doubt in his heart, but believes that those things he says will come to pass, he will have

> whatever he says. Therefore I say unto you, whatever things you ask when you pray, and believe that you receive them, and you will have them."(Mark 11:22-24, NJKV).

In James, it also says you ask and receive not because you ask wrongly with intent to fulfill godless desires or desire something in a godless manner. This qualifier is only applicable when asking something from God. Notice that this spiritual law of believing, speaking and receiving applies to everyone, not just believers. The qualifier whosoever is all-inclusive of humanity and not new.

> "And the Lord said, "Indeed the people are one, and they all have one language, and this is what they begin to do; now nothing that they propose to do will be withheld from them" (Gen 11:6, NJKV).

Here the first human government rebels against God in building the Tower of Babel and refusing to go forth and multiply. It is never completed because the Lord stopped them by creating the multiple ancient languages and imposing them upon the people. You can't build if you can't communicate.

Hundreds of years later after the Hebrews are out of Egypt and in the wilderness, they sent scouts into the Promised Land to spy it out for their attack. Ten spies spoke evil, and the people believed their report. Then the people murmured against God. God had to repent (change His mind or actions) because of **what they said** about not going into the Promised Land, going back to Egypt, and **dying** in the wilderness. The forty years of roaming in the wilderness were waiting until the last of that generation died, **as they spoke over themselves.** Here it is revealed the power of unity and speaking what you believe, even against Gods will. These guidelines are lessons learned from people's mistakes. Seeing the power of believing, speaking and receiving. --- "And all the children of Israel murmured against Moses and Aaron, and the whole congregation said to them, "if only we had died in the land of Egypt! **Or if only we had died in this wilderness**! Why has the Lord brought us to this land to fall by the sword, that our wives and children should become victims? Would it not be better for us to return to Egypt?" So they said to one another, "Let us select a leader and return to Egypt..."(Number 14: 1-4). ---'Say to them, As I live, says the Lord just **as you have spoken in My hearing**, so I will do to you: The carcasses of you who have murmured against Me shall fall in this wilderness, all of you who were numbered, according to your entire number, from twenty years old and above'" (Number 14: 28-29).

> ---"For their heart was not right with him, neither were they steadfast in his covenant. He, being full of compassion, forgave their iniquity, and destroyed them not: yea, many a time he turned his anger away and did not stir up all his wrath. For he remembered that they were but flesh; a wind that passeth away, and cometh not again. How oft did they provoke him in the wilderness, and grieve him in the desert! Yea, they turned back and tempted God, **and limited the Holy One of Israel.** They remembered not his hand, nor the day when he delivered them from the enemy. How he had wrought his signs in Egypt, and his wonders in the field of Zoan: turned their rivers into blood..." (Psalm 78:37-43)

The Holy One of Israel is the Lord Jesus, through the Holy Spirit. They are limited by fear, unbelief, and doubt, just as the enemy is empowered by them. If you do not believe you are called by God to execute the profession of arms, in its many capacities, He will still use you as best He can. But He may not always be able to protect you. Learn and remember what God has done for so many others; the reason I cite so many scriptures is for your strengthening of faith.

What He did for them, in principle and or similar action, the Lord will do for you. The Holy Spirit is the same power today which parted the Red Sea. He is the same power today which raised Jesus from the dead. But, this makes little difference if we are not aligned with how he does things. We limit Holy Spirit power by our unbelief. Without out him, we fight with hands tied behind our backs; we just don't know it. It's time to come unshackled. It's time to take back the ground the enemy has in your mind and take the fight to him. What you say is what you get. The battle is for control of your tongue through shaping your belief to distract you from using or developing your faith. Or worse yet, speaking on behalf of the Enemy unknowingly.

Taking back the battlespace

There are two strategies for retaking control of your life and possibly the lives around you for their safety. On convoy, you had a jamming system which is designed to cause interference between a signal and a remote detonator of an improvised explosive device (IED). One believer praying before a mission allows God to protect most if not all non-believers also on that mission. Keeping them alive and helping them fight is one of the innumerable ways the Lord can facilitate the protection of the Covenant warrior. The first strategy is intervention or interference. Interrupting the process steps from James, so things are not planted, to begin with. The second strategy is to uproot or poison an evil crop to avoid or at least minimize any evil fruit.

> "For though we walk in the flesh, we do not war after the flesh: For the weapons of our warfare *are* not carnal, but mighty through God to the pulling down of strong holds; Casting down imaginations, and every high thing that exalteth itself against the knowledge of God, and bringing into captivity every thought to the obedience of Christ; And having in a readiness to revenge all disobedience, when your obedience is fulfilled"(2 Corinthians 10:3-5).

The revenge of all disobedience pertains to the aggressive attitude we must have toward ungodly thoughts and the spirits behind them. We are not to be passive concerning enemy spirits. An idea, image, philosophy that has presented itself has one of three sources: divine, self, or demonic. Some loosely interpret this to refer to church discipline, which if more churches followed it the Gospel would spread much faster. The harshest punishment for a believer is banishment from fellowship. This is not to be confused with the Catholic tradition of excommunication. No one can sentence another person to Hell.

Ultimately the only sin which sends you to Hell is a rejection of Jesus payment or redemption for your sin, accepting him as your savior. Evil behavior can cause a believer to die physically (sleep). Christians are referred to as asleep in Christ until the resurrection. Death is equated not with physical death, but eternal separation from God. When a believer dies they go to Heaven. When you die as a believer, you will be reunited with your loved ones in Heaven. There are no reunions in Hell.

A special note on my suggestions and examples: I'm not trying to put you under law or in some kind of spiritual bondage with my personal suggestions and examples, actions on contact, illustrations, etc. My personal prayer suggestions now and in later chapters are just to illustrate concepts of praying the word of God in different circumstances. You don't have to follow or repeat what and how I say it exactly. Let the Lord lead you. Start with my suggestions as templates and then speak your own, over yourself.

Actions on Contact

Someone says something wicked stupid to you.

The first thought crossing your mind is yours because you are conditioned to respond a certain way. Maybe it started as a fiery arrow from the enemy trying to influence you to react a certain way, with profanity or vulgarity- which you proceed to say to the individual immediately (there is emotional/mental response memory not just muscle memory). Then you remember you are the righteousness of God in Christ. A covenant warrior of honor. Swallow your foolish pride. Never mind what they said to you, you are the noble soldier, rise above petty squabbles, and let your light shine. You are a Christian, still working on a lousy language habit.

Ask the Lord to forgive you, and then thank Him for it. Praise Him for His forgiveness, and declare this is the last time you use profanity because you are delivered from profanity or evil speech, gossip, slander. You get the picture. Apologize to the person for the way you spoke to them and ask them to forgive you, if the situation allows. They probably will not let you, or not even care, and might laugh or say something else wicked stupid, but you have maintained your integrity and positively witnessed for the Lord. You have also gone one-step closer to full deliverance and cleaning up your foul mouth. When you commit to self-accountability, and hopefully you also have a good accountability partner, this process starts out tough, but by His grace gets easier.

Eventually, you will find your self-awareness of saying something foul, is heightened. The next stage is catching it on the tip of your tongue. After that, you will start catching the thought before reaches your tongue, (before you say it). Next, you will sometimes literally feel the demonic insertion of a view or vulgar response like an arrow going into your mind. Other times it's just your former highly developed answer resurfacing into your mind. Either way, this is where you capture the thought and cast it back out.

When you begin to feel the enemy placing a thought and or image in your mind from the outside, this is a good sign that your soul and spirit are tuning in with the Holy Spirit. If something comes up into your mind from the enemy or yourself- speak to the thought or image. Plead the blood of Jesus over an image to white it out or wipe it out of your mind. Command both the image and the thought to depart from your mind; to be uprooted and cast into the ocean. You cannot fight thoughts with thoughts. You must speak to them, command them. After a while, your firewall or hedge will very seldom even allow a crazy image or thought to get through.

Simulation

- Thought X enters your mind under duress or some other situation.
- If the thought is entertained and mulled over, considered, or meditated on- repent. If it is caught, and evaluated, and cast out, there is no need to repent, as you have not sinned.
- After evaluation reject any ungodly thought or images
- Plead (apply) the Blood of Jesus over image or idea.
- Command X not to take root (from the enemy) or be uprooted (from yourself) and cast into the sea.

- Thank and praise God for the blood of Jesus and power to take captive every thought. Additionally, thank Him for the renewing of your mind and new sensitivity discerning between good and evil.

I do not always do every step consciously, although it is important to work on in the beginning. You do not have to follow this like a wicked spell or something. The point processes Catch, Decide, Respond, Command, and Praise. In the application process, you do not always have to say you apply the blood. I do not always apply the blood, but always respond with the word of God about the thought, taken from Jesus example at the temptations of Satan in the wilderness.

Another point is power and authority. The **power** of the resurrection is from the Holy Spirit, who raised Jesus from the dead. The **authority** to call upon, or expect Holy Spirit or holy angelic assistance is in the name of Jesus. His name is above every name and every named thing. Jesus name is not magic it is authority and power. Invoking His name apart from His will, expressed in His word is useless. Jesus rejected and cast out each temptation of the Devil by responding with the truth of the Scriptures which applied to the situation.

Another example:

- Thought X (some angry emotion, or angry expression)
- I say "I take that thought captive in the name of Jesus" then I say, or I just skip to this part "the wrath or anger of man works not the righteousness of God" a quote from James.
- Then I may say, also to myself under my breath, or if I cannot speak, repeat it in my mind; 'the wrath of God works not…' Then I cast the thought out verbally, and may say "therefore I will not act upon this anger." I (and you will be too) am empowered of the Holy Spirit after declaring the scripture to submit to what it says to do. The Holy Spirit empowers through the spoken word of God. Early in my walk, I would quote the word over my thought, and not feel like submitting to it, just quoted it because it was true, but I still felt like doing something else. I would ask the Holy Spirit to help me not only want to be obedient but empower me to obedience. He will; He loves you. Trust Him.

Locker Room Evangelism

Do not go around telling everyone to not curse around you etc. You are not the profanity police. Do not turn judgmental toward them making faces or remarks about their conduct. It is not your place to judge non-covenant people. Politely, do not participate in evil jokes, speech, and gossip. Offline, when appropriate, when the opportunity comes in the natural course of a conversation, mention you would like people to **try** not to use the Lord's name in vain around you. Any person who does, say nothing, let the Holy Spirit handle it. Your anointing will draw out people's true self for good and evil. If they hate Jesus they will surely hate you, for His spirit, the Holy Spirit is in you.

The reason you choose to draw a line in the sand with using God's name in vain is that it carries a particular warning from the scriptures. Whoever takes his name in vain will not be held guiltless. While other curses and cursing are bad, the Lord's name is in a category all its' own. Remember we are not the profanity police. The world will speak as it speaks, we've all been there. Don't get offended no matter what is said; it is what it is.

Some people will get worse on purpose, pray for them privately while disregarding their remarks publicly at that time. Many will catch themselves by using profanity and apologize. This is respect for God through you. Be sure each opportunity to thank them for apologizing and trying not to use his Name or profanity. Let them know you appreciate it. Your witness, shining His light just got brighter through sincerity. You emphasize - to try- so as not to put them under a lawful spirit for the strength of sin is the law. You will be setting them up for failure if you do not focus on trying or attempting. If you demand they watch their mouths explicitly or implicitly, you will look judgmental (because you are judgmental if such is the case) and not represent Jesus well.

I did this for years on active duty and on every field problem one or two of my fellow soldiers would approach me asking to pray to receive Jesus as their savior. I'm not saying this will happen to you. I am saying as a Christian, a Covenant Warrior, we owe it to the Lord, those around us, and ourselves to take a positive stand for Jesus.

Tearing up a bad harvest

The trees and mountains symbolize multiple things depending on the context or type of tree. The fig tree which dried up from the roots after Jesus cursed it. Jesus taught on the demonstration of power and authority.

> "Assuredly, I say to you, if you have faith and do not doubt, you will not only do what was done to the fig tree but also if you say to this mountain, 'Be removed and be cast into the sea, it will be done. And all things whatever you ask in prayer, believing, you will receive" (Matt 21:21-22 NJKV).

> "So the Lord said, "If you have faith as a mustard seed, you can say to this mulberry tree, 'Be pulled up by the roots and be planted in the sea,' and it would obey you"(Luke 17:6, NJKV).

In context, here the trees are thoughts, images, and strongholds of behaviors that are wicked. They also represent our perspectives on situations, which seem impossible to be fixed. You can command a seed to die and not come to fruit, drying up from the root. You can command imaginations, thoughts, etc. to be gone from your mind, cast out like the mulberry tree. A mustard seed is smallest in its class and is unalterable. Our faith is to be the kind God has when He speaks he believes, and it happens. Having faith in God's word is also having faith that your faith-filled words, God's words will come to pass.

Out loud, alone or with a trusted prayer partner speak to the stronghold, whatever it or they are, repent asking forgiveness for speaking/doing whatever. Then apply the blood over its' power over you declaring you are now free (repeat these if you fall back, just get back up and keep fighting in the new mindset). And command that any words you have spoken regarding those issues and any words remembered or not (words are spirit and continue until they come to fruit or are plucked up/destroyed) commanding them to all fall to the ground. This phrase means to be canceled and no longer attempt to come to pass. Then speak that you cancel a word when you catch yourself misspeaking.

You are retraining your spirit to bring to pass all you say and learning only to say what you mean, and what is in line with the word of the Lord. The reason many people speak evil and it happens so quickly is because we have believed for it, and developed our faith/fear to the point, that when a negative thing is spoken is happens quick, by the hand of the enemy. We need to stop this, and re-develop our faith and spirit to bring forth what is good, not evil- quickly.

CHAPTER 7

Fighting Mindset

You follow orders wearing your body armor and helmet into conflict. You are qualified with one or more weapons systems, knowing when, and how to use them effectively. Putting on your physical armor and trusting in your training is an act of faith in the men who designed and tested the physical weapons and armor and developed your training. Your faith is placed in the word of a human that the protective gear and weapons systems, when it all breaks loose will perform as promised. Food for thought is that all the substances and combinations of substances which make up our armor and weapons come from raw materials and elements which the Lord created by and with faith - the primal essence and force.

> "…'In righteousness, you shall be established; you shall be far from oppression, for you shall not fear; and from terror, for it shall not come near you. Indeed, they shall surely assemble, but not because of Me. Whoever assembles against you **shall fall for your sake**. Behold, I have created the blacksmith who blows the coals in the fire, who brings forth an instrument for his work; and I have created the spoiler to destroy. **No weapon formed against you shall prosper**, and every tongue which rises against you in judgment you shall condemn. This is the heritage of the servants of the Lord, and **their righteousness** is from Me' [yours and my righteous

> standing before the Father because of Jesus qualifying us], says the Lord" (American Patriots Bible NJKV, Isaiah 54:14-17 em ad).

The second is the attacks of the enemy. It is a war, there are and will be casualties, but these can be drastically limited in our personal as well as professional lives. Make no mistake our Enemy, who is behind our enemies, is supernaturally intelligent, exceedingly powerful, and has been around since before humanity. He knows the system laws of the universe; we're learning them. Don't be hard on yourself. Imagine the payoff once you are on the same track as the Lord. Victory over the Enemy, and our enemies at a remarkably reduced cost to us. We are trained not to give up when things do not go as expected. Lessons learned is in the spiritual aspect of war and life as it is in the physical. Don't blame the Lord and don't give up.

If you are going to be mad, be mad at the Enemy and his forces. Attacks from the Enemy never stop. They only subside and return at opportune times. His most vicious attacks come when you first start on the way of the Covenant Warrior. When Satan experiences a defeat, he often does one or both of two things. He launches a swift and vicious counterattack designed to regain immediately lost ground, or he strategically withdraws for a more opportune time. These attacks target you personally and professionally through and aiming at friends and family, even using strangers in your life. The enemy literally has no heart, no mercy, and no compassion.

We are on the offensive, taking back our lives and helping others reclaim their lives, protecting them, even if it means killing another. Remember, Satan as powerful as he is, is terrified of Lord Yeshua (Jesus). Satan is terrified of you learning and exercising your covenant rights and power. All Satan's moves since Jesus rose from the dead, are defensive attacks and sneak attacks designed to thwart God's plan for all our lives.

Holy Spirit will instruct you in the purposes and use of His armor and weapons, in conjunction with physical, financial, and intellectual assets, training, and education provided in this world. The mission is to retake territory occupied by the enemy. Retake, retain, and aggressively obtain more. To expand Gods influence through you to the benefit of all around you; on and off the battlefield. You cannot help others if you are always in need yourself. You are anointed and ordained too lawfully use authority to bless, help, and protect your nation and its people from all enemies within and without; human and demonic.

Your Spiritual Armor

The armor gives us the spiritual knowledge and the focus we need to help guard our spirit, soul in the decision-making process, hear God and operate by faith and not from our senses.

> "Finally, my brethren, be strong in the Lord, and in the power of his might" Ephesians (Eph) 6:10.

The power and might here are the authority of the believer (being strong in the Lord) for domineering use of His raw and extreme power. Also, remain aware our strength is in His power and might, not ours. Jesus power turned the tables on the Enemy [Ephesian's 4:8] and stripped them to nothing [Colossians 2:15] for the believer who believes and receives. This is the power and authority of the resurrection and ascension. This strength is not only mental, emotional, spiritual strength, but as needed for the dual role of the Revengers, includes physical strength and prowess with weapons.

> "Put on the whole armour of God, that ye may be able to stand against the wiles of the devil" (Eph 6:11).

Self-explanatory, this armor must be put on. We are not to give place or a foothold to the Devil. The place he wants is a foothold in our mind. We are to be aware he has schemes against us. The wiles are the Devils plans against us. Satan cannot accomplish these objectives if we win the war in our hearts and minds, the real battlefield. Sure, there is the physical battlefield, but you must be victorious in the spirit, too be exceeding victorious on the streets and during combat operations. To stand is to hold your ground and not give an inch. Actively thinking, speaking, believing, and dwelling on what is right and good.

> "Finally, brethren, whatsoever things are true, whatsoever things are honest, whatsoever things are just, whatsoever things are pure, whatsoever things are lovely, whatsoever things are of good report; if there be any virtue, and if there be any praise, **think on these things**" (Philippians 4:8).

Generally speaking, having a constant awareness of your identity in Christ, and His love for you that it will never fail helps to cast down and out the spirit of fear(s), unbelief, and doubt. All three try to say you're someone who you are not, and try to make you see yourself apart from Christ. To drag us back to an identity from our past instead of identifying with Jesus and our future.

> "Wherein in time past ye walked according to the course of this world, according to the prince of the power of the air, the spirit that now worketh in the children of disobedience: Among whom also we all had our conversation in times past in the lusts of our flesh, fulfilling the desires of the flesh and of the mind; and were by nature the children of wrath, even as others" (Eph 2:2-3).

A godly military perspective virtually lost among most is in Jude, Zechariah 3:1-4, and 2 Peter 2: 9-11. A snapshot of conflict between celestial also categorized extraterrestrial, beings Satan and Michael. Do not be confused. Extraterrestrial means merely not originating from Earth, 'terra firma' or terrestrial like us humans. Interaction with the enemy is not one of reverence, as unto the Lord, but with respect to position and power of the enemy. This does not equal fear of, agreement with or worship of the Enemy, just acknowledgment.

Satan is the commanding enemy general and king. When the Lord Himself, as depicted in Job, speaks it is still respectfull, even to Satan. Not because he must per se, but because its reflective of His character. In Jude Satan and the Archangel Michael, the Chief Prince and Commanding General of all the loyal angels, are contending. Michael speaks sternly and firmly, yet respectfully not profanely, and not using derogatory, demeaning or disrespectful words. This is an angel reflecting the character of God. This is the Covenant Warriors cue to do the same. This self-control, temperance, or meekness demonstrated throughout scripture by the Lord, His angels, and human prophets is powerful. A principle we should sincerely imitate. God honors the honorable.

How should we speak of all our enemies? Always speak courteously and respectfully. The Lord God is not impolite, even to the vilest of creatures. Neither should we be. Being polite and respectful, not endorsing or bowing to them, is action exercised from a position of strength and power, not weakness. Satan and his ilk are disrespectful to all, but the Lord face to face. They fear Him exceedingly. "Thou believest that there is one God; thou doest well: the devils also believe, and tremble" (James 2:19). They are terrified of Him.

> "Wherefore take unto you the whole armour of God, that ye may be able to withstand in the evil day, and having done all, to stand" (Eph 6:13).

1Peter 5:8 depicts the enemy at a roaring lion roaming, seeking whom he can devour. He is looking for a breach in the hedge of protection, some weakness in our defenses (our lack of knowledge our covenant status and rights, our insecurity, or inferiority) to exploit. Putting on the mindset of *who you are, a beloved son or daughter* of the Lord's. Putting on the mindset armed with the truth of God's word, described through a Roman soldier's armor. It is an act of our will, to depend on His promises based on who you are, in Christ.

Time to Gear Up

> "Stand therefore, having your loins girt about with **truth**, and having on the breastplate of **righteousness**"(Eph 6:14) ;

Truth is knowing and believing what God says about a situation is what it is. Not what it looks or feels like, but what He says it is. Remember the Holy Spirit has the only perfect, unclouded information about what everyone and everything in the universe is thinking, plotting, doing, desiring, etc. He is the true source of accurate information to base our decisions, laws, and social dynamics. Remember that spiritual laws supersede or trump the physical.

Truth is worn as a belt, which connects and secures other pieces of the armor together. You must know the truth about yourself and your situation from the study of God's word, and fellowship with the Holy Spirit, then put it into action. Jesus said to know the truth, and it shall make you free. Truth is what holds all the armor together just as the loin belt held the Roman soldier's armor together.

Without knowledge of the truth of something, you cannot have faith in it and apply it accordingly. Hosea said 'My people are destroyed for lack of knowledge.' The idea of standing is not reactive; it's responsive. It is awaiting an expected attack or counterattack of the enemy. It is a steadfast preparation not to lose any ground taken, nor to back off during the aggressive process of retaking more territory.

Righteousness is about knowing you deserve all Heaven has to offer through the Renewed Covenant because, regardless of the mistakes we make, we are forgiven. They are forgotten by God and paid for back at the Cross before you were born. You are always in right standing spiritually because Jesus righteousness and right standing with the Father is credited to you as a believer. Your recreated spirit is pure (having Jesus nature, not Satan's), cannot sin, and is sealed by the Holy Spirit Himself. It is untouchable. We cannot even screw it up. You have a covenant right to expect God too not only want to help you, but He seeks to help you. Not because of our righteousness, this is counted as filthy, or bloody rags. But, because of the Lord Jesus' righteousness, his work on the cross only, not at all on our merits. This is great news because we cannot mess it up. This is who you are; your identity is in Christ, not who or what other people say you are. Including the voice of the enemy attempting to disqualify you from what Jesus permanently qualified you for.

Righteousness protects your heart or spirit, this permanent standing before God is your identity point of reference. A critical truth you must understand. Know you are the righteousness of God in Christ, in right standing with God, having covenant rights based on Jesus work on the cross, **not** our works - good or evil.

He will perform all things for you- because of your status and faith, not based on your current issues, nor your church attendance lack of attendance. Not because you stopped cussing, or drinking, or sleeping around. All those effect fellowships and carry good and bad consequences, but do not define your right standing with the Father. Your **permanent covenant relationship** is based upon Jesus: thoughts, actions, obedience, sacrifice, resurrection, ascension, and acting as our High Priest and Advocate with the Father- His God and Father, who in Him is also our God and Father. Your status is righteous and pure. God always has a good opinion of you through the Blood payment of His Son. By grace, you've been saved and not of your own works.

How God sees you in and because of Jesus Christ, this never changes, it's how you see yourself, which causes the problem. Our wrong personal perceptions decide how we believe and speak in line with or out of alignment with God's word. Wearing the Helmet of salvation is not merely 'knowing' you are saved. It is walking like a prince or princess- a beloved son or daughter of the King with all the benefits- and responsibilities- of such. Your status is by grace alone. This is the knowledge and power of grace in your life to motivate, transform, and empower you NOT to want to sin (removes sinful desires), and the empowerment NOT to sin, but overcome a temptation.

"And your feet shod with the preparation of the gospel of **peace**"(Eph 6:15); Peace is the understanding God loves you, cannot be angry with you, and the confidence to endure hardship. He endures with you, feels it with you, knows your pain, and is in it with you. Holy Spirit doesn't just lead and empower you; Jesus experiences your pain with you. You are loved and understood. Stand your ground; you are not alone. Do not quit. The victory is sure, do not doubt. This quiet confidence is released by the Holy Spirit into your heart and soul enabling you to be calm, during the chaos, and disaster, **supernaturally** knowing He is with you, and its truly going to be all right. Hold your head up high. You are an ambassador/ soldier of the Kingdom. You are no joke, and the Enemy knows it. The question is- do you know it?

The Roman soldier's shoe is a metal greave protecting the shins and knees attached to a special shoe. It had spikes on the bottom from 1 to 3 inches long. Great to hold your ground, with each step also forward. These spikes enabled you to crush and decimate an enemy beneath your foot. As with most armor, it has defensive and offensive capabilities. The schemes of the Devil try to create crisis and chaos in our hearts and minds, through circumstances, to discourage and distract us from the presence of His love and peace. His peace directed to rule or umpire our hearts enables us to pray, speak, think and receive effectively in the middle of chaos.

Reference this yourself to Hebrews 3 and 4. Be aware when some translation says 'Jesus' instead of Joshua. It is referring to General Joshua and the children of Israel entering the physical Promised Land of Israel. Joshua and Jesus are common names and pronounced the same Yeshua. Spelling is sometimes different and confuses people. This is why when we refer to Jesus the Son, it is commonly Jesus of Nazareth or some other such additional title identifier.

This is our free will submitting to God in crisis and frustration. God, in turn, empowers us too 'remain calm and return fire.' This is us in Him resisting the Devil. Also, this is then the Devil fleeing from us. If there is not free will submission, there is no real resistance, no fleeing Devil. This is the only thing a Christian is ordered to do as a work- this is the 'laboring' into His rest. It is ceasing from striving ourselves, but trusting in and following His leading. This peace is beyond understanding, but experientially real [see Philippians 4:7] fruit of the Holy Spirit.

> "Above all, taking the **shield** of **faith**, <u>wherewith</u> ye shall be able to quench all the fiery darts of the wicked" (Eph 6:16).

Faith is the power of the punch. It is the grease in the wheels. It is the substance of that which is already seen, the material for building and bringing into being (from the spiritual dimension into the physical dimension) what is not seen; except as seen in a promise of God. Faith is substance and faith is an extremely powerful force, able to be aimed or directed. Faith as a shield is a great illustration. The shield is the

Roman shield, which covers wide and long from head to toe, for complete coverage. Additionally, in some Roman attack formations, shields were held in such a fashion as to protect from above and behind. In the spirit, the shield is a sphere of God's favor. The Roman shield needed daily maintenance to keep it from drying out and becoming easy to break. This meant daily applications of oil to the multilayered leather shield. "If the Roman soldier wanted to live a long life, it was imperative for him to pick up that vial and apply the oil to his shield every single day of his military life" (Renner, 2007, Dressed to Kill: a Biblical Approach to Spiritual Warfare and Armor). This is the picture of faith needing a refresher or anointing for each day. As the Lord says "give us this day our daily bread…." This is daily fellowship with the Holy Spirit and study of the word.

"Faith that is ignored nearly always breaks and falls to pieces during a confrontation with the enemy" (Renner, 2007 em ad). The attacks of the enemy will come as the very flammable arrows of old. They would explode on a shield on impact in an attempt to render it useless. For this reason, professional soldiers of old soaked their shields in water before battle. The shield of Faith must always be soaked in the confessed word. The confessed word is the homologeo (Hom-ol-og-eh-o) or saying the same thing as God says. We must soak ourselves in the word renewing our minds. This would then quench the otherwise extremely dangerous and volatile arrows of the enemy. Interestingly the word dunamia is translated 'shall be able.' This word means the power to, or not to, be able to do something. Of note is the Kings English 'wherewith' is more accurately translated 'by which.'

Renner's translation of this verse helps bring out the meaning to the original readers. His portion of the verse reads " …By use of this shield, you will have explosive and dynamic power…" Wow, the combination of water saturation (the Word of God) and application of the anointing oil (power of the Holy Spirit) creates a formidable and versatile shield. No wonder it is written His favor encompasses us as a shield (Psalm 5:12). This encompasses completely from all directions, dimensions, and relations. The shield, besides absorbing and rendering powerless the initial attack, also has an attribute, which retaliates to attacks upon it.

The dual use of God's spiritual shielding is far superior to physical armor and shielding. It seems similar to reactive armor on Russian tanks which reduced the effectiveness of the incoming round. The Shield of Faith has an immediate, almost reflexive counter strike feature. This auto counter strike is executed on our behalf. One of God's promises to Abraham and his descendants is the physical Israel and spiritual Israel (the Body of Christ) is He will curse those who curse us... This is God's promised response to an attack against us. A curse is an empowerment to fail or removal of protection from intended harm.

> "And take the **helmet** of **salvation**, and the sword of the Spirit, which is the word of God"(Eph 6:17):

Salvation is knowing and believing in all the benefits of his/her righteous granted status. You can have on all the body armor, but without the Helmet, you are missing a vital piece. Many Christians **scarcely** wear **only** their Helmet. They know they are saved and going to Heaven... that's about the extent of their understanding of their salvation and God's goodness. They are reactive, not proactive. The other pieces operate based on this one. Without this one, the consciousness of the **Covenant relationship** to God, your **status** in Christ, armor, and weapons <u>will not work to their full potential</u>. The enemy and his power are under our authority on the Earth. When Principalities with Adam's authority in the Earth tried to drown Jesus, he spoke to the winds and the rain, not to the demonic powers controlling them. "Jesus authority over the Earth is greater than Satan's authority. Therefore, He did not have to address the principalities. The Earth responded to a higher authority than the demonic command"(Jackson, John Paul, 2013, Needless Casualties of War).

> "Behold I give unto you the power (in Greek its <u>exousia</u> or authority) to tread upon serpents and scorpions and over all the power (in Greek its <u>dunamis</u> or miraculous raw power) of the enemy and nothing shall be any means ever hurt you" (Luke 10:19 em ad).

Where there is no authority, there is no backup. Since Jesus' becoming sin, and a curse on our behalf (the penalty of breaking the Law), descent into Hell, resurrection, and ascension to Heaven. He was able to obtain all authority from the depth of one to the height of the other, and every dimension in between. Jesus authority is delegated to all who believe in Him. "And Jesus came and spake unto them, saying, All power [this is the Greek word exousia meaning authority] is given unto me in heaven and in the earth. Go ye, therefore," (Mat 28:18-19a)... This authority, and the Holy Ghost power in you and the angelic assistance around you is available through faith.

Your **perceived** status or standing with God changes like the wind. It is **your opinion**, how you **feel**, what you said, did wrong last night, or in the last twenty minutes. Enemy thoughts shot into your mind to confuse, depress, distract, and cause you to condemn yourself. This condemnation and guilt are <u>from Satan, not God</u>.

It is a departure from the reality of your **unchangeable status**- God's permanently good opinion of you- your breastplate of righteousness! A fact, which kept conscious of, kept in the forefront of your mind, enables you to have faith in all the parts of the armor- release your faith for them and receive. A key to receiving from God is in giving glory to God. Glory in this context, of its many definitions, is having a good opinion of God, that He will do it for you because God loves you. You are **pre-qualified** for healing, protection, etc., because of Jesus perfect life. You are beloved, favored, and entitled to all the benefits of Heaven.

You are **never disqualified** because of your sins, or mistakes made in this life. However, if you are not conscious of your status, you will disqualify yourself with fear, unbelief, and doubt. In some cases, we disqualify ourselves because unbelief or doubt says the Lord, might not, will not, or cannot make good on promises; not having a good opinion of the Lord. This is the attack on your mind. Active use of the Helmet is casting down imaginations, and casting out doubt, fear, and unbelief. All the armor interrelates and interconnects. Realizing how much the Lord loves you is key to being able to wear your breastplate and Helmet effectively.

> "And take the helmet of salvation, and the **sword** of the **Spirit**, which is the **word** of God"(Eph 6:17):

The Sword is our spoken, applied or declared the word of God in faith, up close and personal. The Spirit's sword or sword of the Spirit is His intervention. God's sword is larger than our sword, wielded on our behalf when ours is not enough. Our Sword is the up close and personal Roman short sword. The Amplified Bible says "the sword which the Spirit wields." Scholars, preachers, and researchers should pray and consult multiple translations before preaching or writing on this. There are several ways to translate into English. Worth mentioning: remember in English, Greek and Hebrew a phrase or word in different context can mean more than one thing at the same time. This is not a contradiction, its a coexistent reality. Holy Spirit is working with and through us.

The Romans and other foreigners spoke Latin and Greek. Some spoke all three of course. Jesus is a Jew, who spoke to His fellow Jews in Hebrew, though the Holy Spirit inspired the writers of the New Testament to write in Greek to enable greater and easier distribution and understanding of the His word. Jesus may have spoken all three languages. Written above Him on the cross is the charge against Him, in Latin Greek and Hebrew so all could read and understand why Jesus or any 'criminal' was being executed. The sword, being God's word spoken by us or wielded by the Spirit is very powerful.

> "For the word of God is quick (meaning alive or living), and powerful, and sharper than any two-edged sword, piercing even to the dividing asunder of soul and spirit, and of the joints and marrow, and is a discerner of the thoughts and intents of the heart"(Hebrews 4:12). Note: this is the power of speaking God's word in faith.

Other translations have it as the Spirit's sword. The rich and exciting, thing about Greek and Hebrew languages is the multiple complimentary meanings to some phrases. One such concurrent meaning is in Mark 11:22 "And Jesus answering saith unto them, "Have faith in God." This phrase has the dual meaning of also having the faith of God.

> "**Praying always** with **all prayer** and supplication **in the Spirit**, and watching thereunto with all perseverance and supplication for all saints" (Eph 6:18);

Here is a new weapons system classification for modern believers. It is not new to ancient believers but is rediscovered. In my personal studies and research, I found it only in Rick Renner's Dressed to Kill. It makes perfect sense since we speak and pray the word, sending it out to accomplish its purpose. The **seventh piece** of the Roman soldier's armament is the **Lance of prayer**. This is actually in the plural sense seeing there are various types of prayer for various situations. **Lances** are the range attack weapons of prayer similar to javelins or spears. Speaking is powerful. It knows no limits to its range; its effective range is the world. Distance is not a factor, but timing is.

What you say either God's word or the Enemy's word, designates which sword or the effectiveness of the lance you are using, or not using. This is the difference between cutting a swath through the enemy and the Enemy (or enemies) cutting you down. Both are powered by your perceptions of the truth, one clear the other deceptive. God, the Holy Spirit, and His angels operate with our best interest at heart. Satan attempts to rip your heart out and eat it while it still beats.

God 'sends' His word of protection, healing, or other such thing and it does not return void (almost like a boomerang instead of a missile or lance) but accomplishes what it is sent to. God fires arrows of His own. The fact there are actually seven not six pieces of Roman gear. This would be common knowledge to believers at the time of writing. The seventh is also plural - types of prayer. A Roman soldier carried and had available to him different types of lances for different situations. There is one type carried at the ready.

The Amplified Bible puts it like this- 'Pray at all times (on every occasion, in every season) in the Spirit, with all (manner of) prayer and entreaty. To that end keep alert and watch with strong purpose and perseverance, interceding on behalf of all the saints (God's consecrated people).' An application like this of the word of the Lord is a lance launched out at the enemy. This is a ranged attack, whereas other applications are for close quarters combat, up close and personal physically and spiritually in the battle zone of your mind. This is where the sword(s) come into play. This reveals the multiple uses of different scriptures, depending on the situation- covering all situations imaginable, and some we can't imagine until we need it. Praying and sending a Lance at the enemy may result in the Spirit using His large two-handed sword against them in the distance- He fights for you, buffering you.

> "And for me, that utterance may be given unto me, that I may open my mouth boldly, to **make known the mystery of the gospel**" (Eph 6:19),

Paul requests intercession and petition that he might continue to have an open door or platform to speak and witness of the truth and demonstrate the power of the Gospel. Ultimately, all conflict is about keeping the Light of the Gospel of salvation and fellowship with God out of a region, group, people, family, or an individual's knowledge and grasp. Freedom only exists as much as the Gospel is known and the manifest presence of Holy Spirit is. Where the Spirit is, there is Liberty. It is no mystery why, as documented in the historical public record, that our founding Fathers incorporated much prayer to the Lord, and many principles and verbiage from the Bible, in constructing our founding documents founding our Nation upon Christian principles. They credited the U.S. Constitution as anointed and crafted through prayer.

> "For which I am **an ambassador in bonds**: that therein I may speak boldly, as I ought to speak" (Eph 6:20).

Paul is declaring, after requesting assistance from fellow believers to unleash their lances of intercessory prayer on his behalf (a spiritual request for fire support). He is declaring, encouraging himself in the Lord, reminding them and himself he is a representative of the Kingdom of Heaven in a hostile foreign Kingdom- the people under the darkness of the god of this world. He is the Lord's bondservant, knowing he must be valiant regardless of opposition. This is the result of boldness in faith and expectation based upon God's love for you; walking in the miraculous power and grace of the Lord Jesus, making a difference at multiple levels for multitudes of people.

Just as you are an ambassador for the military under sworn oath and accountable for your actions, so too are you an ambassador for Jesus, a soldier of faith. The bonds Paul refers too here and in other places is as an indentured servant, though no one is compelled by the Lord. Instead, Paul is compelled by his appreciation and awe of Gods' love and power. Paul is so intimate in his relationship with the Lord that he couldn't imagine a life apart from Him. This is a mental and spiritual dedication and loyalty, voluntary. Just as we are loyal to our nation, so Paul is loyal to the Kingdom of Heaven, even more so.

Back to the Belt

The belt is neither offensive or defensive, but what all the rest of the armor is connected to holding it together. Other parts of the armor, such as the Breastplate are dual use. A shining breastplate reflects the sun, if behind an enemy, back into his eyes blinding him. Jesus said you should know the truth and it will make you free. Remember, this is operative, it must be put into action, applied. If you do not apply and practice, and sharpen your skill in the word, it will not make you free, and the rest of your armor may not function properly. You will simply be a warrior with a lot of knowledge, but no skill in putting that knowledge to any good use. You've noticed I repeat some things, but this is to drive home certain foundational points.

Recognizing one thing is a fighter jet, another a taser, or rifle, and have read about or seen some people fly, or shoot these, doesn't mean you're qualified to fly or shoot these yourself. You must learn, train, practice, practice, and practice some more, then do it, again, and again. You are learning on a personal and larger scale, use during your force on force training. Not so you can actually hurt your acting red or blue forces training with you (God won't allow that), but to learn to ask and receive from God during training and education preparing you for the real-world situation.

Know scriptures by heart, there's no time to look them up during a fight, and Bibles aren't handy if captured. Develop your faith, let the

Holy Spirit and the angels train with you, just as you train with your fellow warriors. Train like you fight. You won't be able to fight with the Lord as well if you do not train with the Lord. Make your mistakes and experience more lessons learned in training, than on the field of battle. Surely you will do both, but less during a fight means more victories and fewer casualties.

> "A pint of sweat saves a gallon of blood" Gen. George S. Patton Jr.

COVENANT WARFARE

CHAPTER 8
Cold Hearted Prayer

"And let us not grow weary while doing good, for in due season we shall reapif we do not lose heart" (Gal 6:9, NJKV).

There is a time for peace and a time to be relentless in pursuit of victory over evil. The lances of prayer hurled at the enemy and on behalf of our allies and friends should, paraphrasing from the 300, darken the sky so to speak. Only instead of shade, it will be the mighty word and blood of Jesus raining down on them. Lances (not the kind used in jousting), javelins or throwing spears are range attack weapons. Prayer (the lance in spiritual armor) is a spiritual range attack weapon. Their range is across dimensions, physical distances, and time.

There are Lances of intercession, the praying on behalf of someone, and the most common type of prayer, petitions or requests for something. There also are Lances which are preemptive. For example, these are prayers before a mission, deciding on and development of an operation, or speaking the blessing over your children. All operate by grace through faith. Fear is a perversion of, or wrong motivation releasing and misdirecting the force of faith. Fear is contaminated faith. What you have peace for or fear about is likely to happen according to the Law of Faith. What you focus on you empower. We will only be looking at three lances - declaration, agreement, and the imprecatory prayer.

Lances of Declaration and Agreement

A declaration is when you speak the word of God over a pending situation. Praying about having the courage and not being harmed before a mission, or part of your daily prayers in a combat zone. It is speaking boldly then thanking God for doing it before it is needed. Assume the sale. This is boldness of faith which God adores. Servants are unsure, but sons and daughters decree with boldness, knowing their fathers love for them, that He honors His word.

This is how favor at work in relationships, healing, raising the dead, being bulletproof, or walking on water (two people have done this the Lord Jesus and Peter) works by faith. Peter had faith, then was distracted, taking his attention and faith away from Jesus. The storm began to intimidate him **after** he was already walking on water with Jesus. The Red Sea parted for Moses, and the Jordan river was parted three times, once forty years later when the children of Israel crossed over into the Promised Land. Then once for Elijah and Elisha. All these miracles are done by faith.

> "And the LORD said, Behold, the people are one, and they have all one language; and this they begin to do: and **now nothing will be restrained** from them, which **they have imagined** to do."

The principle of unity is important. Jesus also said where two or more are gathered I am in the midst of them, and if two or three agree on something on Earth it will be done of the Father in Heaven, manifesting on the Earth. Unity among followers of the Enemy is apparently essential. Therefore, the reverse lesson is unity among believers is also crucial. Unity, agreement in a declaration empowers the decree. Consequently, the Lance of the prayer of agreement is very powerful. Agreement among believers for God's will to be done on Earth, Jesus promised it would be done of the Father in Heaven. Satan understands the power of this Lance and works to keep you from finding a prayer partner(s) to get with before starting missions, important meetings, etc.

Another description of faith is of dynamite (Copeland K. How Faith Works CD set). A person uses dynamite to blow out a tree stump. The person is credited with the stump removal, even though it was his understanding of the power and way to use a stick of dynamite. He may or may not know the chemical composition, or the way dynamite is manufactured, or even why it does what it does. But he knows if he digs a hole next to the stump, or drills one in it. Then places the stick of dynamite into the hole and lights the fuse Kaboom! The force of the explosion removes or disintegrates the stump.

> "Bless the LORD, ye angels of His, ye mighty in strength, that fulfill His word, hearkening unto the voice of His word" (Psalm 103:20 JPS).

By our words, **spirits** are **authorized** to act. Satan's angels follow his words and the loyal angels follow the Lord's words. We are the voice speaking God's or Satan's words/images; we choose which. A word of faith for those just starting on their journey as a covenant warrior. The enemy often says to us we don't have the faith. As Peter's faith slowly diminished he slowly sank. Even that is miraculous, who slowly sinks in water! As your faith builds, you will rise from underwater to walking on it. So, start building it, for even a little faith is a lot of power. Whether the force of faith, angel's response to your words of faith, or a Holy Spirit response to faith, set the charge and blow the stump! Your statements and agreements of faith will be honored and enforced.

> Matt 17:20 "...And Jesus said unto them, Because of your unbelief: for verily I say unto you, If ye have faith as a grain of mustard seed, ye shall say unto this mountain, Remove hence to yonder place, and it shall remove, and **nothing shall be impossible** unto you."

These next scriptures alone can keep you alive deployment after deployment, after deployment... "In famine, he shall redeem thee from death: and in war from the power of the sword" (Job 5:20) goes with Psalm 103:4 and Psalm 91. Read, memorize, and believe them. Speak them over yourself. God chooses how to deliver you. Maybe through a fight, or from one, or another way. The how is not our concern, trusting God with all your heart is our job.

Launching the Javelin of Judgment

There is a prayer vital to a Minister of Vengeance. It is virtually unused or often improperly used. They are called imprecatory prayers. Imprecatory means to call down upon or invoke a curse, calamity, or punishment upon some person, group, or institution through prayer. To pray an imprecatory prayer is sometimes called an imprecation. Imprecation is also called implacable or cold-hearted prayers against an enemy.

Those who see imprecatory prayers as cold-hearted have not been in the thick of it. They do not truly realize the cost of their freedom or know the viciousness of their enemy. They are not actually cold-hearted. The opposite is true a righteous heart burns with holy anger at the wickedness done in the world. Cold hearted, no not really, but they are merciless. Being able to 'call for fire' upon an enemy spiritually with physical results is good to know. It is too important not to get right. An imprecatory lance prayer pertains to judgment and consequences in this life. Many Christians, even some ministers may find this controversial, so let's look at both sides. I want you to be thoroughly convinced for yourself.

> "Crucial to the definition of an imprecation is that it (a) must be an invocation--a prayer or address to God and (b) must contain a request that one's enemies or the enemies of Yahweh be judged and justly punished"(J. Carl Laney, 1981, Bibliotheca Sacra 138, p35-45).

Laney, a Catholic scholar, defines an imprecatory prayer as well. However, not everyone is in agreement on the moral application of imprecatory prayers in God's Renewed Covenant [Jeremiah 31:31-34] the New Testament. Laney expresses criticism of imprecatory prayer.

> "The Abrahamic covenant (Gen. 12:1-3) promised the blessing on those who blessed Abraham's posterity and cursing on those who would curse Abraham's posterity. Because of the unconditional nature of the covenant, its promises and provisions remain in force throughout Israel's existence as a nation" (Laney, 1981)

> "In light of the fact that the Abrahamic covenant reflects God's promise to Abraham and his descendants, it would be inappropriate for a church-age believer to call down God's judgment on the wicked. One can appreciate the Old Testament setting of the imprecatory psalms and teach and preach from them" (Laney, 1981, em ad).

Imprecatory prayers are based on the righteous status of the covenant warrior, petitioning the Court of the Most High God for a judgment against an enemy. The enemy is your enemy without just cause. To be able to petition the Court of the Most High you must be in covenant. There is a foundational covenant still in effect for this prayer. To qualify, you must be a descendant of the seed of Abraham, Isaac, and Jacob. Who then qualifies as Abraham's seed, the Jew only? Yes. This begs the question, are Christians when they are born-again to Christ now Jewish and in Covenant? Yes, Christians are spiritual Jews, spiritual Israel or covenant people of God.

> "Of this man's seed [talking about Jesus human physical lineage through Mary, King David] hath God according to his promise raised unto Israel a Saviour, Jesus: When John had first preached before his coming to the baptism of repentance to all the people of Israel"(Acts 13:23 em ad).

> "Men and brethren, children of the stock [married into bloodline, born into bloodline, **adopted** into bloodline] of Abraham, **and whosoever** among you feareth God[believes on Christ as Savior, not born a Jew in the flesh, but became a believer in Yahweh (Jehovah)], to you is the word of this salvation sent" (Acts 13:26 em ad).

> "Concerning his Son Jesus Christ our Lord, which was made of the seed of David according to the flesh" (Romans 1:3);

> "Now to Abraham and his seed were the promises made. He saith not, And to seeds, as of many; but as of one, And to thy seed, which is Christ" (Gal 3:16).

> "Having predestinated us [preplanned as available to all humanity- not forced not pre-chosen to be believers though not all will choose it] unto the **adoption** of children by Jesus Christ to himself, according to the good pleasure of his will, To the praise of the glory of his grace, wherein he hath made us accepted in the beloved" (Ephesians 1:5-6 em ad).

As believers in the Messiah Jesus our Lord, we are adopted children of promise, of Abraham's seed and rightful heirs. This authorizes the covenant warriors to pray imprecatory prayers. Even though Laney goes on to say-

> "However, like the ceremonial dietary laws of the Old Testament, the imprecations in the Psalms **should not be applied** to church-age saints. This is clear from Paul's exhortation in Romans 12:14,'Bless those who persecute you; bless and curse not.' Paul admonished the Romans, 'Never take your own revenge, beloved, but leave room for the wrath of God, for it is written, 'Vengeance is Mine, I will repay, says the Lord'(12:19). Paul's words in 2 Timothy 4:14 indicate that he practiced what he preached" (Laney, 1981 em ad).

We have already extensively covered this chapter of Romans, and you know for yourself this interpretation is out of context and incorrect. Personal revenge is unauthorized while self-preservation is authorized. Blessing not cursing those who persecute or abuse you is in the realm of the individual. When it turns to self-preservation, or on behalf of an innocent group or nation, it becomes professional. In both of these areas, a judge or deliverer is the way through which the Lord repays. This is through us the Revengers of the Lord.

The type of judge, in this case, is like Samson or Shamgar from the book of Judges. They were not justices, but bringers of judgment fighting and killing the enemies of Israel before there was a king or standing army. All men were fighters back then, Minutemen, not Active Duty. You ministers of vengeance today could also be called judges of the United States, or whatever nation you come from. Laney makes further attempts using Alexander

> "Rather than calling down divine wrath on Alexander, the coppersmith, Paul simply stated, 'The Lord will repay him according to his deeds'"(Laney, 1981).

This is from 2 Timothy 4:14-15 "Alexander the coppersmith did me much evil: the Lord reward him according to his works: Of whom be thou ware also; for he hath greatly withstood our words."

The One New Man Bible translates verse 15 this way "...and against whom you must continually guard, for he vehemently opposed our message." This guy is actively bad news in the realm of business obviously and implicitly in other ways, not to mention the slander to believers, but not a danger to the innocent. Question: is it not imprecatory to request God to reward Alexander according to the known active evil he is committing against a child of Abraham?

The Holy Spirit did not inspire Paul to record this for nothing. Does this mean Paul simply cowered and gave it all to God, then warned other believers about this mean hardhearted guy? I don't think so! This is not an example of letting it go in the traditional Biblical sense; there are plenty of those. This is an example demonstrating the unconditional Covenant of blessing and cursing still in effect, for Christians as well as natural born Jews.

Paul, with the covenant in mind, is boldly commanding God's hands expectantly. Whether your translation says reward or 'will reward' it is still a declaration of calamity, reaping what they have sown, to come upon a person. Incidentally, in that city silver, gold, and coppersmiths earned much of their livelihood fashioning and selling household idols. The preaching of the Gospel negatively affects Alexander's income, as people turned to Jesus and away from false idol worship. Buying fewer idols from the shop had an economic and spiritual impact.

As for the 'bless those which curse you' command from Jesus. It is a directive at the personal level tied to forgiveness and sowing and reaping. It is 'being watered as you water' and 'the measure with which you measure, it shall be measured back to you.' Imprecatory prayers are specialized attack responses against dangerous enemies of influence and power, not against Joe and Jane unbeliever, or a common hater of the Gospel or the church.

Paul's declaration against Alexander is a combination of letting go and giving it to Christ, being persecuted by Alexander. It is also a declaration of this man's fate while warning believers are to stay away. Persecution is one thing, being reprobate is another. Not believing and rejecting Christ is one thing, while 'doing much evil' to someone seems a notch or two above average levels of resistance, reluctance or hatred of the Gospel and believers. It's one thing not to agree or believe in another person's faith choices or lifestyle. It is another to actively find ways to hurt any person or group, Christian or otherwise which you do not live or believe the same as. The cold-hearted merciless prayer you may be prompted to pray against your enemy is them reaping what they sowed. The seed you are planting is one of obedience and demonstration of restraint in character, praying with right attitude or heart. Praying a prayer of judgment is not a light matter.

Laney continues on- "And John makes it clear that God in the future will judge the wicked for their sin (Rev. 20:11-15)" (Laney, 1981). Yes, He will, however until that time Genesis 9:6 and Romans 12:17-13:1-4 are in effect. The Office of Arms is well intact and gaining strength. Many are the imprecatory declarations or prayers from the Old and New Covenants.

> "And they cried with a loud voice, saying, How long, O Lord, holy and true, dost thou not judge and **avenge our blood** on them that dwell on the earth" (Revelation 6:10 em ad)?

Who says this? The souls of martyred believers. Especially those beheaded for being a Christian. Who executed them? Those influenced by the spirit of and coming actual person called Anti-Christ. These are not the murderous pagans of Islam who martyr themselves in killing innocent men, women, and children. They are not in Heaven, nor do they have 72 virgins, which I wonder what the prize for a female martyr is? I have heard they get to be one of the virgins, didn't research that one, but maybe I should.

Some reading this may say I am anti-Muslim, Islamophobic, xenophobic, or some such thing. Not true at all. I love people. Jesus died for all people. I love Muslims, Hindi, Buddhist, Atheist you get the picture. I make no apology, however, for hating the false religious systems of belief of unbelief Satan has sold and used to enslave and corrupt so many. I'm anti-Islamic teaching, not anti-Muslim the person. The angel who delivered the false teachings of Islam to Mohamad was a Jinn; an angel of Satan's pretending to be Gabriel who deceived Mohammed. In English a Jinn is a demon, dark angel, and also referenced to a genie.

One of the ironies of Islam is one of the names or titles Allah brags about is Al-Makireen (not the only spelling S. 3:54; 8:30). Allah brags about being the greatest of deceivers; also translated planners, liars, schemers, or plotters. All are from the negative root word Makar. Some Islamic Scholars hold that plotting means to plot with an evil purpose when attributed to unbelievers. They also say to a good purpose when attributed to Allah, in the same sentence. Very convenient. Though controversial, it is undeniable the entity called Allah is capricious. Even Muhammad himself wasn't sure of his going to Heaven "By Allah, though I am the Apostle of Allah, yet I do not know what Allah will do to me." (Hadith 5:266). His foster mother Halima, "admitted that she thought he was possessed by the devil" (Caner, 2002).

The Jinn who called himself Gabriel would fall under an imprecatory declaration by the Apostle Paul. "But though **we, or an angel** from heaven [Satan's spheres of influence the sky above, galaxy or dimensions above Earth. Does not include God's loyal angels], preach any other gospel unto you than that which we have preached unto you, **let him be accursed**. As we said before, so say I now again, **If any man preaches** any other gospel unto you than that ye have received, **let him be accursed**"(Galatians 1:8-9 em ad). This pronouncement is a double curse for exponential effect in Hebrew culture. Most elements of Hebrew culture are reflective of Heaven's culture. Actively seeking the harm of a Jew or Christian is dangerous.

Jesus declared several curses or woes. A woe of Matthew 23:15 is in the declaration "Woe unto you, scribes and Pharisees, hypocrites! For ye compass sea and land to make one proselyte [convert to Judaism], and when he is made, ye make him twofold more the child of hell than yourselves[get him believing, but in the wrong manner]". Let's not forget Peter in dealing with Simon the Sorcerer, after Simons conversion, concerning obtaining the gift of the Holy Ghost. Notice also the antidote, or counter to the declaration is repentance, removing his issues. Before conversion, Simon was a famous and sought-after soothsayer while he used his demonic powers.

When to pray for the hammer to drop

> "But Peter said unto him, Thy money **perish with thee** because thou hast thought that the gift of God may be purchased with money. Thou hast neither part nor lot in this matter: **for thy heart is not right** in the sight of God. **Repent** therefore of this thy wickedness, and pray God, if perhaps the thought of thine heart may be forgiven thee. For **I perceive** that thou art in the gall of bitterness, and in the bond of iniquity. Then answered Simon, and said, Pray ye to the Lord for me, that none of these things which ye have spoken come upon me" (Acts 8:20-24 em ad).

The clauses (because, for, perceive) tell us when the use of imprecatory prayers or declaration is authorized. Peter declared or revealed the negative consequences set in motion because of Simon's evil thought of his heart as revealed by the Holy Spirit. Imprecatory lances launched outside of God's will not be honored, and carry a possible lethal backfire counter attack by wicked spiritual forces. If you have no authority, you have no backup.

Peter also declared the death of two unbelievers for lying and deceiving, acting like believers, in the book of Acts. This is from the apostle the Vatican claims is the first Pope. If imprecatory prayers or declarations are not appropriate under the New Testament, nobody told "Pope" Peter. If someone told Peter they're not right (speaking sarcastically), then Simon the sorcerer (Acts 8) would not be afraid of dying, and Ananias and his wife (Acts 5), wouldn't be dead, and Elymas wouldn't be blind (Acts 13).

We must be sure when a situation is person to person (not including interviews, investigations, interrogations) then appropriate 'turn the other cheek' or 'bless those who curse you' response is mandated. We are not to return evil for evil: railing (bullying or accusing), gossip, slander, threats, or disrespect by responding with more of the same. Doing these things is not operating from a position of power, but weakness. Power replies with patience and confidence knowing the words of the others are weak. Besides the promise of God still stands against those who curse you, but this is also one of the reasons Jesus wants us to bless them. They need it to avert disaster for them hopefully. Blessing them is also releasing the soul tie or bond between you and the offending person, allowing the Lord to handle it for you.

Even the curses of enemy covens, Luciferians, other occultists from foreign nations (another topic for a whole book or large pamphlet) who wield raw demonic power, can't hurt you. "As the bird by wandering, as the swallow by flying, so the curse causeless shall not come" (Proverbs 26:2). Their authority and power are not higher than your authority, or more powerful than the Holy Spirit. Shall not come is referring to come to rest in a nest or upon you. Notice the Lord disqualifies it with 'causeless.' Enemy witches, obi-men, or voodoo priests may send it, but to no avail against those with a prayer covering and or who know their covenant. They risk much themselves to do evil to a seed of Abraham in light of the covenant of blessing and cursing with the Lord. The curse will return upon whom it came; it cannot make a new nest.

Call for Fire Examples

The most notorious imprecatory prayer is Psalm 109. It is also the model of qualification. In the first five verses, David qualifies himself before the Lord as innocent in the dire situation. He is the victim of significant attack without just cause. The next verses of Psalm 109 (versus 6-19) are full of almost every curse you can think of, including affecting generations to come. Satan, as seen in the first few chapters of Job, takes every opportunity afforded him. Usually, Satan sees the hedge go/going down, or causes it to drop. Verses 20-31 give more justification for the curses upon the enemy and focuses on David's praise and dependency upon the Lord.

Sometimes God does send an angel of His to execute judgments, such as against King Herod, or against Balaam. At the end of Job God tells the three miserable comforters to ask Job to pray for them, or else He would deal with them according to their wickedness. This shows God is willing to allow those prayed against, the opportunity to repent. Should they not repent God's only recourse is vengeance. For our purposes, we need to know two things: are imprecatory prayers still valid and usable, and if so, what are the criteria for use?

Hedges

Nine times is hedge mentioned in scripture. Hedges are about protection and direction. Protection actively denies the enemy access to an area. Direction functions like the various obstacles, made by engineers to forcibly channel enemy forces. An imprecatory prayer is one, which causes the demonic protective hedge of the enemy, if one exists, to be removed. It then petitions for specific judgments against actions, and the authorization for consequences enacted upon the target of the prayer. "He that diggeth a pit shall fall into it; and whoso breaketh a hedge, a serpent shall bite him" (Ecclesiastes 10:8).

Continuing Examples

Also, Moses, whom God heralded as the meekest (most self-controlled man on Earth at that time) called for God to arise and let His enemies be scattered in Numbers 10:35. Of course, Moses declarations to Pharaoh were devastating. Then there is David the King. To slander him, causing him, through a lie, to lose the throne and or his life, would devastate a nation's security, safety, and economy. Here is a quick reference to the imprecatory psalms 7, 28, 35, 55, 58, 59, 69, 79, 109, 137and 139.

If these are hard for you to accept morally and ethically, then think about this"Every scripture inspired of God is also profitable for teaching, for reproof, for correction, for instruction which is in righteousness" (2 Timothy 3:16). I'm not asking you to violate your conscious. If you don't want to use a cold-hearted prayer you don't have to; there is no penalty. My conscious is clear, I agree with the Lord, as he wishes all would be saved and none perish. However, we all know unfortunately even though we all would like evil people to repent, if they don't they must be dealt with. They cannot be allowed to run amok in society. I believe in capital punishment and evangelism on death row. They must face temporal judgment but still, have a chance to accept Jesus' eternal forgiveness before the Earthly sentence is executed.

Jesus quoted from two imprecatory psalms. Paul in Romans quotes from one of those psalms as well. Quoting from Psalms 69:4 and 35:19. Then there is Paul from Psalm 69:22-23. "But this cometh to pass, that the word may be fulfilled that is written in their law, They hated me without a cause" (John 15:25). Quoted from Psalm 35; "Let not them that are mine enemies wrongfully rejoice over me; Neither let them wink with the eye that hate me without a cause" (Psalm 35:19 em ad). And from Psalm 69; "They that hate me without a cause are more than the hairs of my head: They that would cut me off, being mine enemies wrongfully, are mighty: That which I took not away I have to restore" (Psalm 69:4).

Lastly, we have Jesus on the cross. "They gave him vinegar to drink mingled with gall: and when he had tasted thereof, he would not drink" (Matthew 27:34). From the verse "They gave me also gall for my meat; and in my thirst, they gave me vinegar to drink" (Psalm 69:21).

These Messianic prophecies and their fulfillments are linked to imprecatory prayers. One warning about wanting to pray this prayer came from Jesus. We are talking about the human heart. When praying for the destruction and downfall of the enemy God is being invoked to act on your behalf, not out of bitterness, envy, jealousy, or vindictiveness, but injustice. In the parable of the unjust judge; he finally gives the woman her justice (Luke 18:1-8). The point Jesus is making is <u>unlike</u> the unjust judge, God wants to and will answer his children in distress speedily. Great satisfaction is expressed and expected when God overthrows the wicked as in Psalm 137. There is no conflict between love thy neighbor and speaking against the enemy forces. Both are in the New Testament. Both have their proper place and time. Loving your neighbor is protecting them from threats by hostile forces. These forces only understand greater force exerted on them to stop.

> "Put me in remembrance: let us plead together: declare thou, that thou mayest be justified" (Isaiah 43:26)

> "Thus saith the LORD, the Holy One of Israel, and his Maker, Ask me of things to come concerning my sons, and **concerning the work of my hand's command ye me**" (Isaiah 45:11).
>
> "And the Egyptians shall know that I am the LORD, when **I stretch forth mine hand upon Egypt** and bring out the children of Israel from among them" (Exodus 7:5).
>
> Notice in these examples, and there are several more, that the first time God stretches forth His hand one group is judged and blessed, while the other is judged and cursed.
>
> "Though I walk in the midst of trouble, thou wilt revive me: **thou shalt stretch forth thine hand against** the wrath of mine enemies, and <u>thy right hand shall save me</u>" (Psalm 138:7 em ad).
>
> "He shall **stretch forth his hand** also upon the countries: and the land of Egypt shall not escape" (Daniel 11:42 em ad).

Remember who the true enemy is. Do not be fooled into thinking this is just between factions of humans with different worldviews. Treating them with respect is also a way of retaining our own humanity. Before employing an imprecatory prayer, try to ensure personal revenge or hatred is not in your heart. Be sure your prayer is in righteous indignation for evil committed, the crisis in the process, or planned- keep it professional. Ask Holy Spirit for help in this. This is not an easy thing to do apart from grace.

David was able to keep it professional and demonstrate great passion. He is very emphatic in Psalm 109, so can we be, yet he pleaded his case and justified the cause and justice of the curse. Pray in faith, ask the Holy Spirit if it is appropriate, and His guidance on this. Keep this in mind when imprecatory praying. "Rejoice not when thine enemy falleth, and let not thine heart be glad when he stumbleth: Lest the LORD see it, and it displeases him, and he turns away his wrath from him. Fret not thyself because of evil men, neither be thou envious at the wicked; For **there shall be no reward to the evil man**; the candle of the wicked shall be put out" (Proverbs 24:17-20 em ad).

This does not mean you cannot celebrate in victory. David's victory over Goliath of Gath is celebrated by parading his head on a pole from the battlefield back to Jerusalem. A personal favorite of mine, for there is nothing like a public statement of victory; where God gets the glory. Finally, his skull is buried in a mound outside the city. The name of the mound is Golgotha or place of the skull. You might know it better as Calvary, the place of Jesus crucifixion. It speaks to the final judgment of the wicked suffering in an eternity of Hell; which is not a reward.

> "The curse of the Lord is on the house of the wicked, but He blesses the dwelling of the righteous" (Proverbs 3:33).

> "He who returns evil for good, evil will not depart from his house." (Proverbs 17:13).

Jesus warns-

> "And it came to pass when the time was come that he should be received up, he stedfastly set his face to go to Jerusalem, And sent messengers before his face: and they went, and entered into a village of the Samaritans, to make ready for him. And they did not receive him because his face was as though he would go to Jerusalem. And when his disciples James and John saw this, they said, Lord, **wilt thou that we command fire to come down from heaven**, and consume them, even as Elias did? **But he turned, and rebuked them**, and said, Ye, know not <u>what manner of spirit</u> ye are of. For the Son of man is not come to destroy men's lives, but to save them. And they went to another village" (Luke 9:51-55 em ad).

The point Jesus is making is the primary reason for imprecatory prayer is not a vendetta because you have been rejected or disrespected. It is not a personal issue, but a professional one. Nor is it appropriate when you are prejudice against someone. The Samaritans were hated by most Jews in general. Though of course, Jesus hated no one. Peter's motives above are not about righteous anger. When the bigger picture is involved, Gods honor, national security, our battle plans, and operations, or innocent lives are at stake. Petition the Court of Heaven for a ruling. Put the Father in remembrance of His covenant as He says to do.

Merciless

Yes, the scripture says to love your enemies. This doesn't mean like them. It also does not mean you must have mercy on them: humane treatment and respect, yes of course, always. However, you cannot always be merciful in sparing their life. Launching imprecatory lances is merciless. The Enemy is coldhearted, and so are many of his human servants. They have chosen a path of resistance and rebellion against God to the point their hearts are hardened to Him. They are dangerous to civilization let alone a community or society desiring peace. Professionally speaking these humans must be put down like rabid dogs. There is no choice. To protect the flock, the wolves must be killed.

The Bible talks about a few groups of people who have become unredeemable. In many cases, if not most, the wolves killed in battle fall into one of them.

> "For the invisible things of him from the creation of the world are clearly seen, being understood by the things that are made, even his eternal power and Godhead; so that **they are without excuse**: Because that, **when they knew God**, they glorified him not as God, neither were thankful; but became vain in their imaginations, and **their foolish heart was darkened**"(Romans 1:20-21 em ad).

> "Wherefore **God also gave them up** to uncleanness through the lusts of their own hearts..."(Romans 1:24 em ad)

> "For this cause **God gave them up** unto vile affections:" (Romans 1:26 em ad)

"And even as they did not like to retain God in their knowledge, **God gave them over to a reprobate mind**..." (Romans 1:28 em ad) Reprobate means degenerate or good for nothing; an unfortunate state to be in- a hard heart.

Do not hesitate to do what must be done if forced. If the enemy is allowed to live, is not imprisoned, or stopped in some manner, but allowed to continue. It is unknown the death and damage enemy operatives, soldiers, terrorists, or criminals, might do. Pray and listen. The Holy Spirit will teach you when and how-to pray imprecatory prayers. He will also tell you when not to shoot.

Hesitation is not the same as Holy Spirit saying stop. Your conscience should be clear. If you do not do it. If no one does it. Someone innocent will die, be abused, kidnapped, etc. It is His vengeance, but our duty; peace-loving law-abiding innocent people, and God depend on you. You are entrusted with a sacred and very tough duty; to take the shot, make the arrest, protect the innocent, get the information, defend the defenseless, free the oppressed.

Danger Close

In 2 Kings 1:1-18 a new king is over Israel who does not respect God. It is King Ahaziah who serves Baalzebub. He becomes sick and sends for a messenger from whom to inquire of Baal. On the way, the prophet of the Lord, Elijah, encounters the messenger sent to inquire of Baal. He gives him a message for the king, similar to that of the spirit of the dead prophet of Samuel gave to king Saul long ago; you're going to die because of what you do, concerning Baal.

The king doesn't like this and with no respect for God or Elijah dispatches fifty men with their captain of the fifty. They obviously mean harm to the prophet and are sent to bring him into custody. They summarily order him down from the hill, mocking him calling him 'oh man of God', to come with them to see the king he declared a curse over (imprecatory prayer or prophetic judgment?). Elijah 's reply was if I am a prophet of God let fire (lightning) fall from heaven. It did and killed all the soldiers (now that's imprecatory wow!!).

The king sent another fifty who suffered the same fate. And a third fifty, whose captain, with reverence for God and respect for Elijah, asked for the lives of him and his men, who asked, not commanded, Elijah to come. An angel of the Lord told Elijah he may go with them; no harm will come to him. A very different situation than what Peter and Jesus dealt with. Maybe not so different from a person downed behind enemy lines, or a unit in an ambush, or bottled up in a corner. Perhaps a little fire from Heaven might save the day? You can't pray something you know nothing about.

What God did for Elijah He will do for you in the sense of protection and vindication. Who knows maybe fire may fall on an enemy unit in front of your eyes. Do not limit God's choice of responses, but remember as a warrior in the covenant you are also an anointed one and prophet under and in Jesus. God defended and protected Abraham, Isaac, and Jacob and he'll do this for you. It is written, "Saying 'do not touch My anointed ones, and do My prophets no harm:" (Psalm 105:15). Elijah is the first spiritual forward observer who calls for fire, danger close and scores two direct hits. Of course, the Lord never misses. Now Elijah declares the death of a king, and God honors the prophet's obedience with angelic assistance, killing a hundred and two soldiers and of course, the king dies. You are no joke to the enemy when you walk in the Spirit.

How God will choose or inform you of His assistance is up to Him, but know you are not alone, and out of bullets doesn't mean out of ammo. Ammo can supernaturally multiply as the fight continues. Do not limit the Lord by unbelief. Think and pray out of the box. Multiplication of ammo is no different from the multiplication of fish and bread, or an unlimited supply of oil and bread to bake during a three-year famine. We see here angels playing a part in human affairs and warfare. How far does this go?

Guardian angels, a believer's personal security detail (PSD) is from Psalm 91. Verses eleven and twelve state "For he shall give his angels charge over thee, to keep thee in all thy ways." And "They shall bear thee up in their hands, lest thou dash thy foot against a stone." These are the angels who cause the fire to fall among many other things. Jesus spoke of this in the Garden of Gethsemane. All believers have a legion of angels of all sorts- warrior, worship, and working, healing, labor, finances, academic, research, science, angels for all our situations.

Some sample implacable prayers

> "Lord I thank you for your favor which encompasses me as a shield. As you confused and turned the enemy upon itself for Gideon, do so or more for us. I forgive my enemy their wickedness determined against me, You Lord are my Helper, I am not afraid; oh, that the enemy would repent and turn to you and no longer be my enemy, but as long as they hate you, they must fall. As you promised, let my enemy fall for my sake. Glorify Yourself in delivering our enemy into my hand."

> "Let the winds and storm level their tents in the field. Let your fire from Heaven consume them. Let your angels slay them in their sleep even as one slew 120,000 in one night as they laid siege to Jerusalem. They say You cannot deliver. They say God is not with us, but trust in demon gods and Satan himself pretending to be you. Let God arise and glorify Himself, let His enemies be scattered, let the fear of the sword of (whoever you are) and the sword of the Lord fall upon them."

> "Lord, slay those who lie in wait to ambush us, attacking us as cowards through suicide bombing missions. Let them explode prematurely, or not all, harming none which are innocent. Let the bomb makers' error in their making, falling into the pit they dug for us. Let the stones they have set to roll upon us, roll back upon and crush them."

No teaching on the cold-hearted prayer would be complete without also mentioning a famous and true story of prayer (among many) during WWII. The request is implacable because what is being requested is to enable them to defeat the enemy completely. If the prayer had not been answered the outcome of the battle of the Bulge, let alone the fate of Bastogne, might have been very different and not in a good way.

The weather was forecasted dismal as far as could be seen. But, a few days after the division had that prayer and Training Letter no. 5, the weather inexplicably cleared December 19, 1944. Then the push to free Bastogne, and on into Germany, victory after victory commenced. The weather was so good our air support forces could fly mission after mission of air superiority, as the Third Army pushed back the Nazi war machine. In January 1945, Chaplain O'Neil recounted Gen. Patton's words in Luxemburg. "'Well, Padre, our prayers worked. I knew they would,' Then he cracked me on the side of my steel helmet with his riding crop. That was his way of saying 'Well done'" (O'Neil, 2004).

At the order of General George S. Patton Jr., his Chaplain Monsignor (Msgn.) O'Neil, of the Third Army in Europe, wrote a prayer concerning the weather which was favoring the Nazis. The order also stated 250,000 copies to be printed on 3x5 cards, to be sent to everyone in the Third Division to pray for this breakthrough. The cards had a signed message from the General on one side and the prayer on the other.

Side One

To each officer and soldier in the Third United States Army. I wish a Merry Christmas. I have full confidence in your courage, devotion to duty, and skill in battle. We march in our might to complete victory. May God's blessing rest upon each of you on this Christmas Day
(General Pattons Signature)

Side Two the Prayer

Almighty and most merciful Father, we humbly beseech Thee, of Thy great goodness, to restrain these immoderate rains with which we have had to contend. Grant us fair weather for Battle. Graciously hearken to us as soldiers who call upon Thee that armed with Thy power, we may advance from victory to victory, and crush the oppression and wickedness of our enemies, and establish Thy justice among men and nations. Amen.

CHAPTER 9

Serpents and Scorpions

Jesus said. "Behold I give unto you the authority to trample on serpents and scorpions, and over all the power of the enemy, and nothing shall by any means hurt you. Nevertheless, do not rejoice in this, that the spirits are subject to you, but rather rejoice because your names are written in Heaven" (Luke 10:19-20, NJKV).

Situation Report

Many of God's people are not operating at full or even half potential supernaturally. People operating supernaturally, trained by demonic forces, have almost unchallenged battlespace at times. Fallen angel fields of fire are littered with victims mowed down by the Enemy like the grass. We should be the lawnmowers, not the lawn. Blades whetted and honed in the blood of the Lamb should be cutting down enemy forces.

We network at conferences and other functions for various reasons such as gaining a helpful relationship to someone in authority, or for a resource to accomplish something. Yet we do not network with the Holy Spirit. And often when we do, we neglect to labor into His rest and let Him and the angels handle the situation for us, through us, or with us.

There are twelve empowerment giftings, specials giftings for occupations and callings, and a separate gift of tongues. Tongues are very controversial, because of false teachings from the pulpits, courtesy of the Devil's propaganda machine. Satan attacks it because of its power which he cannot overcome. Through the bodily indwelling and sealing (protecting our spirits from sin) of the Holy Spirit, we exist in multiple dimensions at once, unlike when we were in our fallen state, before being born-again. This is part of what is meant by we are seated with Christ in Heavenly places.

We are spiritually extended into Him, and He is spiritually connected and extended to and through us into this physical dimension. This is how a legion of demons can possess one person. The metaphysical soul and spirit dimensionally extend beyond the limits of the first four dimensions: length, width, height, and time. They reach into the depths or other heavens. Time and space also extend through the dimensions or depths, but their interactive properties alter with each dimension.

For example, the Heaven of Heavens also called the first Heaven, is where the Fathers Throne is. It is outside of space and time as we experience it. Your lances and words can reach ahead in time before you get there, your faith can compress time, and have a residual effect through time after you have died and gone to Heaven. Your words and prayers outlive you unless you cancel or uproot them yourself. To verbally cancel what you have said which is ungodly, you can simply say "I cancel those words in my life." You can also plead the blood over what you cannot remember you said in your past. The Lord knows what you said and wants that evil canceled.

The Enemy doesn't want it canceled because then he can use it against you, your family, and friends at any time. Jesus said his words were spirit and life. This reveals all words are spiritual. But only speaking Biblically are the words life. If you speak the enemies words, you are speaking destruction and death.

Synopsis of Gifting's

If we believe in the gifts, we can increase our faith, and ability to receive their operations in our lives from the Holy Spirit. Not believing in them does not entirely nullify their working in your life, since we all have experienced help from the Holy Spirit, but not always recognized it was the Spirit helping. The full effectiveness is inhibited. We must believe to receive. These gifts can be the difference between life and death, victory, and defeat to a commander, strategist, intelligence operative, or average

Joe and Jane. The Lord wants us to understand these gifts to manifest them in our lives, for His glory, and our benefit.

> "Now concerning spiritual gifts, brethren, I would not have you ignorant. Ye know that ye were Gentiles (remember gentile means a non-covenant person or - not of Jewish birth), carried away unto these dumb idols, even as ye were led. Wherefore I give you to understand, that no man speaking by the Spirit of God calleth Jesus accursed: and that no man can say that Jesus is the Lord, but by the Holy Ghost" (1Corinthians 12:1-3 em ad).

In the Old Testament, not just the New, God did many miraculous things through and for His people by Holy Spirit power, and angelic means. Some examples are Elijah made iron float; a person is raised from the dead touching the bones of a dead prophet, which Holy Spirit anointing still lingered upon them. The prophet did not do that, the anointing of the Holy Spirit upon that person worked through them to do that.

Do not confuse power gifts with giftings or callings to a specific office or job. A minister of vengeance is an office, a calling. An anointing is supernatural ability to do something. Think of being smeared or covered with the power to do specific things. Gifts are also callings in that you have a supernatural gifting to do one or more things such as a gift of governments from 1 Corinthians 12: 26. "For God has appointed these in the church: first apostles, second prophets, third teachers, after that miracles, then gifts of healings, helps, administrations, varieties of tongues."

After this Paul asks the Corinthian church in this letter if all are apostles, or teachers, etc. The other offices or positions God has instituted don't concern us. We are focused on those called to the Office of Arms. "For he is the **minister** of God, an **avenger** to execute **wrath** upon him that doeth evil" (Rom 13:4 MJKV). No matter what the office or position, all believers should and are benefited by believing and receiving gifts of empowerment, personally, professionally, and for the local church body.

The gifts and callings of God are irrevocable. God does not take them back, whether you use them or not. What we are focusing on is the supernatural power gifts. "Now there are **diversities** of gifts, but the **same Spirit**. And there are differences of **administrations**, but the **same Lord**. And there are diversities of **operations**, but it is the **same God** which worketh all in all. But the **manifestation** of the Spirit <u>is **given to every man**</u> to profit withal" (1Corinthians 12:4-7 em ad).

The gifts enable the believer to endure, avoid, and overcome hardships which will come in this life. Some of our problems are self-made, some demonically made, some come from living in a fallen world with fallen people or carnal Christians. The world is not user-friendly. It is a hostile work environment. Since the Kingdom of God is in us. We are the spiritual portal, the way through which Heaven can positively influence Earth. Be aware the enemy will attempt to use the gifting's from God to people for his own ends. Satan trains his people to put to use the laws of the spirit to his advantage. He works to develop people who can wield demonic power for evil in the family, business, governments, and on the battlefield. Nothing happens in a vacuum.

Anti-Gifts

First, let's define anti. It is not merely 'against' something. The Anti-Christ is a false substitute. Anti is about illusion, replacement, and deception designed to distract the mind and spirit while mimicking, the truth. It also deals with half-truths to appear sincere, when it indeed is not. The spirit of Anti-Christ is a master deceiver, often looking good and helpful, while being extremely evil and dangerous. False religion, doctrine, and deceptive miracles are his specialties.

Satan and his angels have inherent power, but no righteous authority. Yet what is this power? Two angels of the Lord using local fault lines activated seismic activity destroying the cities of Sodom and Gomorrah. Angels appeared to Daniel imparting revelation knowledge of the future and spiritual warfare dynamics information. Angels have sat and eaten with humans and interacted with them as messengers. Other times angels are seen delivering judgments of God on people or places.

Peter the Apostle is rescued out of prison by an earthquake and additional angelic assistance. The Bible says treat strangers well for some have entertained angels unknowingly. Satan's angels are equal in raw power to the Lord's, but not identical in numbers. The authority given to demonic forces is by humans through their worship and actions and speech which is ungodly. Only loyal angels can bring genuine healing and protection. Fallen angels have a chain attached to their 'healings' actions. (Michaelsen, 1982, The beautiful side of evil)

Only God can resurrect you. Satan can, as will happen with his false messiah the Anti-Christ, reverse the effects of a mortal wound. This is psychic or supernatural surgery and manipulation of the flesh. What appears to be healing is really a trade. Your physical health for the poisoning of your worldview, keeping you from receiving Christ as savior and further enslaving your mind with evils influence, appearing as good. Our saying a person is dead is not necessarily the spiritual definition. The point of no return is not directly revealed. However, Lazarus was raised from the dead after four days.

Angels never need anything from a human, except permission; granted authority to operate in their life. Similarly, if a person petitions a false god (since the before Noah's flood Satan's minions portrayed pagan gods, and presently as aliens with godlike power, ability, and knowledge), they are calling demonic forces to intervene for or against another person. Financial prosperity, popularity, all the authority and power this world can offer, Satan can dangle in front of a person. Satan legitimately tempted Jesus with the three categories of sin. You can't offer what you don't have. Real wealth, health, and worship are with the Lord only.

It's a Bird! It's a Plane! It's a UFO?

Not all evil spirits have wings. They must travel using portals, natural, and mechanical means just as we do. UFO's are not intergalactic beings or aliens. They are interdimensional demons. Notwithstanding, they've had since before we were created to master the skills of interdimensional travel of various sorts. It goes without saying our enemy has an understanding of dimensional physics beyond us. That knowledge has caused many commotions for thousands of years, even to this day. Never mind their knowledge of physical and spiritual laws. Follow the leading of the Holy Spirit who created all them, and all the laws of physics. (Putnam & Horn,

2013) As for the power of the enemy which we have authority over, Jesus warned "For false Christs and false prophets will rise and show signs and wonders to deceive, if possible, even the very elect" (Mark 13:22-23). But there are plenty of well researched books by Thomas Horn, Cris Putnam, L.A. Marzula, and Dr. Chuck Missler on this subject, and outside of our focus on the covenant warrior. I included this as side information with scholarly references because there is much controversy and confusion about aliens and UFOs, and it is a stumbling block to many people's faith.

Examples of Demonic power

King Saul consulted a medium who through demonic assistance could call up a person from Hades to talk with and through her. This is called a person who has a familiar spirit. Hades is the Greek for Sheol (a Hebrew word for Hell, the Pit, the Grave, etc.) or Hell in English. It is the land or dwelling place of departed spirits. Unredeemed (not born again) spirits descend the land of the dead called Hades. They reside there tormented in flame (Luke 16).

A spirit in Hades can be brought up with demonic assistance to speak with the living. A spirit not in Hades, but in the Heaven of Heavens cannot be brought down by demons. Incidentally, your soul and spirit stay together. Demons are very good at mimicking people past and present. This helps perpetuate the reincarnation deception. Simon the Sorcerer, before he was saved (Acts 8) used demonic power. The fortuneteller (Acts 16) had a demon of divination cast out of her by the Apostle Paul. She earned much money for her master before that.

Demonic forces tried to gain credibility by saying Paul, whom God was working many miracles and healings through, served the Most High God. This is not intended to give Jesus praise as it appears. It is the Anti-Christ spirit attempting to connect her evil prophecy with true Holy Spirit power. Demonic prophecy sometimes works because what we fear we empower. What we worship has influence and authority in our lives. What we speak and believe, according to spiritual Law- happens. Remember in Psalm 103 angels are listening for and obeying our speech lined up with God's word. The fallen angels try to get us to speak prophetically over ourselves believing the wrong, to our own destruction. They listen for and bring to pass the words spoken in line with Satan's word.

Paul got rid of the spirit by casting it out in the name of Jesus. Peter confesses that Jesus is the Christ, the Messiah the Son of the Living God in Matthew 16. A careful reading of the passage shows Jesus next statement "upon this rock, I will build my church (the called out ones), and the gates of Hell would not prevail against them" is a reference to belief in Jesus as Messiah, the Son of the Father, is the cornerstone of faith and authority- the rock. The gates of Hell are the authority and power of darkness which will not be able to keep out or contain the actions of the Body of Christ, fulfilling the Holy Spirit's will and exercising their authority over the serpents, scorpions (demonic and evil human minions) and all the power of the enemy.

In Matthew 18:18-19 Jesus is teaching on binding, loosing, and the prayer of agreement. Whatever we forbid or bind on earth God enforces that in the heavens. When Paul cast out the demon of python out of the fortune teller, he was commanding it to leave. It obeyed Paul because, just as you give a message to a commander (with more rank than you), but the message is from a commander with more rank than them, they must obey. The demons and angels only obey the word of the Lord spoken with authority.

It's not magic. In Acts it is recorded, there were seven sons of a Jewish sorcerer who witnessed the power of Paul's to cast out demons. They tried to deliver, or exorcise a demon out of a person, by saying they command him to come out in the name of Jesus whom Paul preaches. The reply from the demon acknowledged Paul and Jesus authority, their right to command him and expect him to obey. Then the demon stated he did not recognize who they were. Translation; saying in Jesus name only counts if you're a believer in Jesus. If you are not, then you do not have the authority to speak in Jesus name and expect anything to happen. The demon possessed person then proceeded to attack all seven men, sending them running from the house. If you're not saved, never try to exorcise (also called deliver or deliverance) a demon.

Balaam was hired to curse what God blessed. It could not be done. He was hired because it was known if he cursed (empowered to fail) something it failed. It was widely known the most powerful god wins for his or her people. When God Almighty let His people be overrun or defeated there was always a reason. God did not like allowing them to be crushed. The reason is one they brought into being by their actions: or the effects of their leadership, causing a breach in or lowering of the hedge. God judges the conquering nation for their crimes against His people. A recent example is the defeat of Nazi Germany, and the rise of a new German government.

God transformed Moses staff into a snake, then the sorcerers of Pharaoh, through demonic power, literally transformed their staff's into living deadly snakes also. God's snake most likely is bitten and injected with the venom of many snakes, suffering no damage, as it swallowed each of the Sorcerer's snakes one by one till all were devoured. In short, you cannot overpower, nor hurt what is under God's power and anointing. The Magi of Pharaoh never got the symbols of their power back. Moses snake devoured all the other snakes then turned back into a staff. This shows the complete dominance of Holy Spirit power over satanic power. This also reveals the limits of fallen angelic power. Of the next ten plagues (miraculous judgments on ten primary gods of Egypt), the first three are duplicated on a smaller scale by Pharaoh's sorcerers. They cannot duplicate any more miracles after this. They are left in the dust.

Remote viewing is not a new concept either. Remember what the demons pervert and teach is not as powerful as what it substitutes for. Ask a sorcerer of Pharaoh or Saul's witch. Dreams and visions originate with the Lord. Of course, you can jump into a pagan made portal of Buffalo skins, or be moved by the Holy Spirit. Just ask Philip who was teleported in Acts 8:39-40. All occult power is a perversion of the gifts and empowerments of the Holy Spirit and loyal angels. When psychics say they know where the bodies are buried or have supernatural incite enabling the cracking of a case- it may be true. The Devil knows where the bodies are buried, who did it, and when. Of course, so does God. The difference is demons know because they were part of committing the evil act. God just knows everything. To appear benevolent Satan will sometimes sell out a murderer or rapist, tipping off someone to look helpful. Careful, this is not what it seems. Satan works to promote false beliefs as true, even giving false credit to God through false prophets.

There are many people in witchcraft, who are good people. They would give you the shirt off their back. However, deception is a deception to the core. Satan does not care if you do a multitude of good works or not. Some of the most effective false prophets and demonically inspired charismatic leaders seem to be some of the nicest people, denying themselves possessions, or donating mountains of their possessions and throwing their name in with self-exalting causes.

However, when demonic power is used to prevent an evil action, it is a bait and switch. The lesser of two evils has occurred. Witchcraft and all the spiritual arts and prayers of false religions are spokes on the wheel. This wheel with all these spokes has a hub they are connected too. The hub is demonic power. You may not know its evil; most don't think its evil, but that they are using evil. Many consider the blessings, potions, rituals, and spells (prayers to demonic powers) are helping people. They are not. This is a deception and not the worst to come. A coming great deception is warned about in the Bible.

It's worth saying again: your charms, incantations, or invocations of a false god kept you alive… Healed through spells, potions, crystals, spirit guides, a person under the influence of a spirit during operation… They are not really healed, or protected, but brought further into the mindset of bondage blinding their minds to Jesus. Satan does not heal; he commands the evil spirits causing the physical affliction to be withdrawn, this is not the same. What is withdrawn can be ordered to return worse, at the Devils will. Satan's angels can protect similarly to the loyal angels if it serves their purposes to keep some people alive miraculously. Not everyone or everything is as they seem.

> "For such are false apostles, deceitful workers, transforming themselves into the apostles of Christ. And no marvel; **for Satan himself is transformed into an angel of light.** Therefore, it is no great thing if his ministers also be transformed as the ministers of righteousness; whose end shall be according to their works"(2 Corinthians 11:13-15 em ad).

The Gifts of the Holy Spirit

> "For to one is given by the Spirit the word of **wisdom**" (1Cor 12:8a em ad); Supernatural guidance - knowing

what to do next, a keen understanding of situations, helps in making command decisions, strategy and policy…

"to another the word of **knowledge** by the same Spirit" (1Cor 12:8b em ad); Knowledge: supernatural information- what the enemy is doing, where you left something, understanding when someone is lying, personal information about detainees or interviewees, where to find a missing child, Intel, or evidence for the prosecution or defense. Additionally, a word of knowledge may carry a word for healing. Gifts complement each other and often manifest together.

"to another **faith** by the same Spirit" (1Corinthians 12:9a em ad); A supernatural boost of faith to accomplish something, believe for something beyond your current ability or level of faith- little, great, strong, shipwrecked, mustard seed sized… This is temporary supercharging of your faith so you can believe for something you otherwise may not be able to.

"to another the gifts of **healing** by the same Spirit"(1Cor 12:9b em ad); Conducting healing crusades or services. Supernatural healing empowerments of anointing oil, laying on of hands, speaking God's healing word for and to yourself, or and communion... Do not limit the multitude of ways the Lord can get His healing to you. His will is for you to be healed…anointed music has healed people… His presence of glory has healed people…Jesus healed the maimed, the blind- every type of affliction known to man…God has augmented the hands of surgeons, field medics, nurses, EMTs, and ordinary folk to save lives. Luke the apostle who wrote the Gospel of Luke and the book of Acts, is a physician. One of Jesus titles is great Physician. Gifts of Healing and Miracles are both in the plural. This gift is also seen in operation along with Faith, Knowledge, and anointing oil.

"to another the working of **miracles**" (1Corinthians 12:10a em ad); Supernatural raw power activated and directed by faith to do common, uncommon, and out of the box actions, often appearing to defy or accelerate the known physical laws and medical knowledge or ability; from the greatest (global) to the least (personal) levels... In Acts, we learn that through Paul God did unusual or special miracles. "so that handkerchiefs or aprons were brought from his body to the sick, and the diseases left them and the evil spirits went out of them"(Acts 19:12).

"to another **prophecy**" (1Corinthians 12:10b em ad); This is not demonic fortune telling. Though the Spirit does give prophetic words or dreams. It is also the testimony of Jesus which is the spirit of prophecy (His past physical first coming and resurrection, soon appearing, then the later physical second coming) there is more to all these gifts. Ask the Holy Spirit Himself to help and guide your study of and walking in His gifts.

"to another **discerning** of spirits" (1Corinthians 12:10c em ad); This is supernatural information on demonic and angelic activity, or its presence, sometimes its influence. Sometimes it includes seeing or sensing into the spiritual realm (hair stands up on back of the neck, really saw something out of the corner of your eye, temperature drop for no reason in a room), an open vision of a spirit, or something maybe no one else noticed. It might be supernatural, it might not. Always ask the Lord if you think something is not natural. The Holy Spirit seems to manifest this gift through women often. We call it women's intuition about situations.

> "to another **divers** (old English for diverse or various) **kinds of tongues**" (1Corinthians 12:10d em ad);

Supernatural speaking human languages fluently you do not know in the presence of those who do. Also as Peter who spoke Hebrew, but was heard by those listening in their native languages. This is God-glorifying, powerful evangelism... Sometimes you speak in an angelic or unknown tongue which is supernaturally interpreted, a fresh living word for a congregation, or group: news flash from Heaven (this equals an aspect of prophecy). IF no person is manifesting the gift of interpretation: DO NOT speak in tongues publicly among unbelievers- this causes confusion. Moreover, we are not to preach in tongues. If a group of believers who all pray in the spirit, their personal prayer language, are together they certainly may pray about an issue together in tongues, and may not have an interpretation, this is a private setting. This the gift of tongues for each person, used by each in a small group. Sometimes People confuse the two separate gifts thinking the public use rule applies to all.

> "to another the **interpretation of tongues**" (1Corinthians 12:10e em ad):

Primarily coupled with speaking in many kinds of tongues- interpreting them- either naturally or supernaturally- is prophetic and tied to tongues in general; also, its interpretation may reveal secrets of unbelievers or believers unknown to anyone else, but God and that person for example. This is evangelistic, and spiritually strengthening to congregations and small groups. It may include gifting with natural languages study, interpretation or translation.

> "But one and the same **Spirit works** all these things, **distributing** to each one **individually as He wills**" (1Corinthians 12:11 em ad NKJV).

Ask for their operation, and you will receive. What people call their sixth sense are their spiritual senses. If you doubt supernatural gifting's or miracles is for you, don't doubt--believe. Jesus said in John 14:12 "Most assuredly, I say to you, he who believes in me, the works that I do he will do also; and greater works than these he will do because I go to My Father." The Spirit will do it. For it is the Spirit which worked through Jesus to work miracles and manifest all the gifts. The Holy Spirit will do as Jesus promised you.

The Unstoppable Lance

> "For he who speaks in a tongue does not speak to men but to God, for no one understands *him*; however, in the spirit, he speaks mysteries... he who speaks in a tongue edifies (strengthens) himself (his/her spirit), but he who prophesies edifies the church." (1Corinthians 14:2, 4, NJKV, em ad).

It is obvious Paul is talking about a different type of tongues since the divers tongues he talks about in chapter twelve is as the Holy Spirit wills. Unlike the gift of Chapter Twelve, this gift we can choose to use or not. So, what is the difference in types of gifts or gifting's that Paul is talking about? The Greek word translated 'gifts' in chapter twelve is charisma. Verse 4 of chapter twelve looks like this "Now there are diversities of gifts [charisma-endowments-miraculous faculty], but the same Spirit..." In James 1:17 the word for gift is dosis and dorema. The verse would be "Every good gift [dosis-giving of gifts] and every perfect gift [dorema-bestowment or present] is from above...." In Acts chapter 2 verse 38, the word translated gift is dorehah. It reads like this "...and ye shall receive the gift [dorehah- gratuity or gift] of the Holy Spirit." These are different types of gifts. The "gift of the Holy Spirit" is like a bonus or extra, such as a personal gratuity or tip.

In chapter nineteen of Acts Paul meets some disciples of John who after talking with Paul believed in Jesus as the Messiah. At that point, they were saved- indwelt of the Holy Spirit, but as yet had not accepted or received the extra, the power. After they believed, Paul laid hands on them and then they received the gift of the Holy Ghost, speaking in their prayer language, a New Covenant gratuity of power offered to believers. It is not mandatory, but voluntary.

> "For if **I pray** in an unknown tongue, **my spirit prayeth**, but my understanding is unfruitful. What is it then? **I will pray** with the spirit, and **I will** pray with the understanding also: **I will** sing with the spirit, and **I will** sing with the understanding also" (1Corinthians 14:14-15 em ad).

The operation of the gift at the will of the believer is also described in Jude. Keep in mind edify and 'to build you up' mean the same thing. This is building or strengthening of your own spirit which overflows into your soul and physical body. Praying you interpret back to yourself is also important for growth in the spirit and soul. Understanding is for the soul. This is communication between you and the Lord Himself in the Spirit.

Physical food feeds the physical body. Knowledge and understanding is food for the soul man. Praying in the spirit, not just speaking, or study of the word of God is fuel and food for the spirit man. Most of us starve, or 'diet' spiritually, and wonder why we are weak supernaturally. This is one time the more you eat, the better you will be mentally, emotionally, physically, and of course spiritually. Remember you are a spirit (body), with a soul (body), in a physical body. You must feed them all the right food for complete health.

> "But ye, beloved, building up **yourselves** on your most holy faith, **praying** in the Holy Ghost, Keep **yourselves** in the love of God, looking for the mercy of our Lord Jesus Christ unto eternal life" (Jude 1:20-21 em ad).

You do not have to be in trouble or under stress to do this. Habitually praying, with a specific person, or situation in mind, or just for the day to come, this helps 'keep' you on track in the Lord (keeping you in His love). Moreover, this is a way of praying for surprise situations, or attacks of the enemy set against you today. We are not, and reasonably cannot be informed about every little thing all the time, this would become scary and overwhelming. If you know too much about what the enemy or a boss at work is about to do ahead of time, you might make it worse, by speaking fearfully about it. Trust Him and listen. He will let you know what you need and when you need to know it. Praying in the Spirit is no substitute for reading your Bible.

Catching the Fire

"And when he (Jesus) had said this, he breathed on them, and saith unto them, Receive ye the Holy Ghost: Whosoever sins ye remit, they are remitted unto them, and whosoever sins ye retain, they are retained"(John 20:20-23 em ad). This is after Jesus resurrection but before His ascension back into the Heavens, which was witnessed by around five hundred people by the way. This is His first appearance to the disciples in the upper room. Only Thomas was not present the first time. All of them believed and were born-again and indwelt at that moment.

Thomas later believes, but since the Holy Spirit has already been dispatched into the Earth to believers, Jesus doesn't have to breathe upon Thomas for Him to become born-again. Otherwise, Jesus would have to breathe on everyone personally, which would be hard since He won't be back down here for a little while longer. So Peter is indwelt by the Holy Spirit in John chapter twenty but, is baptized about a month or so later after Jesus ascends, on the Day of Pentecost. It is clear these are two separate events.

> "But Peter, standing up with the eleven, lifted up his voice, and said unto them, Ye men of Judaea, and all ye that dwell at Jerusalem, be this known unto you, and hearken to my words: For these are not drunken, as ye suppose, seeing it is but the third hour of the day. But this is that which was spoken by the prophet Joel, And it shall come to pass in the last days, saith God, **I will pour out of my Spirit upon all flesh**: and your sons and your daughters shall prophesy, and your young men shall see visions, and your old men shall dream dreams"(Acts 2:14-17 em ad):

Great say some, but that was for them and not for us in the future. Miracles died out after the apostles and disciples died out. A crazy belief believed by far too many people. Not only are miracles in abundance documented in legal and medical and other records around the world as this is being typed. Even in the Scripture, we of today, who were the future yesteryear when this was written were written about.

"Then Peter said unto them, Repent, and be baptized every one of you in the name of Jesus Christ for the remission of sins, and ye shall receive the gift of the Holy Ghost. For the promise is unto you, and to your children, **and to all that are afar off**, even as many as the Lord our God **shall** call" (Act 2:38-39 em ad). We are those afar off, who come later in time as we experience it, whom the Lord has called, and who have answered. The Lord called all people and had a preordained mission or purpose for them. Unfortunately, many do not hear, or if they understand, they reject the call, some for a little while, some forever.

Keeping it clear

Once you are born-again, you have authority, and you can receive power. The Holy Spirit does not come in a rushing wind each time, though He may do whatever He wills. These are two separate events in scripture to make it easy not to get confused. There are several other places in the book of Acts touching on this subject. The indwelling of the Holy Spirit and the baptism of the Holy Spirit are two separate things. There are numerous doctrines of demons surrounding tongues. Here is the Biblical bottom line up front.

- You can be saved, and not walk in the power of the Spirit
- It is untrue you must speak with tongues to be saved
- You cannot lose your salvation if you don't pray in tongues
- Fruit of the Spirit is not same as the gifts of the Spirit
- You are not less of a Christian if you don't pray in tongues
- You are not more of a Christian if you do pray in tongues

Some depend upon their works to show and bring salvation. Nonsense, actions should be seen, but may or may not be, even when they are Christian. A believer choked by the thorns will not manifest much if any fruit. The thief on the cross, others saved on death row, on their death beds, have no works or fruit. They may not have been baptized in water, and most did not speak in tongues, but they are still saved by grace through faith.

For those who cry out 'one baptism'

All believers are indwelt, not all believers receive (though they can) the power/fire. John the Baptist mentioned this separate baptism before Jesus is revealed as Messiah. It is important enough to say again. When you think of a pool of water. Being baptized is to be immersed spiritually or physically in a pool of water or spiritual substance or empowerment. In the Old Testament this was unto repentance. In the New Testament it is still a symbol repentance, but is the public profession of faith in Jesus (when you were born-again and already baptized spiritually). When you are dunked in water and then come up this is a picture of the death and resurrection of the Lord Jesus. That we are buried with Him in baptism and raised with Him in newness of life. Here is a scripture on only one baptism in Ephesians.

> "There is one body, and one Spirit, even as ye are called in one hope of your calling; One Lord, one faith, one baptism,"

Of course, this is true. But many who say this is water baptism, also believe there are no other baptisms. This belief rejects the additional aspects of 'the one' spiritual baptism occurring at the point of salvation, which opens the door to so much more in scripture.

> "I indeed **baptize** you with **water** unto **repentance**: but he that cometh after me (Jesus) is mightier than I, whose shoes I am not worthy to bear: he shall **baptize you** with the *Holy Ghost*, **and** with *fire*" (Matthew 3:11 em ad).

There are blatantly more than one baptism experience for the believer. The first is unseen happening at the moment you believed and are indwelt by the Holy Spirit. Another is in water which is your public profession of faith, a work of man not the Spirit. The first baptism opens the way for the baptism with fire (power) with the evidence of speaking in personal tongues, and for other gifts of the Spirit. Some receive the gift of speaking in personal tongues or Baptism of the Holy Ghost before being water baptized. There is a common order, but it is not a set-in stone order, of experiencing or receiving gifts.

Moving in the Power of the Spirit

> "So then after the Lord had spoken unto them, he was received up into heaven and sat on the right hand of God. And they [the apostles and disciples or believers] went forth, and preached everywhere, **the Lord working with them,** and **confirming the word with signs following**. Amen" (Mark 16: 20-19 em ad).

Any Christian, especially a Minister of Vengeance, needs to be receiving the baptism of the Holy Ghost, and exercise the gift. It's your choice, and the Lord will always be with you regardless of your choice. But you are on the edge, and in the thick of the warfare in the natural and supernatural. You should be fully equipped with all Spirit gives you. The Enemy is wicked, merciless, and devious beyond imagination or comprehension. Without Holy Spirit help, and a working knowledge of the word, we are unnecessarily vulnerable.

You may have been doing very well without this gift. Satan's resources, though substantial is still limited. He allocates them as needed. Being a wise commanding archangel, if you are no threat to him, little or no direct resources are dispatched against you above the normal allotment. Why waste resources, if you are not a threat to his Kingdom. Prayer of all types is important. A statesman named Donoso Cores said, "Those who pray, do more for the world than those who fight, and if the world is going from bad to worse, it is because there are more battles than prayers." A French Bishop Jacques Bossuet said, "Hands uplifted, rout more battalions than hands that strike." For a warrior perspective on prayer refer to the appendices with Gen. Patton's Training Letter No. 5.

Receiving the gift of the Holy Ghost

If you already pray in tongues or are not interested, you may skip to the next chapter.

It is not mandatory to have someone lay hands on you, though it is common, to receive the baptism of the Holy Ghost. Many pray and receive it at home, some at crusades, and some through praying with a person on the television. One believer, who I know personally, received it while praying over the phone in the middle of a deliverance situation. Here is a suggested prayer for you, paraphrased from Perry Stone's Code of the Holy Spirit.

> "Father God in the name of Jesus I am hungry for Your promise of power, the fire, the dorehah gift of the baptism of the Holy Ghost. I want to operate in my personal spiritual prayer language and be able to receive from the Holy Spirit, any and all of the charisma gifts, according to His will. It is your will and promise to me to have and operate in these."
>
> "I sought and asked and thank you for them by faith. For Jesus said, seek and I shall find, ask and it shall be given. I have not asked amiss, for this is your express will for me to have these. I therefore thank you for them provided by grace, taken through faith."

God inhabits the praises of His children. It will come up from your spirit in your belly, not from your soul in your head. Ask the Holy Spirit to help draw it out like water from a well, manifesting His gift. He will not violate your free will or be pushy, He is polite. Ask Him if you are nervous or fearful, or doubting, to overcome these for you, He will do it. This is not some crazy emotional outburst. One person in the Gospels asked Jesus to help him overcome his unbelief that he might receive from Him, and he helped him. Holy Spirit is your Partner and Helper.

The New Normal

It may feel a bit odd **at first** on your tongue since the source is a spirit, not a soul. Keep your mind on Christ. Now with your mind on Christ lift up your hands and begin to praise Jesus for all He has done, is doing, and will do for you. Just lift your hands in worship to Him, praising Him aloud with your mouth, believing His gift will manifest, that you have it now. The more you use this gift, the easier it becomes, and the more you build yourself up in the spirit. It becomes natural with time and use.

It is strange when it first comes up from your spirit (belly area) into your mouth and tongue. Your brain tries to interpret and make sense of it. Check out the University of Pennsylvania's study on tongues. (Newberg et al, 2006) and (Penn State). That while speaking in tongues, test subjects portion of the brain for audio is markedly less active. It is because your soul is not controlling your tongue to speak your native or another learned human language, it is your spirit controlling your tongue, at your will. In the natural, our soul can learn new languages difficult for the tongue to speak at first. It is the same with our spirit. It is a new language for our tongue, originating from our spirit man, our inner being, not the conscious or unconscious mind.

CHAPTER 10
Politics of War

To properly engage in war you must sententia (think) correctly about war. In thinking about war (*Sententia In Bellum*), philosophical, military, and religious leaders have struggled and debated for ages about appropriateness in war and use of violence. What it looks like initially may not be what it really is. Some early Christian theologians are non-committal in their theory of *Jus Ad Bellum* (just resort to war), and *Jus In Bello* (the law during war). Another translation of Jus Ad Bellum is the just cause for declaring war. Another translation for Jus In Bello is the rules of conduct during war.

> "Jus Ad Bellum principles which identify requisite conditions for resorting to war. These are **just cause**, **right authority**, **right intention**, **public declaration**, **last resort**, **reasonable hope**, and **proportionality**. Also considered are the Jus In Bello principles of proportionality and **discrimination** (noncombatant immunity), the criteria for determining just means." (Davidson, 1983)

Laws and regulations are boundaries of conduct, conferred rights and obligations agreed upon within a society by its participants. Rights are assigned by those with authority to do such. A person can lay claim to a supposed right, but this does not make it lawful or binding in and of itself. The same authority that gives permission for a soldier to take leave also gives orders telling the solider to go to war. It is an authority which dictates morality, or immorality disguised as morality. In the founding documents of the United States of America are found the precursors and revealers of the Bible as a primary source of the concept of our government. Other influencing works are the Magna Carta, Mayflower Compact, and John Locke's Two Treatise of Government. An early example of the authority of We the People can be seen in this excerpt from the Mayflower Compact (original spelling).

> We, whose names are underwritten...having undertaken, for the glory of God, and advancement of the Christian faith...a voyage to plant the first colony...by these presents, solemnly and mutually in the presence of God, and one another, covenant and combine ourselves together into a civil body politick, for our better ordering and preservation and furtherance of the ends aforesaid; and by virtue hereof to enacte, constitute, and frame such just and equall laws, ordinances, acts, constitutions, and offices, from time to time, as shall be thought most meete and convenient *for the generall good* of the Colonie unto which we promise all due submission and obedience... (em ad)

Though the Mayflower Compact declared loyalty to not separation from England, and the King, God's grace is the cited source of sovereignty or authority. Primary loyalty or submission is still to the colony itself, its preservation, and the furtherance of the stated purpose of settlement. The from time to time clause includes any future government structuring authority's right to make constitutions or other declarations which might break association with King and country, should the purpose of the colony or its general good be threatened.

In the case of the Declaration of Independence, rights and the right to become independent are asserted directly from the Creator, who holds accountable all rulers of all peoples. The Declaration is a list of 26 cases of abuse of the King's authority. The injuries and refusal to address these abuses of power by the King are the justifications to no longer recognize the Kings authority under God over the American Colonies. This is Biblical just cause for breaking away and becoming independent. The general good (welfare) of the colonies is at stake. Treason to one nation is the last resort to another. What we call the War of Independence, others called rebellion or insurrection.

> "The Declaration of Independence...[is the]declaratory charter of our rights, and of the rights of man"Thomas Jefferson, 1819

The Declaration cites the source of the Peoples authority, rights, and entitlement as from Natures God. Then the over twenty reasons which force them to action. Of the fifty-six signers of the Declaration, twenty-nine held seminary degrees. Do the Declaration and Revolution stand the Biblical test of justice? Is Just Cause criteria (the justified act of revolution for the preservation of something threatened) met or not met? If not then they are acts of rebellion and treason; unlawful and criminal no matter who won. Note: Because of revisionist historians seeking to erase the Christian heritage and history of America through and economic only view of the nation's history. Taxation without representation seems to be the only reason for the Revolution people know. Ironically it is not in the top ten or even the top half of listed abuses. It is number seventeen of twenty-six. The root cause is explained in this excerpt from the Declaration. It is to gain freedom from oppression.

> The history of the present King of Great Britain is a history of repeated injuries and usurpations, all having in direct object the establishment of an absolute Tyranny over these States. To prove this, let Facts be submitted to a candid world. He has refused his Assent to Laws, the most wholesome and necessary for the public good...

> ...and that all political connection between them and the State of Great Britain, is and ought to be totally dissolved; and that as Free and Independent States, they have full Power to levy War, conclude Peace, contract Alliances,

establish Commerce, and to do all other Acts and Things which Independent States may of right do. And for the support of this Declaration, with a <u>firm reliance on the *protection of divine* **Providence**, we *mutually* pledge to each other our Lives, our Fortunes and our sacred Honor.</u> (Declaration, 1776, em ad)

We need more of that kind of patriotic devotion and faith. The signers, in signing, morally, and legally obligated themselves to the task of instituting a new government, a new nation. In the process, they became enemies of the State. Reliance upon divine Providence (God) shows the authors and signers of the Declaration of Independence, the United States Constitution, and Bill of Rights knew their covenant with God. They knew they could not win their war for freedom without God, nor without prayer. Prayer was commonly conducted by our Founders during the meetings and discussions creating the Declaration, U.S. Constitution and Bill of Rights. Many read through the Bible each year.

The mission statement of the United States of America is the Declaration. How the mission is accomplished or worked out is in the United States Constitution. Parameters or in analogy the by-laws are the Bill of Rights (first ten amendments). The Preamble to the U.S. Constitution connects the intent for freedom in the Declaration with how we will live free. We are the first nation to do this. God is the primary source of authority. It is American exceptionalism - the great experiment.

WE THE PEOPLE of the United States, in Order to form a more perfect Union, establish **Justice**, insure domestic **Tranquility**, provide for the common defense, promote the **general Welfare**, and secure the **Blessings of Liberty** to ourselves and our Posterity, do ordain and establish

> this Constitution for the United States of America. (Preamble em ad)

The secondary source of authority who God delegates authority to: WE THE PEOPLE. It is derived by divine right in the Declaration with the outlining of the oppressive acts done by the King to his subjects in the American Colonies. Purpose: form a more perfect Union. To manifest the purpose, a domestic enforcement force along with supporting organization(s) needs assembling. Culture is determined by We the People and therefore not always right. Might does not make right, the majority does not make it right- ask anyone lynched by a mob or Jesus with the crowd shouting crucify Him! Culture is guided by ministers, and or whoever the people are listening to for guidance. We change culturally according to whom we pay attention to.

The farther our values move from the Bible, the less integrated we are with the culture of Heaven and more integrated we are with the culture of Hell. It is obvious which culture brings blessings and protection and which causes the spiritual, moral and economic downfall of a nation. As the preamble paraphrases and uses Biblical principles (2 Cor 3:17), the Founders wanted their government, our government, to "secure the blessings of Liberty" through godly administration. You and I are WE THE PEOPLE who delegate the responsibility to govern well.

Two things our Founders understood from the Bible. Liberty refers to God who is the source of all blessings and only one who can be judge, lawgiver, and executor all at the same time, without becoming corrupted. Separation of powers is a protection against a sole person waging war, and oppressing his or her own people unchecked for personal gain. A President may enact policy actions and engage in warfare to a point. It takes an act of Congress to declare war. A judge may declare a thing unconstitutional saying a President is acting beyond their Constitutional duty. But, in the end if any person desires a jury trial. We The People judge the law, not just the facts. (John Jay, 1st Chief justice of the Supreme Court, Georgia v. Brailsford 1794).

Two scriptures Jeremiah 17:9 and Isaiah 33:22 are where we got our Biblical precedent for the separation of powers. Because the heart of man is wicked, separating the powers or functions of government among three branches and many people are the checks and balances designed to compensate for the deception or wickedness in the hearts of a few or many. Since the Lord is not susceptible to evil, the three functions of government, lawmaking, judging, and ruling He does righteously alone. Our Founders divided the authority of delegated responsibility among us as branches of government. Yes, history buffs also know of John Locke and Charles Montesquieu's contributions, but my primary focus is on the Biblical precedent. A summary of the Founding Fathers thoughts and Biblical roots of our government structure is in George Washington's farewell address, declining to run for a third term as President.

> The spirit of encroachment tends to consolidate the powers of all the departments in one and thus to create, whatever the form of government, a real despotism. A just estimate of that love of power and proneness to abuse it which predominates in the **human heart** is sufficient to satisfy us of the truth of this position. The necessity of **reciprocal checks** in the exercise of political power by **dividing and distributing** it into different depositories and constituting each the **guardian** of the public weal (*prosperity or good*) against invasions by the others, has been evinced (*demonstrated*) by experiments ancient and modern, some of them in our country and under our own eyes. (Washington, 1796, p.22, em ad)

Just Cause

Two of the three primary aspects of war from which our features or sub-aspects of war are derived are Jus Ad Bellum and Jus In Bello, the justice in going to war, and methods of conducting war. The grounds or the legal reason for the justification to go to war is called Casus Belli. Though we Americans find it hard to agree on some specific definitions, we have a very good sense of what justice looks like. Equal opportunity for and equal treatment of all is justice. What are some commonly held acceptable reasons for war?

> (1) Differences in religious or political ideology are not in themselves justification for war or intervention.
>
> (2) Nations should hold strong presumptions against intervening in the internal affairs of other nations or taking sides in a civil war.
>
> (3) Nations are justified in coming to the aid of another nation when that nation is unjustly attacked by a third nation.
>
> (4) Intervention is justified on the request of the government to balance support given by a third nation to an insurrection or insurgency movement.
>
> (5) Intervention is justified on behalf of a revolutionary force seeking to overthrow an extremely oppressive regime, provided that this force has general popular support and has requested intervention.
>
> (6) Intervention is justified to stop the massive abuse of human rights
>
> (7) Intervention is not justified if definitive determination cannot be made as to whether or not the unrest in another nation is a justifiable revolution with broad popular support or unjustified intervention by a third nation with little popular support. (Davidson, 1983)

Retired Colonel Thomas McShane adds a twenty-first-century twist to Just Cause. "A violation of sovereignty still constitutes casus belli or grounds for war..." There is a paradox of sovereignty. To attack without direct threat or provocation is to violate another nation's sovereignty which is not a just cause for war. Yet if the issue is humanitarian is that an exception? If another holocaust of the Jews or another people group is occurring, or ethnic cleansing such as happened in Rwanda 1994, a nation who had not threatened us. Is this cause to intervene and violate another nation's sovereignty? McShane further comments on the legal status of this ethical dilemma and public opinion. Intervening because of human rights violations is a very controversial subject with no two situations entirely alike.

> "It is unrealistic to expect consensus on actions such as forced regime change, intervention to prevent genocide, and even severe sanctions, all of which constitute violations of sovereignty" (McShane, 2012).

Interestingly McShane incorporates sanctions as a type of sovereignty violation. I do not agree with Col. McShane, that sanctions violate sovereignty. They are consequences for threatening actions taken by a sovereign nation. They are attempts to pressure a country to change its behavior without force. Sanctions are also forms of protest which may not apply real pressure in execution for several reasons, but send the message to another nation of our disapproval. Sanctions can trigger a war if the country they are imposed upon declines to change, but instead retaliates. There is no obligation on the part of one government to trade with or not restrict travel to or from any other country. Trade tariffs and travel restrictions are based on a nation's economic goals, cultural values, and or security factors, and are sovereign acts. No state is obligated to accept persons of other nations for example. Our American history, culture, and policy of immigration are impressive, but at the same time, legally speaking, (at the time of this writing) it is dangerous and foolish.

As we touch on principles of causes of war, justice, and how to act during the war, we refer to a seasoned Prussian German combat soldier and master strategist of the late 18th and early 19th centuries, Carl Von Clausewitz. In Principles of War, he teaches the objectives of war. Objectives, Clausewitz says if they are not accomplishable, or even projected attainable would assumedly undermine just war theory. Additionally, a humanitarian reason for conducting a war doesn't exactly fit the objectives of a traditional war.

> "Warfare has three main objects: (a) To conquer and destroy the armed power of the enemy; (b) To take possession of his material and other sources of strength, and (c) To gain public opinion" (Clausewitz, 1812).

God is an honorable God. Though He knew the children of Israel had the right to the Promised Land, they still did not draw first blood. They eventually are provoked by a rear attack, from a faction of the enemy Canaanite tribes occupying the Promised Land. The just cause of the aggression on the tribes occupying the Promised Land came from their drawing first blood. Even when God has just cause to destroy a people because of rampant child sacrifice, for example, He doesn't just do it immediately. He always waits until the Covenant is attacked, or rather a Covenant person or leader is attacked justifying God's intervention and participation in the retaliation. The Lord put Sampson in a position which entangled him with a Philistine woman to provide God just cause for war. God did not pick this fight using Delilah, but another woman before her. God set the enemy up.

> "Then his father and his mother said unto him, Is there never a woman among the daughters of thy brethren, or among all my people, that thou goest to take a wife of the uncircumcised Philistines? And Samson said unto his father, Get her for me; for she pleaseth me well. But his father and his mother **knew not** that **it was of the LORD**, that **he sought an occasion against the Philistines**: for at that time the Philistines had dominion over Israel" (Judges 14:3-4 ONM em ad).

When the Lord sets up the enemy, they still have the opportunity to make the right choice, but He already knows they will decide wrongly and give Him just cause. This is not making the enemy look like it's their fault, it truly is their fault. God is sneaky as we shall see, but to fabricate a pretense for war is dishonorable. God is wholeheartedly honorable always. To paraphrase General Patton's famous statement in Berlin, perceiving Russia as a future threat said, "In ten days I'll have a war on with those Communist...and I'll make it look like their fault." Patton would have been fabricating a just cause for attacking a perceived threat which is outside of Biblical parameters and not the same as God's use of Sampson. General Patton's foresight as to the threat of Communism is to be commended. General Patton's proposed method of 'making it look like their fault' to cause a war is not acceptable in this context. If no real just cause exists, then so be it. God created a situation in which the enemy would give Him just cause. I respect General Patton considerably, but we all make mistakes with good intentions.

Notwithstanding, conspiracy theorists citing the timely movement of some critical ships out of Pearl Harbor, before the attack. Radio traffic transcripts from December 8th throughout the war in the public domain. However, radio transcripts dating from December 7th and earlier are supposedly still sealed. If indeed we were reading the mail of the Japanese, we knew the attack was coming. The attack is possibly provoked by the United States embargo of resources necessary to their Asian war machine which was a good move.

Some say Imperial Japan took the American embargo against the Japanese before entry into WW II as an act of war. It is initially publicized as a gesture of non-support of Imperial Japan's advancements in Asia. U.S. politicians and military advisors already perceived the threat posed by the Nazi and Imperial Japan war machines. However, lacking the support of public opinion, and the ability to sway Americans into joining the war before it was too late, something drastic had to be done. If America hadn't entered the war when it did German would have been our new national language instead of English.

We could have had a similar effect meeting the Japanese airplanes over the Pacific before they reached the harbor. All we needed was too coincidentally have a plane ordered on a flight of some kind, which would coincidently see them coming and report it. Or send a naval ship on a maintenance run, or some such thing, who would report after spotting the swarm of Zero's headed to Pearl Harbor. We would not have tipped our hand in the communications area, saved more service member lives, and possibly some ships. Public outrage would have been the same.

Decades earlier, losing 120 civilian Americans on the torpedoed passenger ship Lusitania fueled the fire causing America to enter WW I.

We were warned by the Germans about this possibility before submarine U-20 in 1915 sunk her in the Atlantic. It was allegedly smuggling war materials to England our ally already at war with Germany. Both incidents caused public outrage and gave just cause to join in the battle. Either war whose victory if not achieved would have meant the end of civilization as it was known, especially WW II. An outraged public will support vengeance. For the record, I do not believe the 9/11 attacks were permitted in any fashion by our government, but a result of part of our hedge of national protection being breached from within.

In the cases of the Imperial Japanese and Nazis, an 'occasion' against them needed to be found. God didn't want these attacks against us to happen. I'm just speculating, but is that what it took to realize the threat of Radical Islam? The Twin Towers had been bombed once before, we've had citizens held hostage at the embassy in Tehran, passengers were taken hostage on planes, along with other incidents around the globe. Only after 9/11 did we as a nation rise up and fight back. Now, at the time of this writing, thanks to President Trump, ISIS is decimated, and respect for America returns.

Right Authority

Right Authority and Just Cause as with other facets of just war theory overlap. Having the ability to use force does not automatically mean you have the right to use force. If the right to use force is not from lawful authority, there is no lethal force authority. King George ordered troops to blockade Boston Harbor after the Boston Tea Party; considered an act of domestic terrorism by some. When he gave this order, it is before the Declaration of Independence. It is under lawful authority as the colonies were still submitted to the crown at that time. Lawful, yes, though arguably an abuse of power, an overreactive use of force instead of addressing the underlying problem.

In the case of the War Between the States, the Confederates had the ability, but no authority to conduct war. They previously submitted to the rule of law under the Republic when they signed the Constitution. They did not like the way things were going and stated they are separating or ceding from the Union claiming sovereign nation rights. They had no lawful authority to leave, nor right to claim independent statehood. Their cited reasons for forming their own nation are not recognized by the Union. Their Declaration of Secession from the Union attempted to mimic Declaration of Independence but was not Biblical. It is culturally grounded, and they did not have the authority to leave. It was selfish economic interest masquerading as a moral right to self-govern.

The Southern States downfall starts with being led astray by the thirteen-page outline of the Confederate States of America's (CSA) right to wage war, written in 1860. Statute violations cited seem to mirror the reasoning founding fathers used asserting their right to conduct war, and the authority for the War of Independence from England. The flaw in their logic was their perception any grievance, this one being the ending of slavery as being a violation of states' rights. The Articles of Confederation were how the government was structured during the Revolutionary War. After the war, a new structure of government is created superseding and replacing the Articles upon the majority of states ratification of the United States Constitution. A document not signed by all states, but ratified by nine of fourteen by 1790. Two of the nine ratifying states are the chief instigator states of Virginia and South Carolina. The three holdouts Massachusetts, Georgia, and Connecticut signed by the end of 1939.

The Southern states signed over their authority until it did not suit them. The Tenth Amendment and last amendment to the original Bill of Rights was essential to South Carolina. It states "The powers not delegated to the United States by the Constitution, nor prohibited by it to the States, are reserved to the States respectively, or to the people." They used this as a right to the return of slaves from free states, and as a pretense to the right to revert to a sovereign nation of their own. Their supposed authority came from the wording of the Treaty between England, and the United States of America joined in their minds to the Tenth Amendment.

Britain stated the colonies are "Free and Sovereign and Independent States" meaning the mother country, an established and universally accepted sovereign power now recognized them as independent sovereign powers. However, we just broke away from them, and the King no longer determines the way we organize or view ourselves. Whatever their apparent independence, they gave it up by consent through signing and participating as a member state of a Union under the United States Constitution. The two most influential states in starting the Civil War, Virginia, and South Carolina had been functioning under the U.S. Constitution peaceably for **seventy years**.

Our Republican form of government, unlike the Articles of Confederation, is a government founded upon the principles of the Declaration of Independence. By their own admission, the consent of the governed elected a President hostile to slavery. An approval process of election of leaders they agreed and submitted to until it no longer served their preferences. Though elaborate in its attempted paralleling of the Declaration of Independence. The Declaration of Secession still falls short of the right or authority to wage war. Therefore, they became rebels instead of revolutionaries.

Right Intention

The South did not have the right intentions. They were breaking covenant without just cause. Their founding document of immediate cause for secession cited no real authority, even from the Divine. The Divine whom they called upon in their conclusion. They assumed God to be on their side instead of checking to see if they were on God's side.

> *..."We, therefore, the people of South Carolina, by our delegates, in Convention assembled, appealing to the Supreme Judge of the world for rectitude of our intentions, have solemnly declared that the Union heretofore existing...is dissolved, and that the State of South Carolina has resumed her position among the nations of the world, as a separate and independent State..."*

Their appeal to God is heard. Four years later His ruling from the Divine bench manifests at Appomattox Courthouse. Right intentions are crucial to the Warrior. Now I must say, many a warrior has gone to war with right intentions, while their leadership did not. Such is the case of the South. We may be sent on an illegal mission unknowingly, yet can rest that our hands are clean of blood guilt, the same cannot be said of those who knowingly ordered an immoral use of force. Then there is the mission which is technically illegal, and the participants know if caught, the State cannot claim them. There are many variables in these situations, but these actions are often justified out of necessity. Don't worry; the Lord knows enemies try to hide behind many laws, attempting to shield their dangerous activities.

When the Rebels fired upon Fort Sumter April 12, 1861, they used lethal force without moral authority against a lawful government. The outcome of the war was decided in Heaven immediately. Once shots are fired, you have reached a point of no return except through surrender or being defeated. Conversely, when the British military fired upon the American militia, it was decided in Heaven against the English that day, but it took years to manifest in our reality. England had drawn first blood without justification against us.

Why didn't they have justification; because the Declaration of Independence listed the abuses of authority by England. Abuses the colonies unsuccessfully attempted through lawful means to stop. The King was informed legally of the Colonies no longer recognizing his rule. Instead of replying with answers to twenty-six violations of colonist's rights, or an offer of some relief, he sent the military. The British army is sent lawfully by the Kings authority to enforce unlawful rule over a newly sovereign people, whose obligation to submit to the King, expired upon his continued abuse and neglect of them. If the right to fight and means to resist are present, are not a people duty-bound to conduct war for peace? Yes.

The King of England chose not to use diplomacy when he could have. The South saw it could not win legislatively against the growing abolition movement. Their decision, attempt to break the covenant and assert a personal power base in human misery and degradation. Ironically, to fight the Union, the South made its own Constitution mirroring the one they rejected. Of note is another difference, recognition by an established international country- the Vatican. At this time in history, the Pope is the King of the Papal States. Yes, France allied with us in the War of Independence, a critical event- militarily and politically. And the Vatican did not support the Union because the American Revolution contributed to weakening power of the Papal States. International recognition by an established power was necessary for the Confederate States of America (CSA). Though lacking formal recognition, the letter of Pope Pious IX King of the Papal States, to President Davis of the CSA informally recognized the CSA as a legitimate sovereign nation.

The Pope's letter to Jefferson Davis caused widespread desertions from the Union among the Irish and German Catholic soldiers. Moreover, upon the assassination of Lincoln, the majority of nations sent condolences at the loss of the United States. Conspicuously none came from the Vatican, as a Catholic priest gives sanctuary to fugitive John Surratt. Surratt is hunted in connection with the assassination of President Lincoln. He is then moved to the Vatican joining the Papal Zouaves, (the Popes personal guard) under an alias. John Surratt is finally apprehended in Alexandria, Egypt. His trial in the assassination ends in a hung jury.

Formal Declaration

A government should declare its intentions officially to the enemy nation. Both the Colonies and the Confederate States adhered to this custom. However, some make declarations of war within their own borders, to its own citizens, while attempting to appear publicly friendly. Iran among others is notorious for public chants of "Death to America." In The Law of Land Warfare (U.S. Army Manual, FM 27-10) is American accepted practices.

> "The Contracting Powers recognize that hostilities between themselves must not commence without previous and explicit warning, in the form either of a reasoned declaration of war or of an ultimatum with conditional declaration of war...nothing in the foregoing rule requires that any particular length of time shall lapse between a declaration of war and the commencement of hostilities."

Notice the phrase lapse in time. A lapse could be minutes. Not officially declaring war is then the use of preemptive strikes. Remember the attack on Pearl Harbor came as an 'official' surprise because after the attack commenced was their declaration of war pronounced. Israel's preemptive strike against Egyptian Air Forces is justified because multiple hostile actions on the part of the Egyptian and other military's in the region confirmed their intent to attack. At this point, a declaration would cause Israel to lose the initiative and any chance of winning. Notwithstanding God who did help them as documented by many military miracles during battle. Therefore, a preemptive strike is permissible if war is inevitable, for the attack may serve two purposes. First is to gain and retain an advantage over opposing forces. Second is the possibility of stopping a war through the strike. Such as a raid on an ICMB or other facility preventing a nuclear attack.

> On the morning of June 5, 1967, Israel launched a preemptive strike against Egyptian forces in response to Egypt's closing of the Straits of Tiran. By June 11, the conflict had come to include Jordan and Syria. As a result of this conflict, Israel gained control over the Sinai Peninsula, the Golan Heights, the West Bank, the Gaza Strip and East Jerusalem. Israeli claims on these territories and the question of the Palestinians stranded there posed a long-term challenge to Middle East diplomacy. (Israeli War, 1967).

Japan possibly felt our embargo of resources against them was an act of war, not using force, but through actions hurting their war efforts in Asia. Equally debatable is the closing of the Straits of Tiran (a major source of trade), and military buildups along Israel's borders, from openly hostile nations. A preemptive strike is not a breaking of the Laws of War and Conflict when a formal declaration is withheld while aggressive actions were undertaken. In such cases, it is legitimate to preemptively strike in defense of national security and peace where the targeted country is in all ways belligerent toward the preemptively assaulting nation. A preemptive strike is not always from a vulnerable position, but to avoid becoming vulnerable. It does not violate the avoidance of first blood if honestly waiting for official first blood means losing the war or any chance of victory. Covert preemptive assault is the preferred option.

Preemptive would also constitute the first strike nation doing so to ensure its probability of survival. The probability of success here equates with continuation as a sovereign state, self-preservation, not domination of another state. A preemptive strike is not justifiable if the intent is to surprise an enemy to gain a tactical and strategic advantage when the target nation poses no threat. That would be a sneak attack without justification. A sneak attack is an aggressive action; a preemptive attack is a defensive action. A sneak attack is drawing first blood without a declaration of war. For example, one country does not like the religion or ideology/resources controlled by another nation. It decides to eradicate the opposing religion through military means and annexing the non-hostile country without actual threat from that nation.

Probability of Success

> "Or what king, when he sets out to meet another king in battle, will not first sit down and consider whether he is strong enough with ten thousand men to encounter the one coming against him with twenty thousand? Or else, while the other is still far away, he sends a delegation and asks for terms of peace." (Luke 14:31-32, NIV)

If you know you cannot do anything about a given situation you continue to pray, listen to the Holy Spirit, and bide your time. An opportunity will arise to correct the situation. Should the cause be right such as with John Quincy Adams constant abolitionist overtures, the right time will come. Adams brought up his anti-slavery motions to Congress repeatedly and were struck down repeatedly. He never stopped trying, saying his duty was to keep trying and God's duty to bring the results. In the case of the Revolution, logistically the Colonies had no chance of victory against an established world superpower. Yet they did prevail, a testimony to Divine Providence, providing.

I believe the South not only thought they had the right to break the covenant but additionally thought they would succeed. Should or would you like to have a high probability of success, of course. Will the likelihood of success always be there? No. D-Day is an example. A lot could have gone wrong, and the invasion fail, but the attack had to happen. As Jesus said, who doesn't count the cost: is defeat less than the cost of not even trying.

Last Resort

Self-explanatory, if given no choice then you fight, or you submit to oppression. This is the tactic of Islam. Submit, convert, or die. If you are a convert and you abandon Islam, you are sentenced to death. I mention Islam again because Islam is a political, military and religious system all wrapped into one. The true separation of church and state in the Constitution is not for the government to be against religion, only to prevent the government from establishing a nationally enforced State Religion. Islam is state-sponsored religion. The church and state are the same in Islam. When repeatedly assaulted eventually you must respond or submit. You truly always have the choice, but last resort is the final decision to capitulate or resist, too submit to shackles or attempt to break loose of the shackles. Scriptural considerations for Last Resort: Romans 12:17-18 (NIV) "Do not repay anyone evil for evil. Be careful to do what is right in the eyes of everybody. If it is possible, as far as it depends on you, live at peace with everyone". Unfortunately, as we well know is it is not always possible to live at peace with everyone.

Proportionality

Several instances in the Bible the spiritual and moral decay of people or groups, like a virus was about to spread, or His own people rebelled terribly, and the consequences were dire. When children will be raised serving false gods, and false prophets are leading people to hell as a culture extreme measures had to be taken. They were all wiped out, a proportion equal to the seriousness of the problem. It must be brought back to remembrance, that at that time the Lord Jesus has not yet defeated the power of the enemy. His authority and power had not yet been delegated to all who would believe.

The Jews, the people of Yahweh, were not born-again at that time. So, before you point the finger at them and others of that time, recall you were a sinner once too until saved by grace through faith. An opportunity not afforded them in the same sense. Salvation came by dying in faith believing for the coming Messiah. Once Jesus ascended into Heaven, then they all gained entrance. Their former residence in Hades was a protected oasis called Paradise (Luke 16). Thank God the battle is no longer defensive on our part.

The principle of proportionality evaluates the effects or means of war in justifying the end. It does this by calculating the value of expected results. In this regard, proportionality is counting the costs, doing a cost-benefit analysis, and or a risk assessment. In ethical decision making, there is frequently a tension between ends and means, between the result desired and conceptions of what is the right action. Those who consider results the only valid criterion for selecting a course of action is saying the end justifies the means.

The just-war tradition incorporates elements of good results and right action, in making decisions about war. In the Jus Ad Bellum sense, this principle insists that there be due proportion, that is, **less or no evil** following from *acting* rather than *not acting* in the manner contemplated. What is acceptable is often up to public opinions pressure on the decision makers which is not always a reliable moral gauge to measure a decision by. There are examples in the Bible of total war and limited war agenda in operation. It cannot be overemphasized that at critical times prayer and searching for an answer which will not violate your conscience is always in order. Less evil is better than more. Decisions which weigh heavy on a conscience do not mean you should feel guilty. Some decisions should be hard.

Discrimination

A cost-benefit analysis distinction is made between total war and limited-war decision making. In limited war, extra care is taken to minimize all damage to property and people. In total war, the only agenda is victory and domination. Political agenda determines rules of engagement more than victory often times when limited war theory is misapplied. Any way you look at it public opinion usually rules the roost. Limited war theory places greater emphasis on protecting the innocent, or discriminating between warriors and noncombatants. Just War theorists today tend to view noncombatant immunity as an absolute principle, whereas other theorists view it as a relative principle. Both are valid views. The challenge comes in deciding which one applies when.

Total War

Total war philosophy uses all possible lawful and moral means to affect the complete victory, conquest or domination of opposing forces, militarily, economically, politically and culturally. Such was the fate of Imperial Japan and Nazi Germany. While today total war does not sit well with public opinion, during World War II, when nations and cultures were threatened, including in the United States, it was the opposite. The waring Axis nations of Germany and Japan enjoyed public support from their citizens for their aggression and tactics. Our initial goal was not to annex Germany or Japan or make them future allies and democracies, it was to defeat them and dominate them in defense of the threats to our own way of life, and the lives of our allies. Becoming allies is a different type of domination in this context than the traditional taking over of the losing nation. Our occupying of Japan and Germany after the war offered protection from the Soviet Union and helped with the reconstruction of the nation.

> The Allies viewed the German and the Japanese civilian populations as enemy populations and did not hesitate in treating them as such...the Anglo-American strategic bombing campaign against Germany and the American air war on Japan. In both cases, the aim was to terrorize noncombatants, to lower their morale, and to abolish their will to fight. The planners of the Allied bombing campaigns tried to maximize not minimize, the killing of civilians. (Goldstein, 2010)

Traditional Total War philosophy rejects the **absolute** immunity of people, places or things under certain conditions. Biblical Total War philosophy mandates conquest of opposing force with the least amount of noncombatant casualties or destruction of property as possible. This does not mean ignoring the improper use of people, places, or things ordinarily exempt from targeting. Violations such as storing ammo in a hospital nullify the exemption turning people, places, and things into possible targets. There is a level of complicity or consent among civilians which must be maintained for any aggressive action to continue. Total war, and to an extent limited war theory, have the same objectives they only use different methods.

Bombing Hiroshima and Nagasaki, as well as the carpet bombing raids over Germany annihilating industrial and residential areas, had a two-fold purpose. One to materially cripple the enemy war machine in manufacturing and transportation of equipment or ammunition to the front lines. Secondly, make the cost of war so high that the will to fight of the civilian population diminish, resulting in the ruler of a nation to surrendering. As horrible as the air raids of Great Britain and Germany, or the bombing of Hiroshima and Nagasaki, more lives are saved in quickly bringing the cost of war to a height unmanageable by the enemy. As we waited, hoping Imperial Japan would surrender after the first bombing, they didn't. It wasn't until after the second bomb dropped about ten days later that they surrendered. They could have avoided the second attack.

Sometimes a ruler becomes more dangerous and erratic when faced with defeat. Such is the case with wicked rulers who have no heart for their citizens. A glaring example of this is once adult soldiers were killed toward the end of WWII, the Hitler Youth were forced to fight the losing battle for Berlin. Alternatively, if that doesn't work the devastation to the civilian population may cause some military leaders and rank and file warriors to rethink their position and duty to their citizens. Desertions during battle, and attempts to overthrow or assassinate a dictator (Hitler for example) from within to end the war are hoped for second order effects. The sooner the war ends, the fewer people must suffer, and reconstruction and reconciliation can begin.

Priority of Noncombatant Immunity

> "Wisdom *is* better than weapons of war: but one sinner destroyeth much good" (Eccl 9:18).

Even in total war, non-combatant immunity (NI) discrimination still has a place. There is never a justification for killing civilians as punishment for partisan or underground activity. Using civilians as human shields surrounding military targets is also always unacceptable. As is the using of traditionally non-targeted sites (churches, synagogues, mosques, museums, schools...) as a hidden weapons cache, HQ, or staging areas for military operations. Sending children or other NI into battle suiting them up with explosives is also forbidden. Once a violation of the laws of war is executed (killing innocent civilians as punishment, human shields, HQ in a hospital...) then the dilemma arises as to the right response to these actions.

Even if considering the population as supportive or consenting to the actions of their military or other organization. The unlawful use of sites, children, or human shields and the people around specific places do not make those lives less valuable than the lives of the civilians you are sworn to protect. The issue is who are you personally responsible for, or accountable to. Your own citizens and service members are your covenant priority. Of course, you should only attack these sites if truly warranted. Collateral damage is always unfortunate, and sometimes unavoidable.

Avoid such attacks or pre-emptive strikes involving human shields and civilians when at all possible. Always warn the enemy using human shields that you are willing to attack anyway if provoked. Use of a human shield is primarily for baiting another nation with idle threats and protecting potential targets. If the threat of use of force is determined valid, you must publically warn the country or group using human shields that you believe they intend to sneak attack or in other ways attack from those shielded sites. Say that you are reluctant to hurt their civilians, but will if you must. Hopefully, in the world court of public opinion, you will win, pressuring them to stop using human shields. If not, then you must do what you must do. You have a covenant responsibility to your own people first. If you decide not to strike back, you are not wrong either, the risk is yours to take or not. Each situation is different.

> "Thus saith the LORD; Execute ye judgment and righteousness, and deliver the spoiled out of the hand of the oppressor: and do no wrong, do no violence to

> the stranger, the fatherless, nor the widow, neither shed innocent blood in this place" (Jer 22:3).

If avoiding possibly killing, or killing enemy citizens will result in the death of your fellow warriors or put at risk your own citizens, where is the justice or sense in that? When your hand is forced, the blood guilt for a violation of the above scripture is on the head of the enemy, not you. Being a minister of vengeance is not a natural calling. It takes a special person for full or part time, in for a few years or in for life.

CHAPTER 11
Black Bag and Spec Ops

> Just as consent restrains what human beings may do to one another, so it also enables what they may do to one another." (Pfaff T., Tiel J.R., 2004, The Ethics of Espionage)

Accepting equality of freedom and rationalism allows for a common foundation of the virtuous. Virtuous action is what is agreed upon which doesn't violate free will. It also provides for freedom of choice within culturally acceptable boundaries, unless consent is given to be additionally controlled. A criminal act is an act committed against someone without his or her consent, such as murder and theft. No one freely consents to being murdered, coerced, blackmailed, or to the theft of his or her property.

Consent helps determine justification for an action. Ignoring moral law is a violation because it is action without the permission of God. God emplaces the ethical boundary because the action harms the lawbreaker and victimizes others. A lawbreaker does not always perceive immediate consequences to the immoral act. Not all moral violations are criminal violations, and not all criminal violations are moral violations.

Recall the law enacted to stop praying to any god except the king was an immoral civil law. Daniel broke a civil law, upholding the moral directive to pray only to the Lord. He submitted (as morally obligated) to the punishment for breaking the immoral civil law. God honored his faith in obeying the moral code on all fronts and delivered him from death. Those responsible for putting Daniel in a life-threatening situation unknowingly endangered their families. The conspirators' and their families suffered the fate they planned for Daniel.

The reverse is also valid on some points. In ancient Canaan sacrificing your son or daughter to demon gods Molech, Ashtaroth, Chemosh, or Baal was the law of the land. It was socially acceptable and in some ways mandatory. God expressly forbids the practice of human sacrifice. The law of the land endorsed and in some cases mandated moral violations. Punishment comes to those seeking to uphold moral correctness. This type of abuse of the role of government by people is just cause for the Courts of Heaven to sentence a nation or people to judgment.

A person has a right to self-defense and reasonable expectation of defense by the military. In free societies, citizens reasonably empower through consent. In dictatorships, consent is still present since someone is supporting the tyrant ruler. Though not empowered by the public, public opinion is still important to support, or else there will be another hostile takeover. Support for or demand for action (both forms of consent) from a leader can be inspired, induced through fear, or erupt because of an event: a credible threat of attack, attack, outrage from humanitarian violations, or a disaster.

Pfaff and Tiel categorized degrees of consent or participation. Adopting and adapting these levels of involvement, which denote what you can reasonably expect as vulnerability or protection is within Biblical boundaries. Being vulnerable is not always because of weakness or mistakes, but the principle of mutual consent. The permission for yourself or others around you to become a target of some sort given through your actions. Additionally, it is referring to the amount of legal and other safeguards active or available as a target.

Level I

The average citizen is a lowest level consenter or participant. They know clandestine activity must take place, but are also assumptive they are not targets, knowing nothing of value to a hostile power. By virtue of being a citizen some risks are unavoidable. These dangers are becoming a political, military or terrorist hostage, and subject to collateral or direct attack by enemy forces. These risks are inherent to citizenship and unavoidable. Notwithstanding, it is assumed respective governments and their agencies will do their utmost to prevent, diminish and at the very least prepare for such occurrences. An average citizen possesses no knowledge of value to the enemy and no threat; unless a domestic attack is being planned. Then some key individuals in research, utilities, security, etc. may become targets of unlawful combatants.

Level II

The next level is the person possessing valuable information, yet unaware of its value. In the military, during the Cold War, in Germany, we were briefed about talking to foreign nationals. Urged to warn our spouses about nightclub chatter. Former Soviet Union microphones, collecting parking lot chatter on posts. People are usually talking to each other while going to and from their cars in the parking lot of the Post Commissary . Things like training activity, what's the latest, when and where, how long a spouse will be gone. These innocent conversations held bits and pieces of information.

Information individually which held little if any value, collectively and in the right hands is used to derive much information on weapons caches, deployment operations, morale of troops, and soldiers or their spouses disgruntled or having an affair. This information is used to target a person or persons and possibly force or sweet-talk them into treason against the United States. For the most part, these people, not including service members, are soft targets of the enemy, not active participants. Possible targets are disgruntled government employees, or those whose worldview is hostile to the United States, or concerned nation. Some deception, emotional manipulation, and possible bribery might be used against them to obtain information.

Level III

Level three of participation is the average soldier specifically, or law enforcement officer, and their families. They are targets and participants. They possess some valuable information and may know some of this information is valuable. They accept the risks of the duties of their jobs: being killed in the line of duty, killing in the line of duty, or a possible threat to the family because of their sworn duty. They may or may not be targeted by hostile intelligence operatives, depending upon their knowledge. They might be used as hostages, but civilians usually are better targets for their public opinion impact. Revengers accepted the risk, and the public is less outraged at their plight than a basically non-consenting non-participative citizen.

Level IV

After this is the person, who is an undercover agent, spy, special operations service member, etc. They know their information is valuable and guard it well. Even concealing as much as possible what they do for a living. Yet some are willing, for several reasons, to share their information and commit treason. These are double agents. Double agents are useful and dangerous.

Double agents are useful because they can be used to disseminate false information as well as reveal truthful information. There are people like the escaped slave King David and his men came across. He had critical information about their kidnapped families and possessions. He lacked loyalty to his former masters and freely talked in exchange for asylum. Similarly, there will be people in a position of some sort, for one reason or another, who are willing and wanting to share otherwise sensitive information; a good thing when it is the enemies secrets they betray. A person authorized to become a double agent is valuable when achievable. Be careful you are not the one being played; higher risk, for higher rewards. Pray and ask the Lord to reveal enemy agents in your midst. He will cause them to be killed, caught, recalled, or rendered ineffective.

Level V

The deep cover mole; a trusted advisor to an enemy leader, more dangerous and subtle than a double agent. This is the case of Hushai and King David. Hushai is David's double agent. He is loyal to David, though trusted by the rebel forces. Hushai is not as much a double agent as a mole.

A real double agent is Jonathan, King Saul's son. He was loyal to David, lied to protect him, and gave false information to his father the King, who wrongfully was hunting David to kill him. Jonathan did not advise his father against David, just gave false intel. David turned Jonathan after a conversation and test, which proved the wickedness and violence of King Saul. This level of consent and involvement opens the ethical door to intrusive action and coercive actions taken against a person(s), to obtain information.

Hushai is an example of one of the highest or deepest levels of participation in the protection of government secrets. These are the game players consenting to the stakes of the game at the highest, or in the darkest places. Information gathering through deception, by the sanctioned theft of documents (digital or hard), using moles, double agents, and turncoats is found in the Bible.

Police, for example, arrest and imprison people against their will. The difference is they have commissioned authority and training to use lethal and non-lethal force to arrest or attempt apprehension of suspects or criminals. Therefore, use of lethal and non-lethal force or detention of people without consent is not automatically a moral or legal violation. The precedent for interviewing criminals started with Gods' questioning of Adam and Eve. People are to be questioned to verify or obtain the truth of the matter. Interesting to note is God already knew the answers He wanted to see if He could get a confession out of Adam and Eve. Adam confessed in the form of blaming God for giving him Eve who is his alleged cause for bowing to Satan and rejecting God's only law; sound familiar- the blame everyone else game. There were even ceremonial procedures in place to inquire of the Lord concerning unknown perpetrators for known breaches of the Law. Also, mandatory appointing of judges implicitly means someone has to obtain and impart information concerning lawbreaking, and someone needs authorization and training too physically enforce penalties.

The Biblical precedent for long distance spying is in the case of Elisha and God. God personally passed on information only He could obtain. Not forgetting electronic and other means of interception and procuring of information, or disseminating false information precedents are also in the Bible. In modern times we still need God's help; even though modern technology has undoubtedly made information gathering especially in real time, easier. But, don't forget God's intelligence personally given to Elisha was in real time.

An enemy King was secretly plotting against Israel. Each time he came up with a plan, God literally told Elisha via a word of knowledge. Elisha would then relay this to the King. The King then talked to his commander to execute a counter plan ambushing and defeating the enemy king repeatedly. Frustrated and confused, the enemy King asked who the mole on his staff was. The reply came that the prophet of the Lord, Elisha was telling all his secret plans to the King. Realizing if he killed the prophet, then there would assumedly be no one else hearing God, then his next plan would remain secret. The enemy king sent a contingent military force to capture and kill Elisha. They surrounded the town and called out for him.

Elisha's servant was frantic until God opened his spiritual eyes and he saw the angelic host surrounding the physical enemy military detachment. Elisha walked up to the military commander asking who he was looking for. The Lord concealed Elisha's identity supernaturally. Elisha told him he knew where Elisha was. Elisha led the enemy forces into the Israeli army ambush.

In all of these examples God's consent seems pretty standard or acceptable, but to what degree is He consenting on some of the more sensitive issues? As we are about to see, God consents to many delicate and morally tricky actions by ministers of vengeance, also called judges from the Old Testament book bearing the same name. One example we examined was the agent Hushai. Another is the sleeper agent Esther. Undercover work is dangerous, can be lonely, but is essential. Where does God stand on the moral lines crossed in clandestine ops? What is the liberty of our valued agents in the field? Before we look at that, one of the common denominators of various covert operations is lying in one form or another.

The Good Lie

In the realm of disseminating false information, is lying and deception always immoral? Is there a difference ethically or morally? Jonathan lied to protect David, Rahab lied to protect the Hebrew spies, Joshua and Caleb. Hushai lies to a rebellious commander, and Elisha lies to an enemy commander. In all of these situations God is helping the deception to work. There are also believers helping Paul escape arrest by letting him down out a window on a wall. I'm sure when the guards came to their house asking for Paul they didn't say "We heard you were coming for Paul, so we let him out and down a back window of the wall to help evade capture."

Apparently, not all lying is in the category of the 9th commandment "Thou shalt not bear false witness against your neighbor." Maybe all liars having their part in the Lake of Fire has an exception clause. The exception is dependent on who's lying to whom and why. The false witness commandment is to protect a neighbor from unprovoked or unwarranted harm. To foster trust in the people you live with and depend on. Our examples were not of people lying as selfish acts to protect themselves or hurt the innocent. Neither is the false report designed to implicate an innocent person in a crime. Nor were they to protect a guilty person from just judgment. Therefore, not all lies or deception is a sin. Yes, I really just said that. Don't worry; there is one more shocker to come before this chapter is over. I have prayed and am solely responsible before God for the contents of this book. I am hoping not to lose my ordination in how I address this and other controversial topics. Even if I do, I stand by my words.

> "Nazi massacres—especially of the Jews—were thought to legitimize the harsh actions of resistance fighters. Similarly, when the Cold War set in, supporters of the CIA argued that any notions of "fair play" had to go out the door. Thus, we may be led to believe that successful acts of subversion and espionage can admit to no strictures...Such thinking is unjust on the face of it and dangerously close to the sort of language we hear from modern terrorist groups" (Cole, 2008, Whether Spies Too Can Be Saved).

Remember fair is about letting the enemy have a chance. War and Law Enforcement actions should not be fair but must be just and honorable.

Fair would be like letting the criminal get a head start on a foot pursuit, or in not starting to search for an escaped convict for a day or two, giving them a fair chance of not being caught. That would be crazy. But, without Godly limits on what we do, we will act dishonorably and risk becoming godless and inhumane in our actions. This damages our souls, and bodies terribly. The limits God places DO NOT LIMIT our ability to accomplish the mission. These limits protect us, and our enemy from victimization, or wounding in some wicked fashion. On the contrary, accepting Holy Spirit help gives you an **unfair advantage** to be victorious, and remain honorable.

Examples of participation in lying to protect spies, authorization of spies to lie, and the requirement of a spy to lie, has the Biblical endorsement. A woman hid two of King David's spies from Absalom's men. She hid them in a well, covering it with a tarp and corn. She sent the men of Absalom in another direction, thus protecting the spies. In this scenario, the civilian non-participant consented to actively join 'the game' and participate in protecting the interests of the rightful authority, King David. If she were caught, her punishment would be a combatant. She could be considered a partisan or underground operative. She is undoubtedly a patriot of God and country.

Nothing but the Truth

Those who believe as the great Reformation preacher, and founder of Calvinist thought, theologian John Calvin. Stand in opposition to this interpretation. Calvin, speaking about the midwives who lied to Pharaoh, is not convinced of the obligation to lie, even though they saved countless baby boys. Calvin insists that 'whatever is opposed to the nature of God is sinful,' it is vitiosus (morally defective). He adds as an outcome to this theory that all feigning (simulation), whether in word or deed is to be condemned. We have already seen this is not true, but I think it is important to address his objections to a doctrine of violence inclusive of lying because not all lying is a sin.

> "Calvin reiterates, one can only conclude that the midwives lied and that ipso facto, they sinned because

> deception is in itself displeasing to God. The Lord does not reward the midwives for their lying, but only because they feared God and resisted Pharaoh's murderous plot" (Blacketer R.A., 2010).

Of course, I am in stark disagreement with Calvin. The midwives because of their respect for God, did not fear the wrath of Pharaoh, and dutifully lied to protect the innocent. They engaged in lying of the sort spies engage in, protecting secrets or altering of information, which could endanger or harm many innocent citizens. Mendacium Officiosum is Latin meaning the dutiful lie. The dutiful lie is not a sin.

To seal the deal concerning objections of Christians who adhere to Calvinist teaching on lying, consider this. Calvin also addresses a holy lie or dissimulation (to camouflage or conceal). Calvin said that in battle certain kinds of deception are acceptable, which did not break an agreement of peace. So, Calvin backs down and creates exceptions to his blanket assertion all lies are a sin, even the midwives lie. This also relates to the issue of assuming a secret identity, the living lie. Where you not only withhold information, you actively misdirect the perceptions of others to your true nature and intents.

National Secrets, Seduction, and Misdirection

> "Indeed, creating a politically efficacious persona rests, at least partially, on the pragmatic value of dissimulation, a truth John Adams savers when he cautions about the "Damage, Danger and Confusion" that "Enemies" and "indiscreet friends" would wreak if certain information were publicly divulged" (Murray K., 2012).

Furthermore, Heckwelder, a seasoned early American Moravian spy, who started out a pacifist, says after seeing a dark side of humanity "...war makes peace, writing that 'No peace can be made without a Campaign' ".

There was an incident where the truth is told, which should have remained secret. Once told, it cost that person their freedom, eyesight, stopped military action against an oppressive regime, and eventually led to their death. However, in his death, he killed more of the enemy than in his life. Sampson had supernatural strength from God Almighty, rendering him the terror of Israel's enemies. Sampson's girlfriend Delilah, continually accuses him of not loving her because he won't trust her with state secrets. Emotionally worn down he finally gives in and tells her. He revealed a state secret to his foreign national girlfriend, the secret of his anointing, his power from God.

Unknown to Sampson was that Delilah already had taken a bribe from the Princes of her people the Philistines. She sold him out. Sampson's orders from the Lord were not to tell anyone; this includes parents, and Delilah his current girlfriend the secret of his strength. Pay attention: God knew the potential for betrayal by Delilah before Samson met her. The standing order not to talk had this in mind. All Sampson should have had to say is 'the Lord said I could not tell.' A person who doesn't have a hidden agenda would understand and not have accused you or would stop pressuring you.

Samson is the first recorded male to fall prey to the Honey Pot ploy of a sparrow. A sparrow is an enemy operative using sex to compromise your integrity and cause you to give up state secrets. The honeypot ploy is usable against male and female targets. There is an acronym- MICE used to remember the reasons a person becomes treacherous. MICE: Money (financial gain), Ideology (politically or religious reasons), Compromise (getting caught doing something you don't want anyone to find out about, or leveraged in a relationship and emotionally coerced), and Ego (feeling unappreciated etc. becoming a traitor to prove their worth, or as an act of revenge for feeling slighted in some fashion).

He revealed a state secret, for Samson was a judge of the Lord's, a minister of vengeance used by God through his supernatural strength. He became spiritually, emotionally, and sexually entangled with a foreign national citizen which cost him his freedom, his calling, his sight, his honor, and eventually his life. This is called being unequally yoked, which God warns against. Once the information is known she betrayed him to the rulers of her nationality, the enemies of Israel. This is not to say every foreign national spouse is a traitor, of course not. It is a Biblical example why governments are wary to impart clearances for similar security risk concerns and serves as a lesson on being a potential target through relationships according to your level of participation.

We cannot overlook the incident of the lying spirit from the Lord 1 Kings 22:1-40 and 2 Chronicles 18:1-34. This looks like an apparent contradiction. Remember God's character is not in question. The Lord wrote down the situation twice for a reason. Satan can petition the Court of Heaven as our accuser. We see this in Job, and in Satan's petition to sift Peter like wheat as told to him by Jesus. Satan seeks a warrant to harass you and worse. Through our own words and deeds we give him legal grounds that God must honor, and grant Satan's request. Peter boasted publicly of his love for Jesus and that he would die for Jesus. Satan was then authorized to see if Peter meant what he said. The Lord already knew he didn't, and that Peter was thinking too highly of himself. Peter denies the Lord three times the night of His arrest. These are instances of requests to the Court of Heaven.

God asked who would be a lying spirit in the mouth of false prophets (those that either worship false gods or presume on God and prophesy a lie). Those prophets were liars already, and the Lord is looking for a sender of a false message from Him through them. The message is to entice wicked King Ahab to engage in a battle, which will be his demise. This is a judgment for listening to false prophets, to begin with, which carries the death sentence for a Hebrew. Ahab had inquired of his 400 false prophets, and then to the prophet of God, Micaiah. Upon inquiry, Micaiah spoke the truth from God that God had put the lying spirit into the mouths of his false prophets. This was Ahab's way out of trouble, listen to the real prophet of God, which he did not. Even armed with the truth Ahab went to battle anyway following the false prophets and was defeated, just as God said he would do.

God sent wrong information, disinformation, through the ungodly prophets the rebellious King trusted in. This is playing both sides against the middle or turning the tables on the wicked king. The king was already listening to a false spirit of prophecy and not the Lord. The Lord injected through the false prophets what He wanted the king to do. Then God gives an opportunity to repent which he refused. Therefore, using enemy agents in passing false information to the enemy to entrap him is authorized. The reason God must use a third-party angel to deliver the message through the false prophets is that if the Holy Spirit says it, it turns into the truth because God cannot lie.

There is no requirement for us to notify the enemy of a trap since we are not the Lord dealing with His direct servants. It was dissimulation to conceal the fact the spiritual guidance received from the lying spirit is of the Lord. In fact, there is no precedent that it is mandatory to notify the enemy of anything, except a formal declaration of war and the response to human shield warning. Ahab was not a foreign enemy, but a wicked ruler over God's nation, Israel. God handles His own different from the enemy. It is assumed by some that the lying spirit from the Lord is demonic. I believe it was a loyal angel of the Lord's sending information through false prophets. It could be either. Not worth a division over, but not clarified in Scripture either.

Most people have heard about the brave 300 Spartans at the battle of Thermopylae. Led by brave King Leonidas, they along with thousands of allied Greek contingents, fought and died before an invading Persian horde. Most don't know that centuries before Leonidas at Thermopylae, is Gideon and his men of Israel, at the valley of Jezreel. Gideon, a mighty man of valor with only 300 men, fought against and defeated an invading Midianite led coalition horde. Midian is called Saudi Arabia in the present day. The difference between victory and defeat is not skill at arms, numbers or technology, all of which are very important but do not decide the outcome. It is who is in covenant, and have they called upon it, which determines the outcome.

Misdirection is authorized, as are bluffing and psychological warfare. In the battle of Gideon versus the Midianites three hundred men were deployed in a horseshoe formation around an entire valley, spread out over miles of terrain. On a signal, they held up lanterns, blew rams horns, and shouted a prearranged battle cry into a mostly asleep camp. It appeared to the Midianites to be a larger more formidable army attacking at night.

For days before the attack, the Midianites had been experiencing the same recurring nightmares from God about Gideon, a battle cry, and their destruction. Once they are spooked, they are now prepped for attack by Gideon and his three hundred. Using these tactics, the night raid is so successful it sent the enemy coalition armies into such confusion and panic that they turned on each other. Gideon and his vastly outnumbered warriors mopped up the rest. During one of King David's battles, the Lord made a noise through the wind in the trees, which sounded to the enemy like mercenary chariots, reinforcements from Egypt. This deception resulted in superior enemy forces fleeing the battle fearing the tables had turned on them.

God uses dissimulation in His directive to the prophet Samuel to only partially inform corrupt King Saul about his intentions and motives in going to Bethlehem. His 'I'm only going to sacrifice' statement is true but not complete and misguides King Saul. It was a cover story for the real mission. The real mission is of national importance and must be kept secret. It is the anointing of a new King of Israel, while King Saul is still in power. Had King Saul known the truth he would have tried to kill or otherwise prevent Samuel from doing God's will. He might have attempted to kill David before his anointing.

> "Grotius argues that the morality of pretence (deceit with actions) and falsehood (deceit with words) is found in whether or not truth is owed to the person to be deceived." (Laws of War and Peace III. I. XI)

Jesus on the road to Emmaus did not initially reveal His identity as the risen Savior to the couple whom He walked and talked with for miles then ate with them. Jesus concealed His identity until He had talked with them and then said grace over the meal. At which time they could perceive who he really was. Sapphira, when questioned by Peter in the book of Acts, was not informed of her husband's death until she sided with him in their lie. Peter was investigating to see if she would also lie or tell the truth, which she surely would have told the truth if she knew her husband had died because of their lie. There are numerous examples in the scriptures. Suffice to say you do not owe everyone, every bit of information, always.

> "A fool uttereth all his mind: but a wise man keepeth it in till afterwards" (Proverbs 29:11).

Sex and Statecraft

Another Biblical example of dissimulation is in the undercover operation of Jehu. The story of Jehu and the prophets of Baal. God often talks about worshiping false gods, that it is spiritual adultery. This is worship of beings or entities portraying themselves as gods or godlike. They are in reality demonic beings. Baal is a chief demonic god. After Jehu becomes King, he decides he wants to clear out the pagan worship of Baal from Israel. To do this, he calls all the prophets of Baal from around the land to come to a great sacrifice in God's temple to prove their loyalty to Baal. The account of this deception and execution of enemies of God and the state of Israel is in 2 Kings 10:18-25.

Hundreds came to worship Baal. Jehu shuts the doors then he performs a pagan ritual sacrificing a bull on an altar, in God's Temple, all present bowed in worship to Baal. They all proved their loyalty to Baal. In so doing they sealed their fate against the vengeance of a holy God. Vengeance executed at King Jehu's orders. Outside the Temple King Jehu's soldiers awaited. Once he is done with the sacrifice, Jehu leaves. Then Jehu's soldiers entered and killed all the false prophets of Baal, cleansing Israel of her idolatry. This is at the order of the king who pretended to be a Baal worshiper, even sacrificing to Baal in God's Temple. It is a perfectly executed sting operation. Jehu is also careful that no prophets of the LORD were among those he planned to execute.

Undercover operations are authorized as we see in many examples: Jehu, Hushai, and Esther being three of the best precedent setting examples. Lying, deception, procuring information, dissimulation, and disguises are good to go. What about exploitation of sexuality, sex as a blackmail weapon against enemy agents or high-value targets, and sexual relations during covert ops in maintaining your cover? Biblical prohibitions against blackmail include Jer 22:17, Luke 3:14, Ezekiel 18:18, 22:12, and Isaiah 33:15. Whether blackmail for information other forms of bribery, coercion, or deception used against someone. The purpose is in the interest of law enforcement and national security, or it is selfish and causes harm to your neighbor without a cause.

Normal citizens are not active participants. Doing unto others as you would have them do unto you is a principle of participation. To blackmail the innocent, your neighbor, a stranger, or any person for personal revenge, money, a wicked advantage, or unlawful favor, is not acceptable. To blackmail, for example, to gain access to secret information from a hostile nation is acceptable. The targets are participants. In turn, you also become a lawful mark for blackmail according to reciprocal participation theory.

Weaponized Sex

Action taken on behalf of national security (not all actions as we will see in our examination of torture) is and in pursuit of justice in law enforcement, or domestic security we assume is acceptable within lawful or Constitutional limits. It is not for personal advantages or gain and not intended to endanger any citizen it is sworn to protect. There is a wider range of actions available on the international stage than the national, which is as it should be. Therefore, exploitation and blackmail through setting a person up circumstantially - with or without actual sexual contact, to gain leverage over enemy agents, high-value targets, or other assets seem permissible.

You make yourself vulnerable to compromise when you act unethically or immorally. I know adultery is a sin, so is sexual promiscuity and homosexuality. All are Biblically explicit unchanging moral violations, no matter what many cultural voices say; which we know already culture is not always correct. So, it would appear there is no provision for these types of activity during a covert operation of any type, even though they seem permissible and sometimes unavoidable. Still, we must ask the question should we be doing these types of things? Does God give guidance for swimming in these morally murky waters? I found no explicit exceptions to immoral sexual activity (since they are not real relationships) during undercover operations. However, I believe the following examples demonstrate that God implicitly does account for this activity.

Weaponized Sex; Sin or not a Sin

In all undercover situations, you must pray and ask the Lord to give you strength to do what must be done for the good of others. You are putting your life, in some cases your sanity, or real relationships on the line for the good of others. Others who most likely will never know what you did to make the world, and their community safer. Just remember the Lord sees and appreciates your dilemma and struggles. Undercover is one of the toughest jobs of a minister of vengeance. Being someone you are not, **at heart**, that other person usually isn't a good one; you might have to do morally objectionable things.

Here is where you apply a method of Biblical interpretation from silence. Everything mentioned in the Bible is inspired by God for our good. In Job four people are speaking with him in his trauma, then God speaks up. God names three of the people who spoke with Job as speaking wickedly. Therefore, when you read what they said it is an example of what not to say or how to think about God. Nothing is said about the fourth person. From silence, or from not being included in the list of guys who screwed up, you can determine God endorsed what that guy said. Therefore, what he said is a good example of what to say, or think, about God and the situation with Job.

In the case of Abraham when he lied about Sarah his wife to protect himself and slept with Hagar his maidservant at the prompting of his wife Sarah, God didn't scold or chastise Abraham for these mistakes but exercised grace in these situations. Abraham didn't exactly lie. He omitted the fact that Sarah was his sister from a different mother, by the same father. Also in those days, a wife who was barren may give consent to her husband to father a child, through a surrogate maidservant. God neither authorized or forbid these customs, as with other customs. God's lack of comment, besides documenting the action taken, and some specific comments about these actions and others, speak volumes.

Duty Calls

Then there is the Tamar incident from Genesis 38. Judah bore twin sons by Tamar who played the harlot with Judah. Perez, also spelled Pharez, is the firstborn of the two. Two of the three of Judah's sons died being evil before the Lord and could bear no children by Tamar the firstborn son's wife, given to the second born after his death. The third son is supposed to marry her and raise up seed for his two dead brothers, his and her duty. This is the custom to preserve blood and family lines. Judah's bloodline is prophetic and must not be interrupted. Judah refused to give his third son. Tamar had to masquerade as a harlot to get pregnant by Judah, who withheld his son unlawfully from her.

Once her pregnancy was discovered Judah was ready to stone her until she revealed evidence the child was his. Judah said she was more righteous than he was, for she did her duty raising up seed for her first husband. Not only does the Bible indirectly praise Tamar for accomplishing what someone else's honor bound duty to do was, but adds a special note on the relationship.

> "So Judah acknowledged them (his belongings Tamar deceived him out of proving he was the father) and said 'She has been more righteous than I, because I did not giver her to Shelah my son.' And he ***never knew her*** again" (Gen 38:26 NJKV em ad).

God also honors Judah and Tamar's son Perez, son of a single parent per se, who is also born out of wedlock. Both Judah and Perez are in the lineage of Jesus according to the human side listed in the New Testament. Only those accepted by the God are in the lineage of the Lord Jesus. She engaged in technically illicit sexual activity to accomplish a covenant duty. They did not start or maintain a genuine relationship because that would have been unlawful and went too far. She did what was necessary; then it was done. Tamar did not do this with her heart. Tamar did not desire her father-in-law. Tamar didn't do this of her own free will, but out of a sense of duty. In this Tamar did not sin.

Tamar and Judah's relationship resulting in the birth of Perez is unlike the adulterous relationship between King David and Bathsheba the wife of Captain Uriah, while he was deployed to battle. David married her after Uriah was killed in combat. Uriah died in combat because of David, a compelling story, the real Hamlet story, but not relevant to this book. After Captain Uriah's death, David marries Bathsheba. It was an international scandal. That child, born of adultery, died. King Solomon, born after they married is also part of the lineage of Jesus.

The connection between these incidents of sexual immorality is God's comments. Tamar is never reprimanded or shown in any disfavor for her liaison with Judah. The Judah scandal is only mentioned once again after the fact, and that in the form of a blessing. This signifies God's endorsement of Perez and implicitly his birth circumstances. However, in the New Testament God directly mentions the condemned affair between David and Bathsheba, and indirectly points to the murderous circumstances surrounding it.

"And all the people who were at the gate, and the elders, said, 'We are witnesses. The Lord make the woman who is coming to your house like Rachel and Leah, the two who built the house of Israel; and may you prosper in Ephrathah and be famous in Bethlehem. **May your house be like the house of Perez, whom Tamar bore to Judah**, because of the offspring which the Lord will give you from this young woman. So Boaz took Ruth and she became his wife: and when he went in to her, the Lord gave her conception, and she bore a son." (Ruth 4:11-12 em ad MJKV)

> "The book of the genealogy of Jesus Christ...Abraham begot Isaac, Isaac begot Jacob, and Jacob begot Judah and his brothers. <u>Judah begot Perez and Zerah by Tamar</u>. Perez begot Hezeron...King David begot Solomon by her who had been the wife of Uriah..." (Matt 1:1-3,6 em ad MJKV)

Notice the mention of Tamar does not shed a negative light on her but on Judah. Alternatively the mention of Uriah puts a cloud over David. Perez is approved of even though he is conceived and born out of wedlock. Solomon is approved of being conceived in and born in lawful marriage, even though the situation leading up to the marriage is disapproved of. The circumstances in one situation are lust and murder, but the other is devotion to duty.

Where does that leave today's undercover agent?

You are not in a genuine consensual relationship. It is a deception and dissimulation from who you really are and how you really feel, where your heart and duty truly lies. The danger comes in possibly forgetting who you really are and why you're doing what you're doing. When your true identity is blurred with the false temporary identity and lifestyle- it can get worse. Pray not to lose yourself. Pray before each encounter that the Lord help you through, or out of each encounter. Pray it doesn't last a moment longer than necessary. Pray about not developing a soul tie to the person and confusing your real self with the fake life you temporarily need. Disassociation can be very difficult.

You are not a murderer unless you have hatred in your heart. You are not an adulterer unless you have lusted in your heart. Undercover work is not about lust or hatred for another, but working to get evidence and information necessary to bring justice against the wicked and foster the safety of civilians. Your heart is still with your husband or wife back home, not with the person you are faking a relationship with, of whatever sort. If undercover as a couple, this does not mean you have to have sex; you shouldn't be having sex with your fellow agent for obvious reason. Although you may have to conduct some public acts of affection to continue the ruse; avoid doing so as much as possible, again for obvious reasons.

Undercover, and not as a couple is a different matter. Sure, you will have moments of pleasure, your body doesn't know the difference between your true love and the asset or mark. That's not the issue; it's all about your heart, that your true feelings are that you are doing what you're doing because of the necessity of duty - not as a free will affair of the heart. You may be the sparrow on behalf of the United States one day. Pray you are a great sparrow against our enemies, and that your honey pot ploy is successful quickly. Pray to limit your exposure to the emotional, mental, spiritual and conventional dangers of undercover work.

A person who is forced to have sexual relations of whatever type because of a threat to life or limb has not sinned. They are acting for self-preservation, not of their own free will. You are willing to go undercover with all those risks, not because it sounds fun, but because it must be done. Your actions become those needed to preserve your life and get you through an assignment, and back home to those you truly love. They are not of your own free will in the same sense; they are not a sin. My advice is not to tell your spouse about your missions, just be thankful you made it home safely, mission accomplished.

Therefore, sexual liaison to facilitate undercover work is necessary and is permissible for official duty only, for the greater good. Tamar was not involved for her own gain or pleasure, but to affect a righteous cause. This is a serious topic, which must not be avoided, but biblically confronted and fully explored. I am sure many of my fellow ministers will write me and call me something, maybe not brother for writing this section. To be plain for them and you. I'm not talking about staging an event that only looks like an encounter of some sort happened, to turn the enemy into an asset, that is not controversial since nothing really happened. That falls back into the levels of participation. To further clarify, I am also not talking about a wheel's up rings off mentality. That is wicked, not a part of duty, and sinful. There is no excuse for that.

I'm talking about **necessary** undercover operations. I pray right now for those in such dangerous and compromising situations. I pray for their families; may their true relationships endure no matter the circumstances. I pray for you covert agents; Lord protect them from disease and help insulate and heal their souls from the emotional and spiritual liaisons they are exposed to. May their missions be exceptionally successful helping make such sacrifices worth it. I pray they are delivered from having to commit such actions whenever possible, may they find a way out. I also pray to protect them from addictions and from being turned into the enemy.

Revengers qualify for many exceptions in the Lord, clearly. But, even exceptions have limits. There is no reason or Biblical precedent to rape people or abuse children. Indirectly or directly there is no justification or permission granted to do such vile and wicked things. I heard in the South China sea if human traffickers are caught they are summarily executed and kicked overboard for shark food. If that is true, I'm not sure if it is a deterrent, but it certainly solves recidivism problem.

Your conscience, is yours alone, as is mine, and it is between you, and the Holy Spirit. He loves you and me 100%, through the good and the evil times. The exemptions or alternative standard for killing by those who bear the sword verses those who to do not, is no more a license or excuse to kill apart from duty, than being authorized to engage in undercover sexual or drug activity - as necessary, not something to be sought after. The line between sin or not sin while undercover is simple. With the heart or not with the heart. In the line of duty or not in the line of duty. If you slip up. Repent and get back on track, the Lord loves you and forgives you.

Like Jehu, to catch the ungodly in their ungodliness you may have to sacrifice to Baal in the body, but not in spirit or soul. Not with your heart, but as Tamar who had a duty to fulfill. If you must play the harlot, remember you are **not** a harlot. This is an ultimate dissimulation. My heart goes out to all in clandestine situations. I salute your dedication. The Lord bless you, keep you, make His countenance to shine upon you. Accomplish the mission, stay alive, stay safe, come home, live a good life.

Esther the Sleeper agent

Esther is the only book in the Bible where God's name is not mentioned at all. It is a book of international intrigue. If you look closely, you will see the hand of the Lord moving behind the scenes setting the stage to deliver His people still in Persia, who did not return to Jerusalem. The ancestor of an old enemy plotted the first holocaust to exterminate the Jews throughout the empire of Media-Persia.

Every intelligence community warrior should read this book. God manipulates behind the scenes as one coincidence after another reveal there are no coincidences. The book could have started with the pagan Kings call for virgins from throughout the land to choose from to be his queen. But it did not. It starts with the King throwing a party, getting drunk then ordering his queen to parade her body with only a crown on before him and the governors of over 120 provinces. She refused. His regrettable decision under the influence caused a problem for him, but there are no coincidences and no such thing as luck, not really. He fired her as queen, which he could not take back because the law of the land was, once a law is made it cannot be revoked.

Esther was the adopted daughter of Mordecai since her parents died. She was a stunning beauty and was called up as a virgin for candidacy to become the queen. Mordecai told her not to resist the candidacy and not to reveal she was Jewish. Mordecai had a position in the Empire but was under a man named Haman. Haman is second to the King in power, and a descendant of King Agag whom King Saul did not kill as he was supposed to. The Agagites are the sworn enemies of the Jews.

Esther complies with Mordechai's advice and does not resist candidacy for becoming the queen, even though this means she must submit to one night at least, of having sex with a pagan king. If all goes well and she is chosen from among hundreds of competitors, she will have to marry a non-Jew, a non-believer. All of this is forbidden by God expressly, yet the Lord makes no mention against Esther or Mordecai, on the contrary, she is a sleeper agent.

Esther wins the favor of the King and is married to him. The sleeper is now in place as the queen, and no one knows she is a Jew, nor does the King or Haman know of her relationship to Mordecai. All is quiet for about three years. Given the relationship between Esther and Mordecai, her closest servants most likely realized she was Jewish, but it's possible they didn't. If they knew I suspect their loyalty to Esther is why they kept this secret from the King and others. During this time there is no record Esther celebrated any mandatory feasts of Israel. If she had celebrated a feast, this would have revealed her nationality publicly.

In the interim Haman plots against Mordecai and all the Jews. Haman gets a law passed that on a specific day the people can rise up throughout the empire, kill all the Jews and take their land and possessions. Furthermore, Haman, second in the Empire only to the King, has gallows built to hang Mordecai on.

Long before Mordecai or Esther knew of a plot to kill all the Jews, God was working behind the scenes manipulating situations and people to deliver his People and judge those who would hurt them. The day before the hanging is announced Esther, unsummoned, goes to see the King. By law, she could be put to death, but is not. She asks him to dinner, where she will speak her request, worth risking her life for.

She asks that Haman also come to the dinner. They dine, and Esther postpones the request increasing the curiosity of the King. That night the King cannot sleep. He is wondering what the problem is with his beloved Queen. He calls for the minutes of some meeting or event be read to him to put him to sleep. The records keeper randomly chooses the account of how years earlier Mordecai the Jew uncovered a plot to assassinate the king. The King asks if anything was done for the man who saved his life. Nothing had been done.

The morning of the day Haman is about to request to hang Mordecai he is summoned by the King. The King is unaware of Haman's secret hatred and orders him to honor Mordecai the Jew publicly. That night at the second dinner with the King and Haman Esther makes her request known. Esther begs for her life, and that of her people the Jews, whom wicked Haman has plotted to kill. The end of Haman is apparent now. Esther is unaware she is a deep cover sleeper agent commissioned to bring deliverance to her people. God is behind the scenes pulling strings more than most people will ever know.

The point is Esther is put into a dissimulation situation which is a sexually, and spiritually compromising situation. Through her actions and God's silence, her undercover work allowed for certain relationships otherwise forbidden, to accomplish the greater good of national security; the state-sanctioned genocide (an early attempt at Holocaust) of the Jews. God put his endorsement upon the book in that the feast of Purim celebrating when God delivered the Jews from their enemies in the book of Esther, is still celebrated today. Nowhere in the Old or New Testaments, including the words of Jesus, is the Feast canceled or Esther's actions condemned. Jesus would have had to participate in this Feast, which if not sanctioned by His Father, He would not have done.

Assassination

A Nazi German commando Otto Skorzeny ordered his men to wear their German uniforms under their Allied uniforms. They took off the Allied uniforms before attempting to accomplish their mission to assassinate General Eisenhower in his headquarters. Thankfully, Skorzeny and his men were caught, and their mission not accomplished. They are later acquitted at a war crimes trial by an apparent loophole in the writing of the law. We must be careful not to write rules in such a manner allowing criminals to be set free. We must be sure that justice is done regardless of who the suspects are, or how we may disdain them.

> "Skorzeny claimed that he had received legal advice from a colonel who interpreted the 1907 Hague Convention IV, Annex, Section II, Article 23 (f) prohibition on wearing the enemy's uniform as merely prohibiting the use of arms while in the enemy's uniform. Apparently, the legal advice Skorzeny received was correct because he was acquitted in his war crimes trial". (Cole, D., 2008).

Many are the considerations in dealing with assassinations. Who is a legitimate target? If a Hitler type of person is killed, since assassins are often judged by their targets, he or she gets a medal. Yet after Hitler is gone, who fills the vacuum of leadership? Without thoughtful consideration, the alternative might be worse. The Biblical precedent of assassination is Ehud, a judge of Israel. A judge in this context is a fighter or prophet defending the Land. This is the time before the kings of Israel.

The nation had left off following God and was oppressed by her enemies; as every man did that which they thought was right. God raised up judges to get the nation back on track and deliver them from their enemies. Ehud is a diplomat or messenger who arrives with a recurring caravan, with the designated tribute or gift, but with a secret agenda. Deceiving his way into a private audience with the wicked and oppressive King Eglon (also a six-fingered giant like Goliath) then assassinates him. The significance of the six fingers is that is a trait of those with Nephilim bloodline; he is not entirely human; which underscores this leader's human assassination.

Ehud is left-handed and lame in the right hand. Ehud had been here before. He had time to see the way things went and find a weakness in the routine searches of the guards of him. You can imagine Ehud making friends with the guards to encourage their complacency through familiarity. A not so thorough search by guards revealed nothing. And who would suspect the guy with the crippled right had is a threat. Ehud concealed his dagger on his right leg. After delivering the gift, Ehud says he has a special message for the King. This allowed him private access to assassinate King Eglon and escape.

Besides the angelic assassinations of King Herod in the NT, and an abusive husband Nabal in the OT, I would add the death of Joseph Stalin due to the intercessory, and possibly imprecatory prayers offered up when he was moving against the Jews. Back on the human side then there is Jael and King Sisera. After his defeat in battle by Barak, sanctioned by the judge and prophetess of the Lord, Deborah. King Sisera was running for his life when Jael came out to meet him. He thought she was allied with him, because of the type of tent she dwelled in. Her nationality correctly was indicated by the tent, but her personal family House or Clan still allied with the descendants of the long-dead Moses, and his father in law Jethro. King Sisera did not know of this old alliance, and of course Jael didn't tell him (dissimulation). He enters the tent thinking he is safe. Continuing the ruse Jael promises to hide him and gives him milk which puts him to sleep.

Theologians speculate Jael drugged him with the milk. Some say that the milk being heavier on the stomach than the water he requested, plus being tired and on the run for his life put him to sleep. I agree with him being drugged. Why else would the Lord make special mention of it? Either way, she causes him to feel safe, and fall into a deep sleep.

Once Sisera is unconscious Jael gets a tent stake and mallet. Then she hammers it through his head into the ground. When the stake is placed against the side of his skull, you would think he would wake up unless drugged. I am sure this took at least two, maybe three strikes on the tent stake, maybe not. I see this as the use of a chemical or natural substance making a target vulnerable by incapacitating the target temporarily. This sets a precedent for the use of drugs on your enemies in the course of your duties as necessary. It also sets a precedent for woman to be in spec ops. For some of you who think women shouldn't be in the business; Jael (The Old Testament Xena Warrior Princess), Esther and other women of covert action in the Bible say differently.

Just being an evil ruler does not constitute automatic just cause for assassination by a foreign power. The killing of national leaders is to be avoided. A good policy we follow in the United States. If you can't vote them out, then the best is a diplomatic solution. Alternatively, would be overthrown by regime change or other means, letting the new government judge the leader of the old. Being evil justifies the people removing you from office by legal means if possible. If possible, assist and support partisans to take care of their own leaders. It is less messy politically than us summarily doing it, unless we have no other options. Saddam Hussein is a good example of forced removal. Removal from within may solicit assistance from interested foreign powers. Saddam Hussein stood trial and was hung under the new regime. King David would not kill King Saul the Lord's anointed, even though Saul became corrupt he waited for God to do it in His own time and way.

Sabotage

Spies or other operatives sabotage equipment, materials, factories or other facilities to destroy, or inhibit the military threat and capability of a nation or hostile force. Is there a Biblical precedent for sabotaging or obstructing enemy resources or movement? Yes. A well-known situation is the demise of Pharaoh's army in pursuit of the Hebrew slaves halted with their backs to the shore of the Red Sea (western shore of the Gulf of Aquaba across from Saudi Arabia). Cornered until Moses parted the Red Sea. Incidentally, God parted the Jordan river three times. Once at the start of General Joshua's campaign to take the Promised Land. Once for Elijah to cross, and once for Elisha to cross.

There is a choke point, and an underwater land bridge connecting to the shore of Saudi Arabia. It is photographed and still there to this day. An angel caused a pillar of darkness and fire to keep the Egyptian army at bay. The fire illuminated their escape. It took all-night and part of the next day to get everyone across. As the last of the Hebrews was most of the way across the Red Sea, God removed the obstacle. Pharaoh orders his army of chariots and soldiers into the gap following the Hebrews across. This was bait. Once the last of the Hebrews stepped onto the eastern shoreline, all the chariots and most of the soldiers are on the land bridge surrounded by water.

God sabotaged the chariots making the wheels fall off, preventing them from overtaking His people on foot coming out the other side. Then God stops holding up the waters on either side of the enemy army, and they come crashing down drowning both man and beast. Their bodies and the weapons attached to them wash up on the eastern shore. Now the Hebrews previously had no weapons of their own. A brilliant trap playing upon the Egyptians desire for revenge, ending in not just their defeat, but destruction. While at the same time a Hebrew army is created to take the Promised Land.

CHAPTER 12
On Torture, EIT, and SERE

"For he put on righteousness as a breastplate, and an helmet of salvation upon his head; and he put on the garments of vengeance for clothing, and was clad with zeal as a cloke" (Isaiah 59:17).

"It was at SERE school that I met one of the most formative forces in my life, Don Landrum...aka 'the Bearded one'...The particular expertise he taught me... (how to pare a prisoners sense of options down to two: bad and worse.)"

Gregory Hartley: expert interrogator
Author of How to Spot a Liar

Torture brings to the mind an excess of mixed feelings and images depending on whom you talk to, hear, or what you know. You may think of historical or movie accounts of medieval and barbaric methods of information extraction or treatment of prisoners. It revolves around the acceptable moral and ethical tactics for the extraction, access, protection, manipulation, accumulation, and analysis of information; which accuracy can save lives or end them on a mission. Numerous are the opinions on interviewing or interrogating techniques such as waterboarding, threatening the lives of loved ones, physical maiming, abuse, use of chemical substances, environmental manipulation, sensory and comfort deprivation.

War does not have to be morally compromising or damaging to the soul if conducted honorably and in the context of covenant relationship. The enemy shares common denominators. They are a plague on society, a threat to civil order, peace, and prosperity. They have a wicked agenda and members with varying degrees of loyalty, skill sets, and leadership ability. All have command, control, and communication systems with different degrees of influence and effectiveness. In all these systems information is generated, resources collected, and funding transferred

> "There's an old Arab saying, 'Let one hundred mothers cry, but not my mother— but better my mother than me.'"
>
> Michael Koubi
> Shabak Intelligence Officer

Webster's New World Dictionary defines torture, from the Latin verb torquere or 'to twist' as "The inflicting of severe pain to force information and confession, get revenge, etc." Torture includes any severe physical pain or agony. Torturing is the process of twisting, distorting, and permanently or temporarily injuring. Doing the above to a human being is to dehumanize and maim a person in one fashion or another, a person made in the image of God.

Some look at the laws against torture as impractical and restraining of the use of force against reason. Some say Enhanced Interrogating Techniques (EIT) violates no one's human rights. Others say using them violates one person's right to humane treatment. However, with the principles of participation and consent, a person of interest has already consented to the possibility of being interrogated, and therefore her rights are not violated.

Some have suggested even using the fear of something as immoral and dehumanizing. Some call all EIT a form of dehumanization. If all EIT is dehumanizing this is problematic for the Covenant warrior. In dehumanizing one person, you dehumanize yourself. You morally injure your soul. All interrogators must struggle and find the Lord's peace with this dilemma. Many are the thoughts and voices on torture and EIT. The distinction is human vs. inhumane and dehumanizing of the people who are the subject of interrogation. What is the line you cannot, or should not cross?

> "**There is nothing mysterious about interrogation**... sound interrogation nevertheless rests upon a knowledge of the subject matter and on certain broad principles, chiefly psychological...**success** of good interrogators **depends** in large measure upon their use..."(Kubark Counter Intelligence, 1997 em ad).

> "And how does one define "coercion," as opposed to "torture"? If making a man sit in a tiny chair that forces him to hang painfully by his bound hands when he slides forward is okay, then what about applying a little pressure to the base of his neck to aggravate that pain? When does shaking or pushing a prisoner, which can become violent enough to kill or seriously injure a man, cross the line from **coercion to torture**?" (Bowden, Mark, 2003, The Dark Art of Interrogation: A survey of the landscape of persuasion em ad).

> "Epistemic analysis shows that **torture is not a useful and reliable** method of gaining information except in empirically implausible cases...Torture is effective only when two conditions hold. First, the investigators must be able to recognize the truth when they hear it. Second, they must be able to credibly **commit to stop torture** once the truth is spoken" (Koppl R.,2005, Epistemic Systems em ad).

No person can ever be a hundred percent sure all the time, apart from Holy Spirit assistance by gifts of Knowledge, Discernment, and or Wisdom. Unless verified by another source or you have grown to know your subject well enough to tell the difference most of the time. These gifts are often in operation but are often played off as gut feelings, or out of the blue ideas.

> "**Torture works**. It saves American lives. **Argument over**. The problem, however, is that these arguments

were deeply flawed. Torture rarely, if ever, works. And the lives it may save in the immediate present will not equal the multitude of servicemen and civilian **lives lost** because of **torture's power to stoke anti-American** violence worldwide... **Torture violates everything the United States is supposed to stand for**: the sanctity of the individual, human rights, and the rule of law" (Parco J.E., Levy D.A., 2010, Attitudes Aren't Free, thinking Deeply about Diversity in the US Armed Forces; Enjoining an American nightmare, em ad).

"**Interrogators need operational knowledge to be effective**...They need to know the **real** way, not just a **theoretical** one, how enemy and friendly soldiers go about doing their job in order to ask questions that dig out essential facts"(Hartley & Karinch, 2005, How To Spot A Liar).

"**Fear works**. It is more effective than any drug, tactic, or torture device **once interrogators resort to actual torture, they are apt to lose ground**... The threat of coercion usually weakens or destroys resistance more effectively than coercion itself," the manual says. Much useful information is time-sensitive, and running down false leads or arresting innocents' wastes time"(Bowden, Mark 2003).

"Maj. Matthew Alexander, a pseudonym, is a military interrogator who followed the rules in Iraq while conducting 300 interrogations and supervising over a 1,000. According to him, **torture has the second-order effect of increasing the level of insurgents and terrorists in the fight against US forces overseas**. 'I listened time and time again to foreign fighters, and Sunni Iraqis, state the **number one reason** they had decided to pick up arms and join Al-Qaeda **was the abuses at Abu Ghraib and the authorized torture and abuse at Guantanamo**

Bay.' said Alexander." (Parco, Levy, 2010 Enjoining the American Nightmare)

Notes on Torture

- President Ronald Reagan reaffirmed the precedent set by Presidents Washington and Lincoln signing the Convention against Torture and Other Cruel, Inhuman or Degrading Treatment or Punishment in 1988.
- During the Revolutionary War, increased defections from enemy soldiers were because of commonly known good treatment at the hands of the Continental Army, as opposed to the notorious use of torture by the British.
- President Abraham Lincoln outlawed torture to exact confessions.
- The Geneva Convention prohibits any type of mistreatment of prisoners, 'calling it torture lite is still torture, and illegal.'

Additionally, the sin nature in us twists the God-given design to dominate nature, the elements, and the animals- into domination of each other at all costs. It also takes the fear of being dominated or killed and uses that fear as justification to torture captives for information. Torture is a sign of moral weakness and fear. In some cases, torture of prisoners is conducted out of a twisted sense of revenge, as an ungodly outlet for anger, or just plain sadism. Nowhere in the word of the Lord is torture acceptable. Torture is a tactic of the Enemy, used by his minion humans. Some well-meaning patriots are deceived into conducting inhumane acts. What is God's definition of torture? Are Enhanced Interrogation Techniques (EIT) in the category of torture?

Taking the position of the victim as a justification for torture or other war crime is how the Nazi's turned a nation against the Jews. It was all the Jews fault, and they are not human, but subhuman according to evolution... Blaming the Jews for German woes allowed for the creation of concentration camps and the final solution. Playing the victim to justify violence is a fascist tactic. Make people afraid, and they will let you do what you want to make them feel safe. We must remain professional interrogators and not yield to the temptation to use torture.

Tick Tock. Tick To...BOOM!

But what about the dirty bomb, anthrax or some other threat? First, you have to know there really is an imminent threat. You cannot assume there is a threat. Granted our international ports, airports, and checkpoints, stop many daily, quietly, and with good reason. Yet, this does not justify torture. If a person is determined to die a martyr in a suicide blast; torture or threat of death is not always a useful tool. They may be willing to die in the attack you are trying to prevent, according to some Ticking-time Bomb Scenarios (TBS).

This whole subject is a struggle against fear of the unknown or suspected. The Lord's blessing in the intelligence community will bring more timely and actionable information. They do a great job, but the potential in the Lord is exponential. You cannot justify torture for something which may or may not be happening. Biblically you can never justify inhumane treatment of a person. Of course, some do not agree. I am not looking for agreement. God's word is what it is. It is up to the covenant warrior according to his or her own conscience before God. Consensus and popular opinion is not a covenant warriors initial concern. Following the law is.

> "...I take **the moral permissibility of torture** in the ticking time-bomb case to be self-evident; anyone who understands the details of the case would, I think, **consent to the torture**."(Allhoff, Fritz(2005)A Defense of Torture: Separation of Cases, Ticking Time-bombs, and Moral Justification, International Journal of Applied Philosophy 19:2).

> "Gen. Finnegan's mission was to persuade "24"'s makers to stop dramatizing the TBS because the show – wildly popular among U.S. military forces – was leading to abuse and mistreatment of detainees, as the TBS overrode the careful training that the soldiers had in how to treat captives. He brought along experienced interrogators to explain why the scripts are preposterous...The producer

> was another story: a friend and ideological soul-mate of pro-torture politicians; he refused to meet with the general, whose mission failed." (Luban, D(2008) Unthinking the Ticking Time Bomb, July http://lsr.nellco.org/georgetown/fwps/papers/68/).

Fear and anger fuel the desire to torture, not just a sadistic personality. Yes, innocent lives are on the line, when aren't they? But torture is not justifiable when results are sketchy at best, and you are not sure, of what you don't know. In TBS a dedicated enemy may not care to leave the city of the dirty bomb or another device. Such a person, and scenario, if such comes too light, only have to bide their time till their suffering ends, their wicked mission accomplished. You and they are dead anyway. Always pray and trust the Lord. His hedge is the only true security. We have experienced what it's like to breach our national hedge from inside at the Twin Towers, the Pentagon, and in Pennsylvania. "Except the Lord guard the city, the watchmen watch in vain" (Psalm 127).

What does this mean to me?

For the covenant warrior there are two questions: should we capture, and should we interrogate military and or intelligence personnel. Remember, always ask the question should we or may we, not can we. Of course, you can. You are able to do X or Y, but that doesn't mean you should. Don't assume it is a yes just because it seems right the right thing to do. May we capture and should we interrogate? Is there a precedent for military capture and interrogation?

Yes. Judges 8:14 is the precedent for capture and interrogation. It is the account of a soldier of an enemy King. Gideon's men interrogate the captured enemy soldier. He divulges military information, actionable intelligence that sets up the next mission. There are no details given of the methods of interrogation used, just that it took place. This is an endorsement of capturing and interrogation in the military and intelligence arena. Governing principles to judge which methods are permissible is found in other scriptures about the treatment of the enemy. We must remain professional interrogators. We are not to become Grand Inquisitors.

Another interrogation is the secret questioning of an imprisoned Jeremiah (Jeremiah 37:17), concerning the military outcome of a coming critical battle. Here is where a captive sometimes is instructed to tell the truth by God, without compromising security. His statements do not negatively affect the outcome of operations.

In annotating Gideon's interrogation, Holy Spirit is endorsing capture and interrogation, with the expectation of success in obtaining information. It is implied the Holy Spirit through His gifts, or an angel of the Lords is available to assist if we request assistance with expectation. Faith for an expectation of success and support based upon His endorsement of the activity. In the past, the Holy Spirit assisted in others in their intelligence gathering. Therefore it is His will to assist you in your intelligence gathering.

In Hebrew, the word for inquiry or interrogation is spelled Vav Yud Shin Aleph Lamed Heh Vav. Shin, Aleph, and Lamed are the root letters and picture meaning of questioning or asking questions. In Hebrew, each letter has a numerical value and a picture associated with it to detail what is meant not only by what is said but the picture sequences which go with it- the story they tell. Unique to these two uses of the word for inquiry are the bookended letters- Vav Heh and Yud Vav. These designate an intelligence line of questioning not seen in the context of other uses of the word. In proper Hebrew order, they read from right to left with their multiple meanings.

Vav: representing a nail- to be secured or nailed, kept secure. This letter bookends the word for interrogation- someone trying to keep a secret or resist giving information.

Yud: a closed hand; speaking to a deed, work, action of man, to make or force something

Shin: teeth- consuming or speaking/destroying

Aleph: an ox or bull- the 1st, strength, sacrificial, leader

Lamed: Cattell prod or goad, stake- to pry, go toward, tongue

Heh: no picture or a picture of a window/portal to Heaven / God's grace or provision; to reveal

Vav: represents a nail - to be secured or nailed, kept secure. This letter bookends the word for interrogation- someone trying to keep a secret or resist giving information.

Here within the pictures and some of the various meanings are obvious links to getting to the truth through persuasion of some type; gaining information not intended for the questioner. Key to understanding the Heh is that God is represented as the Heh, His grace, presence, provision, person. With His assistance in questioning your subject will crack and reveal or God Himself will show directly to you, what you need to know. The nail pictorial and goad or cattle prod. These pictures are not endorsements to torture. They are clarifiers as to an effort of force made to obtain information as well as an attempt to resist giving up information and the need for good creative leadership to get the information. The resist portion is also the mandate to Survive Evade Resist and Escape capture or interrogation by the enemy.

How far is too far

What then are the parameters in the Lord for interrogations? For these boundaries are what a covenant warrior is charged to maintain. Other scriptures order the humane treatment of an enemy as part of overcoming evil with good. In Proverbs 25:21-22 giving your enemy food and drink, good treatment brings guilt and mental stress to them. In Romans 12:20 humane treatment of the enemy is restated. I saw a documentary on the sinking of the Nazi Battleship Bismarck. In interviews with sailors from the Bismarck, many recounted fear at being 'rescued' by British ships as their ship sank. They had been told numerous stories of the evils the British would inflict upon them if captured. It was all proven untrue.

I am a Cold War dinosaur. We were told stories of the East German and Czechoslovakian soldiers' treatment of Americans if caught or kidnapped and taken across the Border. We were told of the stories captured German soldier's bad treatment at the hands of the Russians during WWII, that, the same would happen to us should war erupt. If captured by the U.S.S.R., we were to expect harsh treatment. I still believe it would have happened because historically they mistreated their own people besides those Germans captured by Russia. And some Islamic States are documented as ruthless to prisoners and their own citizens. Of course, there are also nations in Africa, South America, and Asia where evil reigns, but this is not a surprise to anyone.

On a trolley back in the late 1980's, I met a German Luftwaffe pilot in Wurzburg. The American soldier I was traveling with spoke fluent German. We three talked on a trolley for a little while, a conversation initiated by the old man. This former Nazi, our enemy, started the conversation with praise for America. He said he had been shot down in Africa, captured, and treated humanely, even though he is an enemy. His best friend was shot down on the Russian front, captured, and treated viciously. Both reunited after the war and recounted their stories. He never forgot how well we treated him, our enemy. He went on to say how glad he was the United States took over most of Germany, and that "It was the best thing, which could have happened to it."

Current research, professional interrogator experiences, and expert testimony concur with a Biblical interrogation model. Generally speaking, build report. Rough up (EIT not Torture) when you must, blackmail when you must, bribe or use rewards which yield results. Treat them humanely regardless of their inhumanity. Pray for help and guidance from God before, during and be thankful after the process. God will help you with questioning, the information you don't yet know, but need, through words of knowledge and wisdom to put pressure on your subject to get them to talk. The Holy Spirit or an angel will work over their mind while you are working with them, and when you are not.

To clarify humane, it is what doesn't entail intentional physical, sexual, or chemical dependency or abuse. That which doesn't cause real damage, maiming or distortion to a subject. Unacceptable and inhuman is using electric shock on a person's genitals or a woman's chest. SERE school techniques used to harden our personnel against interrogation are acceptable to use on real prisoners.

Being roughed up and put into fear of something, including the use of the controversial waterboarding is not dehumanizing, but is effective.

Sensory deprivation or overload and isolation are appropriate. EIT is acceptable especially when steps are taken to prevent accidental medical injury, and medical personnel is standing by in case of any unforeseen events, as well as monitors who know the limits of the law on enhanced interrogation techniques. What is legal versus what is allowed varies between administrations. Political bias may cause them to ignore the rule of law being followed and the great results, and hinder interrogations anyway for a foolish political reason.

If for example, you know your Islamic eternal judgment by their standards. This is what God did to Pharaoh. The comment about Pharaoh's heart becoming heavy is a Biblical reference to Egyptian religious beliefs. It refers to the belief at death your heart is weighed to determine your disposition. If heavy, you descend into the underworld. It goes without saying understanding your subject's beliefs is critical. If possible, do as God did to Pharaoh: his own standard convicts him. Convict them in their own cultural context, and they have a better chance of becoming compliant. Just another tool in the bag of speech and dissimulation, the dutiful lie, and other methods. Remember threating is one thing. Abuse is another. In Pharaoh's case, it was not a matter of interrogation, but judgment. Pharaoh's pride was his downfall.

Drug use is not entirely unauthorized but can yield unreliable answers and gibberish. Getting a subject hooked on a drug would be immoral. They will say or confess anything for a fix. You must also attempt to remove from them the reason they are your enemy. You become more so their enemy when you become their drug dealer. Deception tactics are necessary, such as fabricated news broadcasts on a controlled network they have access too. The subject should be in an elaborately controlled atmosphere, a theatre of sorts. This theatrical production is one where we are the directors of their reality and perceptions. The script should not necessarily be a nightmare reality.

If the subjects' religion is known, even atheists have a self-belief system, learn it and use it to your advantage. This is a powerful tool if used correctly. Crack through their worldview, use non-Muslim and ex-Muslim clergy with knowledge of Islam. Experience and understanding the culture and belief system of a person can be used to turn their beliefs against them. Treated right and worked right, a fanatical Muslim can be convicted by their own conscience, and then maneuvered into giving up information. One example, Allah calls himself the most cunning one, a betrayer. How then does a Muslim not know if Allah is betraying him in his capture, wanting him to talk?

A religious expert, a minister, would potentially do well as a trained interrogator. A minister might also do well as a partner or advisor to an interrogator. A minister, approaching the subject, not from an interviewing stance, but rapport building, potentially can make inroads where others have not and sooner. At the same time, some detainees might close up when clergy are present. Having one in the earpiece or reviewing sessions with you could prove invaluable. Psychologists are great, but you are dealing with the spirit, not just the soul of a person. Shrinks can only go so far, especially if out of their cultural element. You need experts in not only Islam and its nuances, but also the counters to it from a religious viewpoint.

However. . .

I am a minister, who also is a former combat arms soldier. I know many of my fellow ministers and certainly most 99% of the Chaplains I've met would make terrible interrogators. Most don't even know to pray implacable prayers, and many have and still preach all killing is murder. Many pray for our law enforcement and military sincerely, but still think their jobs are morally compromised. Moreover, and as testified to by Dr. James Mitchell. You may likely get some evangelistic zealot who screams at or threatens with Hell. I only know of two other ministers who would be an asset, not a liability. I'm sure there are more than three in the world, but I haven't met them. Though EIT is Biblical, these techniques can still be inappropriately applied if established limits are ignored. An account by one expert integrator, working with another expert, is worth reading.

> Bruce and I reminded them that the CIA was in the business of obtaining intelligence, not running a prison where the primary focus was to punish detainees. As long as it was possible to make minor accommodations for a cooperating detainee and as a result elicit answers

> to our questions that were more full and complete, that was what we should be doing. We reminded them that EITs were not authorized for use to punish detainees for acting out or to force compliance with administrative rules. (Mitchell J., 2016)

The job is to get information, not to evangelize or prove some point of doctrine arguing is not a path to rapport building. If they convert so be it, if not so be it. If they convert, be suspicious they likely are trying to play you. You know a tree by its fruit. If they truly convert, only time will tell, the free flow of information should occur. Conversion to Christianity does not earn a free pass. I was one of the very few Christians who did not agree or endorse the efforts of some well-meaning, though misguided attempts to get the sentence of serial killer Karla Faye Tucker commuted. Sean Seller and Jeffrey Dahmer reportedly got saved on death row, but no one asked for their release. I believe Sean and Karla got saved, and hope Jeffrey did.

Sean even worked with the police helping in other occult murder cases in the eighties (Rivera, Exposing Satans Underground, NBC special). These born-again conversions are pardons from an eternal death sentence, same as the rest of us. A religious experience is no justification to commute a lawful death sentence. I would have opposed either Sean or Jeffreys release the same as Karla's. See you in Heaven. Glad you made it and arrived before me.

Rights of Enemy Combatants

Wicked rulers of nation-states support terrorism waged by organizations with no official state origin. This is offering safe harbor to individuals or organizations within a nation. Offering safe harbor is when a nation, which has not formally declared war upon the United States, sponsors combat actions against us. A father of Just War Theory, Grotius, speaks on pirates, which are a type of yesteryear terrorist

> "...war is not the **private undertaking of bold adventurers**, but made and sanctioned by the public and sovereign authority on both sides...— and it is

> accompanied also with other consequences and rights, **which do not belong to wars against pirates**, and to civil wars" (Grotius War and Peace em ad).

Grotius is correct, pirates, today's terrorists, not officially state-sanctioned, enjoy fewer rights in rules of conflict and captivity than officially sanctioned state-sponsored armies, naval personnel under a formal declaration of war. A declaration of Jihad can and often is from a person or a group(s), and not accepted as official by a nation. However, acknowledgment of the seriousness or threat from a faction is a must. Space does not allow to explore all the aspects of the cases of Zacarias Moussaoui, John Walker Lindh, Richard Reid, José Padilla, Yaser Esam Hamdi, or Moazzam Begg just to name a few. Much can, and has been said as to which rights a non-citizen or a traitor possess and what court or tribunal has jurisdiction on a case by case basis.

A discussion should take place concerning retention of citizenship by a traitor. I favor military having jurisdiction over illegitimate enemy combatants not U.S. Courts, unless they are U.S. citizens, depending on the circumstances. Citizens have their Constitutional rights and even citizen terrorists deserve humane treatment. But, I also agree with Grotius that pirates and terrorists do not enjoy the same benefits as state-sanctioned combatants. Those who commit acts of violence, believing they are at war with a nation and its ideologies when that country cannot declare war in return on a state, declare officially unrecognized war by their combat actions.

Does being an unlawful combatant, mean you deserve equal treatment, and equal rights as a state-sanctioned combatant or regular criminal citizen would? Should a U.S. citizen participate with terrorists and committing not just treason, but acts of terror, they have rejected or disavowed their citizenship and the rights attached to citizenship. They should appear before a court and if found guilty of terrorism, stripped of their citizenship and remanded to military for interrogation and sentencing of imprisonment as an unlawful enemy combatant.

As a being created in God's image, equitable, humane treatment of all combatants and common criminals regardless of their participation level or actions toward us is a moral imperative. This enables us to retain our humanity and honor before God and among men. Contrary to popular opinion, this does not block our ability to be effective in war or conflict. Non-state sanctioned belligerents are war criminals, but not U.S citizens should be handled as prisoners of war and tried in military tribunals or civil courts as current policy dictates. When the two intersect- enemy combatant and civil criminal- the military is preferred to process. These are not common criminals.

Common criminals have rights associated with citizenship and are presumed innocent until proven guilty. Presumably, criminals can be rehabilitated then reintegrated into society. Release from prison should be done with care to assess the likelihood of their rejoining the fight. We are not trying to replenish their ranks especially if they are enemy leaders. That would be crazy and reveals another problem with unsanctioned combatants.

There should be no prisoner exchange with a terrorist group which is not mutually beneficial. Still, we must consider; since war is not officially declared and recognized by at least one side, there is no end in sight to the hostilities, no possible peace negotiations. Therefore, a prisoner of war (illegitimate enemy combatant) theoretically never has the right to be released and is risky to trade because the war continues indefinitely. Especially within Islam. Fundamentalist Islam whose definition of peace is being dominated and submitted to Islam. No submission equals no peace. Muhammed taught Muslims to make peace when weak or disadvantaged against an enemy (all non-believers are enemies). Once you regain strength to break the peace and resume attempts to force conversion and submission, not just of people, but nations.

Wrapping up Interrogations

If your daughter became radicalized, a terrorist, or enemy military member, what <u>wouldn't</u> you do to extract information from your own flesh and blood daughter the traitor? What if your wife, mother, or daughter is the traitor? Sensory, and or limited food restrictions, along with the threat of physical damage; I would threaten, but never do or authorize physical damage. Physical damage here does not exclude being slammed against a specially made wall or roughed up in a manner which is monitored by medical personnel and pre-approved as a method of psychological shock and awe. No reasonable person would allow or perform acts of degradation of any kind, such as forced nudity, to be conducted against them. As with her, it is the same with others. Jesus answered some questions from some soldiers in a crowd he was talking to. "And the soldiers likewise demanded of him, saying, And what shall we do? And he said unto them, Do violence to no man, neither accuse *any* falsely; and be content with your wages" (Luke 3:14). Jesus is not referring to their duty as soldiers when referring to violence done by them. He is referring to bullying and abuse of their authority for personal gain. Such as the guards of His tomb, some of whom took a bribe instead of telling the truth about His resurrection, which they experienced firsthand. Remember that back then the military doubled as the law enforcement. A false accusation could mean your life or imprisonment.

Worth repeating is this warning to the victorious.

> "Rejoice not when thine enemy falleth, and let not thine heart be glad when he stumbleth: Lest the LORD see *it,* and it displeases him, and he turn away his wrath from him. Fret not thyself because of evil *men,* neither be thou envious at the wicked; For there shall be no reward to the evil *man;* the candle of the wicked shall be put out" (Pro 24:17-20).

Rejoicing in this context is not referring to a celebration of victory, but the attitude of pride, that you did it on your own. Once that time is done do not forget to return to the peaceful. Don't take it personally. When the opportunity strikes, do as the Lord commands and see the Holy Spirit work your subject on your behalf. "If thine enemy be hungry, give him bread to eat; and if he be thirsty, give him water to drink: For thou shalt heap coals of fire upon his head, and the LORD shall reward thee"(Prov 25:21-22). When we treat our enemies properly, the Lord influences their conscience and minds.

SERE in the Spirit

Survive, Evade, Resist, and Escape in the power of the Holy Spirit. Faith comes by hearing and hearing the word of God. Lord give us ears to hear and a spirit of understanding what we hear. We hear with our physical ear repeatedly, and then it gets into our spiritual ear, the second hearing. Let us not hear a stranger's voice nor be enticed by subtle words, nor be filled with thoughts or images of fear and death, but of life and health. With this in mind, listen, read, remember, and believe. What God has done for others He will do for you in combat, the endurance of capture, evasion of captivity, or release from captivity, even moving you supernaturally to or away from a place. Holy Spirit decides when and how. Philip after preaching to the Eunuch in the wilderness was teleported 20-25 miles away into the middle of a city (Acts 8:39-40). There are testimonies of a minister in Mexico being teleported out of the control of Cartel thugs to a safe place in another part of the city in a moment.

Peter and Paul are released from shackles and prison by an Earthquake. There are no casualties from the earthquake from God. A natural or demonic supernatural disaster has casualties. Peter was also sprung from custody by an angel of the Lord (Acts 12:5-11 and Acts 16:26). Daniel is saved from ravenous lions. Shadrach, Meshach, and Abednego are prevented from being burned alive, after being tossed into a fiery furnace (Daniel 3:20-26 and Daniel 6:19-26). Twice David was protected from an attack by King Saul- at point blank range- for the Lord was with him. David should have been killed (1 Samuel 18-7-12).

Jesus Himself, by the power of the Holy Spirit, escaped the crowd bent on killing Him because they did not like what he was saying. Once they laid hands on Him, they brought Him to the edge of a hill to throw Him down to His death. Jesus passed back through the lynch mob; unable maintain the physical custody of Him they initially had. The second time was at the Temple where a crowd tried to apprehend Him, but He could not be 'suddenly detected' among them (Luke 4:28-30 and John 7:30 and John 10:39). Gaining physical custody of Jesus at the temple was not even possible.

Jesus also could have escaped in the Garden, but it was then His time. When He revealed Himself speaking His covenant name, Yahweh (I

AM) the arresting guards of the High Priest are knocked to the ground, possibly unconscious for a moment and at the very least incapacitated; slain in the Spirit either way. Jesus waited till they got back up then allowed them to arrest Him.

Jesus stated He could have called for the assistance of twelve legions of angels to deliver Him from them [the large group of arresting officers]. This would have been a legion per disciple (11 total), and the twelfth would be Jesus. A legion is over 6,000. What Jesus could have done, is what we can do. He said that for our benefit.

Can you be delivered? Yes. Ask and believe remembering Hebrews 11, verse 35. Is it possible <u>for the Gospels sake</u> you may be captured or tortured? Yes. So, if captured as a soldier or undercover agent by the enemy, what then? Preach the gospel to your captors and use all your training and strength to resist and escape. Remember to listen to the Holy Spirit your divine S-2 (intelligence section). He will give you what to say. Careful, anything you say, true or untrue gives up something so when you must speak to guard against this ask the Holy Spirit to give you what to say. Pray for your captors and their deliverance. It is about Jesus, not you or them. Ultimately, it is you in Heaven and without you, most likely them in Hell. You are in the position of power even as a captive. You know ultimately that you will live here or there!

Tell them you forgive them for their evil in advance. Preach the gospel. Make your captivity about Jesus; bring Him into your situation. Be courteous with your wicked jailers. Sing psalms like Paul and Silas. Encourage your fellow captives. Do not let the fear of death overcome you, for Jesus has those keys, do not despair. Remember the deliverances of John, Jesus, Paul and so forth. Remember Paul in Acts converting his guards at Rome before his death.

They may try to convert you, say to them why you would switch to such a cruel god, based on their actions? Not challenging or insultingly but as a real question. Or say nothing of the sort, use your best judgment. Avoid saying anything if possible. Remember the Code of Conduct Articles. Keep the faith. King David on the run from Saul faked being crazy to avoid death at the hands of enemies. The focus is to pray for rescue, means to escape, to keep the faith, survive, and come home. Pray for your enemy and fellow captives. Making your situation about Jesus and not you is the key to victory in the darkness.

Primary weapons in incarceration are courtesy and forgiveness. Ask God for the grace to love your deceived, going to Hell, inwardly cowardly tormented captors. You will need His grace to make it. In the 'flesh' on our own, we all might wish them dead, etc. Remember you are a minister of vengeance with a covenant of protection, and retaliation against enemies promised by the Lord. Pray against the evil spirits which control your captors. You have no authority over the people, but you do have authority over the spirits controlling them. "NO weapon formed against you will prosper" (Isa 54:17). In a Christian book on testimonies from Vietnam, I don't remember the name of the book. It was twenty years ago when I read it. One was about a Holy Ghost filled, tongues praying, Vietnamese preacher.

His conversions of the youth hurt the Viet Cong recruitment. Eventually, they tracked him down one night, woke him up, then clubbed him unconscious. He came to in an underground complex. The large room was full of Viet Cong, NVA, and a few Chinese officers. They accused him of working with the CIA etc. It was a mock trial, of which there would be only one end. He prayed and remembered God promised He would give him what to say when the time came. Finally, they asked him what he had to say for himself.

Ignoring all the accusations leveled against him, the Holy Spirit, at that moment, instructed him to preach about Jesus and tell His story. The preacher preached it. The enemy kept silent the whole time. There were no altar calls, revival, or shouts of hallelujah. Once he finished, they huddled and mumbled for a bit then clubbed him again. He came to in his home. They never bothered him again.

Only the covenant warrior drawing upon Holy Spirit assistance, using Code of Conduct Articles as a guide is unmovable. When you do not fear death, believe any wound can be healed, and deliverance is available...you cannot be moved. Even if they threaten your family, if they are saved, or not- the Lord can protect them. Do not falter. Do not lose heart or faith. Remain loyal and patriotic to Heaven and the U.S. or your own nation.

There are many stories of missionaries guarded by the angels or the

Holy Spirit Himself. One testimony is of bullets fired at point blank range, but not hitting their target. Peter is rescued from prison while closely guarded by soldiers. He is escorted out of the jail by an angel unetected. Not all stories end in a happy homecoming, though I don't always know why that is. Pray. Become a testimony not a statistic.

The Torture of Jesus

I used to think I was less of an Infantryman if I hadn't killed the enemy or had a combat patch. No one made me feel this way; it was just how I felt. Then I get to combat, go on missions every week or so volunteering as a gunner or driver as needed or requested. Now I realize the patch or combat badge doesn't make you a good or better soldier, just one who has been through or around more than others. Being willing to do what must be done and not having the opportunity too is just how things worked out. My testimony is not the one I wanted to have. Nevertheless, shared experiences are comforting to share, and drawing from each other's experiences is invaluable.

Should you find yourself inprisoned, call upon the Lord Jesus. He withstood immense and cruel torture, yet didn't accept aid and comfort offered by the enemy. He is abused having his beard pulled out, being beaten by a rod, whipped with pieces of bone and metal - 39 lashes tearing all the skin off his back and sides. Jesus is also punched in the face until unrecognizable, has a crown of two-inch-long thorns twisted together then pushed onto his head piercing and tearing him more. On the cross, his arms are pulled out of joint. Jesus understands torture and resisting aid and comfort.

Crucifixion is nine inch long nails impaling you to a cross through the nerves in your wrists and through your feet, on a step. Pushing up for air, then slumping from pain where you asphyxiate; a long, painful death. He could have used His personal divine power to escape but withstood it and the wrath of His Father for all our sins, including your captors. Before crucifixion Governor Pilate asked him why he said nothing to get released? Didn't Jesus know he had the power of life and death over him? Jesus said he had no control over Him except what was given him. This spooked the Governor.

When you pray to Jesus know beyond the shadow of a doubt He is intimate with your pain and suffering, your emotions and fears. Jesus experienced them in the Garden of Gethsemane just before the officers arrived to arrest Him. Knowing what is to happen to ahead of time, the intensity of mental and emotional trauma is to the point blood vessels in his head burst, mixing blood with the sweat from the stress coming off his forehead. His response, He prayed more. He prayed, and an angel strengthened Him to endure the anguish and keep his mind sound and at peace, in spite of the coming torture, death, time to spend in Hell, before His resurrection.

On the cross, Jesus asks for forgiveness for us and those doing this to Him. Forgiveness empowers you and puts your enemy at a disadvantage. Pray, and Jesus Himself or an angel from Him will strengthen you. It's up to you, but making your captivity about your faith changes the dynamic in all dimensions, and puts the Holy Spirit between you and them. Read Hebrews chapter 12 and Fox Book of Martyrs. Maintain an eternal perspective. Turn the tables on your captors. Jesus overcame all in the power of the Holy Spirit. The same Holy Spirit which raised Him from the dead. The same Holy Spirit on Earth and in you, if you are a believer, today.

CHAPTER 13

Guantanamo Bay of Heaven

I mentioned before about how terrorist technically do not have to be released because there is no end to the conflict, only a minimizing of the scope of the war on terror. This is the principle of debtors prison found in the Bible as a metaphor for Hell and the Lake of Fire. I revisit this subject because a warrior must be sure of their future in the next life, to overcome the fears of this life. You should also be doubly sure that the end of the wicked, whether you catch or kill them or not, is inescapable judgment and separation from God and all that is good. This is worth going over again to instill in the warrior that their Heaven is sure, and the fate of the wicked is also sure.

A quick study of death and the afterlife is essential for the warrior who may face death at a seemingly routine traffic stop, an average follow up on a lead, or under fire in a faraway land. Being a useful Christian Covenant Warrior is also about being at peace with the fact you may not make it home. Do you have your affairs in order? You should. This will alleviate a lot of stress if wounded and or mortally wounded.

It is a sad thing; a funeral for a Christian (or anyone) who is the breadwinner of the house but did not have their affairs in order. They went to, and are now enjoying Heaven. What should be a time to mourn the temporary separation and rejoice in the promised reunion at the resurrection. Is overshadowed as left behind loved ones are propelled into poverty. Have you truly thought out the plot, headstone, or cremation, and powers of attorney ahead of time? Have you really done the math on your finances: the amount of your insurance, what will be left for them to live off of, and or invest to assure a good standard of living? I have talked about protection from not dying and believe it wholeheartedly, but it is a good example to others and provides peace of mind for loved ones when the hard choices are already made: pre-paid headstone, funeral plot, cremations, casket, and other possible arrangements. A lot of stress in an already stressful and emotional time and potential family conflicts are avoided.

I also mentioned the fear of death, which many are in bondage under. Furthermore, I put a lot of emphasis on rebuking, rejecting, casting out, and in other ways binding the spirit of fear or intimidation causing us to be coerced and back down on our faith. First, death is not the end, but a transition. If you accepted Jesus substitutionary death on the cross for your sins, and believed God raised him from the dead, said that with your mouth as you believed in your heart- you're saved and going to Heaven. Judgment for you will consist of an evaluation of your works for the Lord. What is from Him is rewarded, what is not of Him burns up in the test of fire, but you do not burn.

Getting into Heaven is a merit-based system. The standard is perfect, life, thoughts, actions, speech according to the Law. **We all fail** the merit test **except Jesus**. Our works are never good enough to earn Heaven. If in Christ, when you physically die you are escorted by angels to Heaven awaiting your resurrected body (1 Thes 4; John 3; and 1 Cor chapters 11 and 15). If you are not saved, you are dragged to Hell which is God's lockdown until your trial. All stand trial or are evaluated for the things they said and did in their body before dying, but only Christians have a defense attorney! Once called up for judgment from Hell (those who did not accept Christ). They are tried on the merits of the works they did in life; their works are never good enough.

The difference is only Jesus merited Heaven and those in Jesus. A Christians works will burn up if not done in Christ, but the Christian will not burn up. What works were done in Christ will be rewarded. As for the wicked, all their works will burn up, and instead of any reward, they will reap whatever torment they've earned. The sentence is carried out and the wicked, along with Satan, and all demons, evil spirits, fallen angels, etc., are cast into the Lake of Fire to burn forever and ever.

This is no Purgatory; the lie that you can go to a place and work off or only have to be tormented for a time and or you can be purchased out of [called Catholic Indulgences] and then get into Heaven. There is no Islamic Paradise with a bunch of virgins (I often wondered what female suicide bombers are promised), there are no pardons, no parole, no reprieve. There is no recycling of your soul to come back here to do it all again, and again, again. The Zodiac killer among many, who do or have done evil, may never be brought to man's justice, but no one really escapes. It is a fearful thing to fall into the hands of the Living God. Nothing is swept under the rug. Your sins are forgiven, but only because Jesus paid for them, if you let him, otherwise Pay Day is coming now or later. Have no fear of death, but be sure to prepare for it.

In Heaven's Guantanamo, the Lake of Fire, the wicked are tormented day and night in flame, their flesh never burning off, and all their senses and memory intact. The memory of each time they rejected salvation in Jesus (the reason they are in the Lake) and all their wickedness replayed in addition to the torment of the fire for eternity. God is all or nothing. Eternity in Heaven, or an eternity in the Lake. For those who would twist my intent, I'm not making the analogy that Guantanamo, like Hell for the wicked, should be a place of torment unlawful enemy combatants. I am saying as an analogy, Guantanamo, for some may be their last stop in this life - no escape.

The fire serves two purposes. First is the permanent imprisonment of the evil spirit, human or other. Secondly, the fire is a way to purge the sin from a spirit, human or other. The catch 22 is only the blood sacrifice of Jesus satisfies Divine justice as payment for all sin. Therefore, you burn forever (debtors prison) since the fire can't ever purge away your sins, nor your torment ever pay for your sin debt. An eternity in Heaven or an eternity in the Lake of fire, it is our choice to accept or reject.

COVENANT SUPPORT

Special Preface to Healing the Fractured Soul parts I and II

As some of you will notice the process of renewing the mind to a new normal, from whichever state it was previously in, is comparable to Cognitive Processing Theory (CPT). CPT is the most common approach to PTSD treatment. An approach not without its valid criticisms and conclusions that in many cases it should not even be utilized (Yehuda & Hoge, 2016). Biblical Renewing of the Mind Theory (BRMT) is not CPT. CPT does not explicitly or primarily incorporate the spiritual component and resources provided by the Living God; BRMT does. This is a difference between pastoral and Christian counseling versus secular counseling. Though CPT is a proven effective and correct model, no surprise since it uses the ancient Biblical model; it simply lacks the comparable spiritual element.

Part of remaining combat effective for the Lord can be involvement of a retired or still serving minister of vengeance in therapy or social groups revolving around their profession. This can help with the transition from duty and trauma back into civilian or garrison life. The key is to remain and flourish in daily functionality without much if any difficulty. You may seek to start or engage in group therapy or support group sessions if none are available in your area. These groups would primarily focus on guilt and shame processing instead of on fear and anxiety. (Vermetten, Jetly, 2018 and Nazarov et al., 2015)

Accepting forgiveness from the Lord is also finding the strength to forgive, if necessary yourself and in accepting forgiveness and understanding from others. BRMT is about your new perspective based on a new identity and moral structure rooted in God's word, His moral framework, and view of you. I've described ideas on taking captive every thought and on other processes. Some of you may feel overwhelmed even though these are all starting points with a light at the end of the tunnel, a light of hope. Don't try to work it all out at one time. First work on a good night's rest, one night at a time.

The idea is to get your mind and body rested first. Then work more on what you say, such as profanity, to gain another victory and an increment of change. Jesus said the words he speaks are spirit and life. The point he is making is our words are spiritual containers and transferrers of power, but not always of life. Then go after the deeper issues surrounding your PTSD experiences. Win the war to reclaim your life one battle at a time: quality, not quantity, no rush, no worry, each person's journey is their own. Don't compare your progress to another person's. Important to remember is to try to be empathetic to the trauma your symptoms may cause your spouse, children, or others interacting with you. It can be frightening for them, as well as frustrating for you to say the least. The family, when possible, is a great source of resiliency and support in recovery, but remember they are also struggling. (Riggs, S. & Riggs, D., 2011)

> What I have argued here is that perhaps the veteran isn't only haunted by the enemy combatants or even civilians she killed, but also by the specter of a world without morals. The phenomenological framework, with its focus on the way that experiences stamp our perceptual world at large, can help us understand what it means to be haunted in this way. Beginning with this understanding of moral injury as a shattering of one's entire moral framework can stand to positively impact both the understanding and treatment of moral injury. (McDonald, 2017).

This section of Ministers of Vengeance is about providing a realistic moral framework is Biblical based that you may fully deal with the various aspects of moral injury inclusive of personal guilt or shame, including survivors guilt, to build a solid foundation in your self-esteem and identity allowing you to do what must be done, and still enjoy your life afterward.

If you are a person who has no desire to change because your hyperarousal etc. fulfills the need for survival, even when not in a threatening situation (Yehuda, 2016). You may want to ask yourself why you want to maintain this comfort zone mentality in an environment which is not threatening. What is the benefit to you, or a tradeoff for keeping a heightened situational awareness? Count the cost: your family, friends or ability to even shop at a crowded mall?

Is remaining in your current comfort zone really adding to your quality of life, or just fulfilling a survival need at the expense of living a satisfying life? My prayer is that Lord will help you change your mind and move out of your current comfort zone of dysfunction, into the comforting zone of His love.

This is not meant to be comprehensive, or exhaustive. It is meant to be a starting point for finding your location in a dark tunnel, then being able to see and take the journey toward the light at the end of the tunnel. I talk about the *time* and *chance* law of Ecclesiastes being canceled out or countered by the covenant promise of being redeemed from destruction. This is my personal confession of faith, but not without controversy. Translation: some fellow scholars would say I am incorrect. If I believe it is fully true I stand behind it. If I don't know I'll say I don't know. If I am not fully persuaded, I'll let you know that also. On the Time and Chance principle being overcome by the promise of being redeemed from destruction I am fully persuaded; although I am always open to correction by the Holy Spirit. You must decide your own confession.

Before we jump into healing, I want to clearly state my position so as not to be confusing or have my words twisted by the Devil and made harmful to you. It is a fact that if a person does not feel the need to get **physical** healing and chooses to live with their injury for whatever reason, that's ok and Biblical. Your tragedy in this life (since in Heaven in your resurrected body you are completely healthy and whole) is a temporary condition. Your faith and trust in God despite the trauma may very likely lead you to someone angry with God who you can positively connect with.

Maintaining your faith in a shared situation means you can comfort those with the comfort you have been comforted by God with. You can demonstrate Jesus love for them despite the loss and pain. You can lead a soul to Christ whom no one else could reach. Saving a soul from Hell is the greatest rescue mission one person can do for another. Each of our journeys in life is our own to travel; I'm just presenting optional trails to take or make.

CHAPTER 14
Healing the Fractured Soul Part I

"We shall attack and attack until we are exhausted, and then we shall attack again." Major General George S. Patton Jr

Enemy spirits relentlessly are scheming against and attacking you, to debilitate you in more than physical ways. If they can't physically wound or kill you, they seek to take you out of play by mortally wounding your mind. They are merciless, to say the least. Even if you are not a Christian you are still a minister of vengeance for the Lord whether as servant or son/daughter and the Devil hates you because they hate Him. We exhibit the same relentless attitude on a mission and in the course of our duties. Warriors getting up each day training and working, day in and day out fighting the good fight. You need this same attitude during the process of healing psychological and physical wounds.

Recovering from a wounded soul is a fight for your sanity and stability. As it is written, "The strong spirit of a man sustains him in bodily pain or trouble, but a weak and broken sprit who can raise up or bear?" (Prov. 18:14 AMP). Ancient cultures and modern times have labeled post-traumatic stress disorder (PTSD) as anything from nostalgia and soldiers heart, too shell shock. Ancient text and classical literature record various symptoms of PTSD occurring in soldiers. Most commonly recorded symptoms are nightmares, but there are others. So, PTSD is not new, but these days it does enjoy some much-needed attention and research analysis.

> Most Soldiers will not attend survival, evasion, resistance, and escape training, or become Special Forces or Rangers operators, yet they deserve elite mental training to endure combat. Resiliency, rationality, virtue, ethics, and Warrior Ethos, grounded in a positive psychological framework that affirms the human spirit, can be integrated together, taught to, and modeled by our military leaders, Chaplains, behavioral health practitioners, and the Soldiers themselves. (Jarrett, 2008)

Breaches in the Hedge- a look at the problem

Moral injury is what strikes at the heart and soul of our being. It can be imagined in some sense as if a part of your nature, worldview, faith, morality, or conscience is severely assaulted by an event or accumulation of events, but you are still alive after the event. Now part of the way you saw things, your coping process, is wounded, gone, or altered forever. Your PTSD may not be from the physical trauma you experienced. An event could be seeing or hearing about another's trauma, sexual assault, or having a sensitivity to blood, injury, and mutilation (SBIM). You may feel betrayed by a morally gray order, or formerly trusted fellow service member, officer, agent, or leader involved in a military sexual assault (MST) incident. You may be dealing with unavoidable and or unexpected collateral, though justifiable, deaths. Traumatic events, which are not dealt with the same by all, must be dealt with or may be used to by the enemy to cause a breach(s) in your spiritual and or psychological hedges.

> Female service members and veterans who experienced MST were much more likely to screen positive for depression and PTSD than those who did not experience MST symptoms of PTSD and depression...The definition of psychological trauma has been rephrased with the DSM V. From now on, witnessing someone else's traumatic event is also accepted as a traumatic life event. (Balandiz & Bolu, 2017)

> "The specific mechanism(s) through which SBIM is associated with PTSD risk is not yet known" (Naifeh et al., 2017).

> "Therefore, it is highly plausible that the interaction of social silencing, the threat of loss of unit support and intense Moral Objection confront the combatant with a strong mental dissonance."(Ritov & Barnetz, 2014).

Post-Traumatic Stress Disorder is the official term, but I don't like it. The term disorder says that something is wrong with you. That couldn't be farther from the truth any more than losing your leg in combat meant something was wrong with you. Your reaction and symptoms of PTSD is a normal response to overwhelming emotional, physical, mental and spiritual trauma. You have been wounded there is nothing 'wrong' with you.

When you have a cold you cough, sneeze, your nose runs, and you may get a fever. This is normal for having a cold, nothing wrong with you personally. If you have PTSD you may avoid crowds, have flashbacks or recurring thoughts, hyperarousal, trouble sleeping, have trouble in relationships, and or feelings of guilt. Now comparing PTSD to the common cold is like comparing shingles to a rug burn, but you get the point- you are normal. You are having a typical reaction to devastating events; trouble handling them.

> The sheep generally do not like the sheepdog. He looks a lot like the wolf. He has fangs and the capacity for violence. The difference, though, is that the sheepdog must not, cannot, will not ever harm the sheep. Any sheepdog who intentionally harms the lowliest little lamb will be punished and removed...He is a constant reminder that there are wolves in the land...The sheep would much rather have the sheepdog cash in his fangs, spray paint himself white, and go, "Baa." Until the wolf shows up. Then the entire flock tries desperately to hide behind one lonely sheepdog. (Grossman, 2007)

LTC Grossman is the first I read or heard compare warriors to sheepdogs. Every good Shepperd takes great care in the health of and invests a lot of time in the training of their sheepdogs; The sheepdog is willing to give its' life fighting the wolves to protect the sheep. Jesus is Shepperd over the sheep and the sheepdogs. When a sheepdog is hurt fighting wolves the sheperd nurses them back to health. Jesus has not left you out in the cold, or conduct mercy killing like a horse with a broken leg in the Old West. Jesus **is** The Good Shepperd. Comparatively, we take great care, patience, and love in the training, care, and safety of our K-9 units. After all, they protect sheep and sheepdogs. They were created able to do what they do for us and deserve the funerals and honors they get. K-9's are one of God's force multipliers.

> It is important to fully understand that there are many circumstances in which we have little control, and these circumstances frequently arise while engaged in a war zone. This is why it is imperative to understand what "normal responses" to uncontrollable or abnormal circumstances may be; these responses provide us with defenses against acute and debilitating reactions when direct control is not possible. (Cantrell & Dean, *Down Range*, 2005)

Because many counselors use phrases like, "you will always be an addict," or you'll always be a recovering alcoholic" that what is happening or happened to you becomes a part of your identity forever. Not true. Whatever you did or what happens to you effects your behavior at first, but only defines who you are, and how you will always behave, if you let it. How you are acting is a result of how you perceive yourself in relation to your trauma. Rehabilitation if part of reprograming your mind and body. To just detox and not fully address the mental emotional, and spiritual aspects are not fully effective.

You can choose to label and limit yourself as 'always' an addict, recovering alcoholic, or as healed, and fully recovered (delivered from) former addict or alcoholic. Both acknowledge the fact you behaved a certain way. The first says you behave differently today, and maybe tomorrow, but it still simmers beneath the surface like a secret identity or personality you are trying to hide, or avoid. The second takes the situation putting it on the shelf of memories, instead of simmering beneath the surface of everyday life. On the shelf puts you back in control, your esteem and identity severed from your past mistakes. Simmering is the experience and appearance of peace between times of violent eruptions, or boiling over uncontrollably. Simmering does not have to be your fate.

This doesn't mean you can go back to drinking or doing drugs with impunity, of course not, don't' be foolish. "All things are lawful for me, but all things are not helpful. All things are lawful for me, but I will not be brought under the power of any" (1 Cor 6:12 NJKV). It does mean you have reassigned value an identity to yourself. An identity no longer based on a chain attached to your past event and still shackled to your ankle as you move into the future. It is ever threatening. Without warning the chain tugs at you to try and drag you back into a mental, emotional, spiritual slavery and maybe physical slavery. Bondage to self-medication through sex, alcohol, and drug abuse or violence.

Instead, your identity is based on what the Lord says about you; who you are to Him and in Him. It means not living in fear of relapse, and if one occurs, you know how to take charge and not let it get the better of you. It means access to total recovery and freedom- no chains attached. It means alternative resources in coping, not simmering in the management of a problem, but complete deliverance from a problem. Even more so, growing stronger than you were before the problem. Remember what you fear, you empower. The severity of symptoms you're experiencing may affect the time it takes to regain control of your mind and life. But, it **doesn't dictate** <u>whether or not</u> you can regain control. Only you decide that. Choose life, and the Holy Spirit is there for you.

As I bring you along a new thought process, let me be clear. I am not saying stop going a group your attending, or other types of behavioral counseling or clinical treatments. I'm not saying that. What I am giving you are alternative ways to view yourself and tools to use to become free from torment. The alternative of renewing and regaining control of your mind and identity in Christ can be done at the same time as whatever else you're doing; to live a good life. A life you deserve more than those who spit on the military, law enforcement, and intel communities. More than the unthankful people who are willfully ignorant of the knowledge you stand on the wall against the hordes of chaos, securing their freedom to be extremely stupid.

In the movie The Great Wall, I found it interesting what warriors who stood guard on the Great Wall of China against the terror of creatures called the Tao Tei, were named the Unnamed Order. People on the safe side of the wall honestly often have no clue as to the dangers others are securing them from and at what cost. Many wolves appear as supposed sheep protesters, self-declared defenders of free speech; very useful to wolves. In truth, these are useful idiots working for and supporting political wolves trying to dress up as sheep. A mark of strength in a free society is seeing ungrateful and stupid people joyfully broadcasting their civil insanity peacefully from the rooftops. If there are no protestors at all, you may not be free. If there are some, you are free. If there are too many useful idiots for too long, with too much influence over free speech, justifying the use of violence to censor or bully the voices of those with opposing opinions. You may be on the road to losing your freedom if their voice becomes law and shapes public policy. Vote, and vote wisely.

Can I really get back to normal?

No, and yes. It is not about getting back to what you are accustomed to, used to, or was comfortable with - a definition of normal. What is considered normal changes with maturity and experiences? What is normal for a five-year-old is not normal for a fifty-year-old. What is normal for a veteran or first responder is not normal for those who have not been either. What is normal for a functional addict or person with mental health issues does not always equate to living a good and healthy life.

Writing to believers, the Apostle John stated Jesus intent for their lives. "Beloved, I pray that you may prosper in all things and be in health, just as your soul prospers" (3 John 2). All things and health include material comfort, physical, mental and emotional health. As your soul prospers is the quantifier or measure. The more of the Word you know and apply, and the deeper relationship with the Holy Spirit you cultivate, the better things go for you and those around you.

I am not talking about your eternal salvation, that is a done deal. I am talking about the full meaning of salvation- of the body (material needs and comfort), spirit (relationship to Jesus, growth in faith), and soul (your mental stability, peace, emotional and relationship health...), all aspects of your life. Jesus came that we might have an abundant life, but of course, we must take it, in the power of the Holy Spirit, from the Devil's grasp. He is working to deceive and trick you out of having all Jesus suffered and died to make available to you- this includes your mind, your whole life. Normal is living a good and peaceable life, which depends on your soul prosperity- how you believe, feel, think in general, and how to interact with God.

Not all PTSD or associated wounds comes from moral injury derived from a betrayal by leadership, or something which a person personally did, experienced or said during an intense situation which caused guilt or shame. It wasn't a controversial order from a leader who tore up my friend's life and dreams; it was what he did. They covered it up to protect him, but he still thrashed and hit his wife in her sleep, she had to sleep in a different room. He confided in me one evening in the field at Hohenfels Training Center what he had done.

It was during Operation Iraqi Freedom when he was fed up with collecting surrendering soldiers. He said a friend of his had been injured and he wanted revenge, not more prisoners. A lot of feelings were racing through him. He described that as a small group walked toward his tank with their hands in the air. Without warning, he opened fire. He told me it was not premeditated, that he hadn't been planning it since he got up or from the day or night before. His emotions erupted and then it happened. It's not justified, or good, but it happened. He permanently changed stations (PCS) not long after that. I never got to talk with him again. I wondered how he and his wife were doing. We were in the same platoon and lived in the same government housing at Smith Barracks. My friend morally injured himself deeply. I pray he got help and forgave himself as the Lord forgave him. I also wonder about the mental health of those who covered up the war crime. I'm not judging. I wasn't there. I am just expressing my concern for those involved in a morally traumatic event.

> How does moral injury change someone? It deteriorates their character; their ideals, ambitions, and attachments

> begin to change and shrink. Both flavors of moral injury impair and sometimes destroy the capacity for trust. When social trust is destroyed, it is replaced by the settled expectancy of harm, exploitation, and humiliation from others. (Shay 2014)

There is no wound so deep you cannot be healed, scarred yes, but healed... yes. Recovery or healing revolves around your resiliency or ability to cope with a situation. This entire book is not just a brief overview of doctrines of the Bible and spiritual context for warfare. It is to renew the warrior's mind, battle hardening the soul. It is equipping you with a predisposition for resistance to experiencing PTSD. A persons self-perception of their ability to process traumatic events and maintain control of their lives is called coping self-efficacy (CSE). Your perception of the event determines your ability to cope with the event. (Benight, 2004).

Not that my faith or yours isn't enough, or that we need secular research to confirm the Bibles principles, but for those of you new to, or unfamiliar with the Bible, and or like me who love research, it never hurts. As the Lord says, let everything be established by two or three witnesses. It instills confidence in the face of other experts who might, for example, have said you can only learn to manage, but you will never recover. Nothing is impossible with God, who designed your brain and your body in the first place. Go back to the Dealer for repairs. The dealership has trained personnel and all the parts to fix you up.

> Results of this study move beyond these earlier studies by showing that even among a group with a relatively high level of PTSS who did not receive treatment, CSE perceptions are still predictive of recovery from post-traumatic distress, over and above the predictive value of those initial symptoms. This means that regardless of their symptom levels, victims will recover if they have high CSE levels. An additional implication is that those with low CSE levels and high levels of PTSS will not recover or will experience a smaller decrease in symptoms. (Bosmans et al., 2016)

> For this reason, moral injury should be assessed in addition to traditional evaluation of war traumatic events among war veterans. Self-awareness of mental states and integration of moral injury events within personal schemas played a nuclear role in recovery from both PTSD and depression symptoms among recovered participants. (Ferrajao & Olivera, 2014).

Another note on the new normal

A new normal is not always what others may expect. A new normal for you for example, **if you are accepting of or content with your situation**, which in turn the Lord respects your feelings and attitude about having prosthetics. The evil the Devil meant for you, to destroy you in some fashion - burned, amputee, etc. – is not God's perfect will for you, but can *become* His permissive will. Your attitude and faith determine the final outcome- to overcome adversity and tragedy or to be crushed by it. It is a decision, but to overcome you need Holy Spirit help. Here are some great scriptures to know about trusting the Lord or in other words submitting to Holy Spirit help and guidance, and an advantage to what others might say is not normal or a disability.

> "Trust in the Lord with all your heart, and lean not on your own understanding; in all your ways acknowledge Him, and He shall direct your paths" (Prov 3:3-6 MJKV).

> "Therefore, submit to God. Resist the devil, and he will flee from you" (James 4:7 MJKV).

> "Blessed be the God and Father of our Lord Jesus Christ, the Father of mercies and God of all comfort, who comforts us in all our tribulation, that we may be able to comfort those who are in any trouble, with the comfort which we ourselves are comforted by God. For as the sufferings of Christ abound in us, so our consolation also abounds through Christ..."(2 Corinthians 1:3-5 MJKV).

When you read this, think not only of Jesus torture, false arrest, the public insults hurled at Him, the betrayal of His closest friend let alone His own creation and more, all of which He deserved none of it. Think about the Apostle Paul who wrote this under the inspiration of the Holy Spirit. Paul who had been left dead by stoning at least once, beaten, whipped, jailed, shipwrecked and eventually executed for the faith. In all these things Paul found ways by grace through faith to endure and still preach the gospel- even getting Roman guards, his jailers, converted to Christ.

There is no mention in scripture of his wife, though at that age and with his prestige as a Pharisee before conversion he must have had one. He even lost his family when he converted. Think eternally, not temporally. This is a temporary situation leading to an eternal destination of peace and love, with no more need for ministers of vengeance. Paul wrote, "But indeed I also count all things loss for the excellence of the knowledge of Christ Jesus my Lord, for whom I have suffered the loss of all things, and count them as rubbish, that I may gain Christ" (Philippians 3:8).

Or remember Joseph. He was betrayed by his brothers, sold into slavery, falsely accused of rape and imprisoned for over around 13 or so years. Then without warning, God promoted him out of jail, and he became the Governor of Egypt, second only to Pharaoh. We live in a fallen world whose god is the Devil. For God to get it done He has to do it through you, a man or woman. Don't feel sorry for yourself or that you are useless. You are not useless but now have a different use. You're still a warrior, only the manner of your warfare is changed.

Many people simply quote "And we know that all things work together for good...", - But forget or neglect to finish the sentence - "to those who love God to those who are called according to His purpose" (Romans 8:28 MJKV). Being called according to his purpose is about the different callings each of us has in our lives. If you are not following God's plan for your life at whatever season of life you're in you are missing many of His blessings in your life. The key to following God's plan for where you are in your life now is in loving God. This is not an affectionate love. Love in ancient near eastern and Hebrew culture is another term for loyalty such as in the ancient Egyptian Amarna Letters, and even Jesus uses the love in the context of this meaning. "If you love Me, keep My commandments" (John 14:15 MJKV).

If you are loyal to and trust Jesus, then He through the Holy Spirit who is our Helper will empower you through that faith or trust in Him to keep His commandments, such as love your enemies and to bless those who curse you. Even in loving your enemies it is not about affection or loyalty to them. It is about respecting them as humans made in Gods image and respecting them, treating them humanely, because of who we are and who God is. This cannot be done in the strength of our fallen nature.

If you do not trust in and submit the God's word, then you cannot resist the Devil. Instead of fleeing he will eat you up and spit you out. The Holy Spirit is called our Helper, Comforter, Advisor, and Counselor. All these titles come from a Greek word Paraclete, which means to come alongside and assist in the various ways mentioned, comforter, advisor, etc.

To Do or Not to Do

It is up to you to give this a try, or not. To do nothing guarantees nothing will happen. To decide to fight to reclaim your life is to increase your odds of success from none to possible absolute victory. You have nothing to lose. Nevertheless, barriers remain. What if it doesn't work for me? Reject that thought; it is for you and you have nothing to lose. How long will it take to recover? Everyone is different. Hopefully, you are planning to be here years from now, and not thinking about suicide.

If suicide, call for help immediately. If suicide you have less to lose since you were thinking of checking out anyway... but don't! Please don't, give the Lord a try. For the rest of us, we plan on living a long time. We can live beaten down, fighting, or victorious. I choose either fighting or victorious. I would rather go to Heaven fighting. If I give up, I may end up there sooner.

I get it; you may feel exhausted or tired of trying. Even when dealing with something like weight loss people get tired of what seems like an uphill battle. Give Jesus a try. Take it one day at a time. There are other reasons people don't seek help or try to live in denial of needing help. Pride or shame may be a factor in not asking for or accepting help. Don't let a sincere, but misguided sense of duty or image you think needs upheld keep you from help. Don't suffer in silence, you owe yourself better than that.

Twenty-two years after his last combat experience in World War II,

> America's best-known hero, Audie Murphy, still slept with the lights on and a loaded .45 caliber pistol by his bed. The only problem is, he couldn't bring himself to ask for help concerning his war stress. After all…he had won The Congressional Medal of Honor. (Cantrell & Dean 2005)

Since you're still reading, I assume you are at least thinking about trying. You are no less brave, less heroic, or less of a warrior for getting help, just the opposite. You go to the medic to get help, and you train to be combat effective. Getting help for PTSD, or any mental, emotional or physical affliction is staying combat effective. Combat effective to pray and serve the Lord even in retirement. More importantly, it is remaining socially active, enjoying time with family, friends, and loved ones.

Spiritual Root to the PTSD Trees

Treating symptoms only, will make you more comfortable, which is not a bad start. Thank God for modern medicine. Luke who wrote the gospel of Luke and the book of Acts was a doctor. Jesus is also called the Great Physician. So, your doctors and medicine available are valuable, and I believe mostly from the Lord. I say mostly because some of the drugs humanity comes up with have worse side effects than the original.

My pastoral recommendation is to pray over all your medicine pleading the blood of Jesus over it and thanking God for it. Thanking God for them sanctifies them. I do it. Pray for your doctors; it doesn't matter if they are believers or not, they are ministering their skills and knowledge to you a believer. Don't stop taking your medicine apart from doctor's orders. It is rare, but there have been testimonies where the Holy Spirit directed a believer to cease their medication to enable them to receive healing, apparently the medicine was adversely affecting them in some fashion.

The emotional events which caused the trauma sometimes opens the door to demonic spirits which specialize in starting a fire in that part of the forest of your mind or throwing gas on a fire that got started due to a traumatic event. This does not mean you are demon possessed or that a demon is operating in your situation. Abuse of medicine can open the spiritual door or put a breach in your protective hedge for a demon of sorcery to begin to influence you. Or different circumstances are used by the demons to pressure us into using drugs in an illegal and unsafe manner. The Greek for sorcery is pharmakia which is the root word for pharmacy, drugs, pharmaceuticals, etc. Sorcery refers to any illegal use of drugs and drugs in combination with witchcraft. Sometimes your root problem is not chemical, emotional, mental, or physical its supernatural.

A Christian cannot be possessed by a demon or demons. Possession is ownership. When you got saved, and the Holy Spirit indwelling you, recreating your spirit and co-habituating with your new spirit, sealing it. He kicked out all evil spirits. The Holy Spirit took possession or ownership of you. Now oppression is another story. Your soul, where your free will, mind, and emotions reside can be affected or oppressed by demonic spirits, believer, and unbeliever alike.

One example is the blindness Satan puts on an unbelieving person's mind, blocking their seeing the light of the Gospel or truth of God's word. The strongholds of your mind are beliefs or perceptions you have. Either your stronghold is a godly belief and understanding or an ungodly one. Remember renewing the mind is about changing your thinking, believing and feeling from the way the enemy wants you to think, believe and feel. Thinking Satan's way gives him influence in the situations and or decisions you will be faced with; give no ground to him when at all possible.

Pulling your Trigger

It could be just the thought of the crowd of people shopping at a mall or at a concert. It could be a sight, place, smell, sound, song, or other things, the list of triggers goes on and on. The variables in each person's personality (good and bad baggage) determine resiliency or lack thereof. The resulting behaviors are similar such as avoidance, flashbacks, etc. Again, just experiencing trauma doesn't mean you will get PTSD, or be oppressed by a demonic spirit, not hardly. Only the possibility these things can occur is there. Don't get obsessed with thinking everything is demonic. You may laugh, but I've seen this unbalanced type of fearful thinking in people and the damage it causes.

Traumatic memories are triggered in various ways which cause us to relive the experience and or re-experience the emotional and mental pain of the event(s). A common symptom besides avoidance of the pain or the triggers of pain is nightmares and lack of sleep. Sometimes the flashbacks come in the night. Your mind is a biological and metaphysical supercomputer. REM stage (rapid eye movement in a deep sleep) or dreaming is like defragmenting your soul. Sometimes the Lord speaks to us in our dreams, the Enemy affects them, or it's just the pizza. Sleep is essential to recovery and healing of body and soul.

If you do not get sound sleep, new problems appear and old ones get worse. The Lord says much about sleeping. Safety in our sleep is a primary promise. If you do not feel safe in sleep how can you sleep unless exhausted? Pray these scriptures, let the Holy Spirit help you sleep well. Let the angels stand watch over you. Psalm 103 is like an insurance policy with all areas covered listed. Psalm 91 is fine print on specifics covered in the policy. The excerpt from 91 has the multiple application of operations at night, vulnerability/safety while asleep in dangerous places, and flashbacks or nightmares.

> "I will both lie down in peace, and sleep; for You alone, O Lord, make me dwell in safety" (Psalm 4:8 NJKV).
>
> "It is vain for you to rise up early, to sit up late, to eat the bread of sorrows; for so He gives His beloved sleep" (Ps. 127:2, NJKV). This pertains to worrying and stressing out leading to loss of sound sleep.
>
> "But You, O Lord, are a shield for me…I lay down and slept; I awoke, for the Lord sustained me. I will not be afraid of ten thousands of people who have set themselves against me all around" (Ps. 3:3-6, NJKV).

> "...Then you will walk safely in your way, and your foot will not stumble. When you lie down, you will not be afraid; yes, you will lie down and your sleep will be sweet. Do not be afraid of sudden terror,"(Prov. 3:23-25, NJKV)

> "He who dwells in the secret place of the Most High shall abide under the shadow (pavilion or tent of protection) of the Almighty...You shall not be afraid of the terror by night...For He shall give His angels charge over you, to keep you in all your ways. They shall bear you up in their hands, lest you dash your foot against a stone" (Ps. 91:1,5,11-12 NJKV em ad).

There is one scripture describing some of the sleep of the wicked. When I first read this, it explained a lot concerning the backward behavior of those whose **lifestyle** is to commit evil. You likely have encountered such people.

> "Do not enter the path of the wicked and do not walk in the way of evil (this does not pertain to undercover work in this context). Avoid it, do not travel on it; turn away from it and pass on. For they (those of an evil lifestyle with reprobate minds) <u>do not sleep unless they have done evil</u>, and <u>their sleep is taken away unless they make someone to fall</u>." (Prov. 4:14-16, NJKV em ad).

The Forest of the Mind

Whether it's the topic of physical healing in the next chapter, mental, emotional healing, or the actions of casting out fear. There is one overarching faith application to all these things - calling something that is not as though they are. Renewing your mind is not just metaphorical or symbolic talk about changing the way you are believing and thinking. It is also about physically changing the wiring of your brain to physically change an issue with your body and mind. A foremost Christian Doctor,

Dr. Caroline Leaf was part of demonstrating in clinical research how the brain can heal itself, how you can purposefully re-program your brain, physiologically.

> Dr. Caroline Leaf is a cognitive neuroscientist with a Ph.D. in Communication Pathology and a BSc in Logopedics and Audiology, specializing in metacognitive and cognitive neuropsychology. Since the early 1980's, she has studied and researched the Mind-Brain connection and did some of the initial research back in the late 80s showing the neuroplasticity of the brain. (Leaf.com About tab) other references from Dr. Leafs book and DVD presentation *Who Switched Off My Brain*

Your brain is made of many parts which physically release or cause the release of different chemicals into your body. For example, if a threat or pleasure is experienced adrenaline or dopamine may be released. If your mind cannot distinguish between real experience and flashback or a trigger causes a re-experiencing of a past traumatic and your mind and body react as if it is happening again, for example, this is our problem. Our memories of the trauma(s) are still raw and are in control instead of us. Our brain does not understand you are not in a life-threatening situation; you are home.

When Jesus taught on speaking, believing and receiving in connection with not doubting in your heart, He talked about plucking up trees. Other places He cursed a large fig tree, and it dried up from its roots dying within twenty-four hours. Jesus said you will know a tree by its fruit meaning by the results of a person's actions you will know what kind of person they are. The metaphor of a tree and its roots, the unseen source of a trees nutrition, and the seed determining the type of tree is not so metaphorical. It is a spiritual and physiological analogy.

The nerves in your mind which contain our memories and traffic our thoughts are called dendrites. They look like trees in your mind whose branches are all interconnected. Depending on the emotional intensity or level of importance of the person experiencing something a branch or dentrites is formed. A branch on a dendrite or dendrites is created to store that memory making it long or short term. Your triggered flashbacks are emotional, and physical reactions to thinking about some situations, or occur because of unresolved or unprocessed experiences, is related to the type of tree planted in your mind, physically, psychologically, or symbolically not just spiritually.

This refers to the neuroplasticity or ability of the brain to regrow or lose dendrites and their branches creating healthy or dysfunctional circuits so to speak in their place. A lot of doctors and counselors engage in journaling and revisiting trauma with the intent to drain the poisonous effect it has on you through sharing and working on setting it aside. I'm talking about rewiring the hard drive. The process of revisiting and purposefully remembering is to rewrite a new memory replacing the old one.

You're not denying an incident or associated feeling, but writing them out, and examining or exploring what thoughts and feelings are produced or experienced and writing those out. (concept from Dr. Leafs Metacog TM) Putting your crisis, and trail of feelings onto paper is not to re-live, but to reevaluate and reassign or rewrite your recollection and allow yourself to change your feelings and thoughts about it; planting new trees while trimming or replacing bad trees.

Yes, you can do this alone, just you and the Holy Spirit. But, I recommend a Christian caregiver, or minister, or counselor, who understands this, and if possible a group which works with the concept of renewing the mind, and not doing it alone. The idea is to resolve internal conflicts, not reinforce a problem through seemingly endless sessions going nowhere. An example of scriptural use is starting with common or general feelings and thoughts, then working on naming the specific symptoms or reactions, and thoughts or feelings. Second Timothy 1:7 says "For God has not given us a spirit of fear, but of power and of love and of a sound mind." Your mind is to be sound. This scripture is foundational in praying, declaring, and receiving your healing, and in protecting you from being traumatized resulting in PTSD. The word here in Greek for fear is di-lee-ah and is used only this once in the Bible. It means being timid or cowardly. Demonic spirits of intimidation attack by shooting evil thoughts into you mind saying its hopeless, you're going to die, give up it's not worth it, you'll never make it, God's not really with you etc. Don't believe the lies.

Jesus last name is not Christ. He is the Christ. Christ means anointed one. Each Old Testament prophet, some non-believing Kings, and every believer is anointed. Walking in power is having the Holy Spirit anointing Jesus used, the same power which raised him from the dead; flow out of and poured onto you. Jesus is not just an anointed-one like General Joshua being anointed to lead an army, or Moses to lead the people out of Egypt. Jesus is the promised, prophesied Anointed One or Messiah with a capital M. Believing warriors walk in the power of the Anointed One and His anointing- the power of the Holy Spirit. What does the anointing or power of the Holy Spirit do? It is the raw miraculous power which gets the job done by faith.

Planting a New Forest

Abraham is the only person in the Bible whose life is chronicled from the time he believes and into his afterlife (Luke 16). God calls him - the friend of God. This chronicling picks up with Abrams being called into a relationship, continues throughout the rest of his life, and concludes with a snapshot of his afterlife. Abraham did some things he should not have. He lied, and even tried to make a promise of God's happen on his own- which failed dramatically. So, Abraham is not only the father of our faith and a friend of God. He is a person with triumphs and failures, just like you and I. His example of faith is to call that which is not, as though it were.

This is not lying or fantasy. It is taking the higher spiritual truth, speaking what God has spoken about the situation as it should be, not as it currently is. You call it the way it should be into existence, by grace through faith, to change the way it currently is. The image or idea originates in the word of God, not our soul or spirit. We then believe what God says about the situation as the *dominant truth* or over our perceived reality, over what our physical senses tell us, other voices interpret, or say is a reality. It is speaking into material existence, what you are not experiencing now, in real time, through your five senses.

We do not ask God to do what He has done; we speak to the situation what God said it should be- **that it now is**. Jesus is the High Priest of His word to perform or enforce His word. You don't have to ask God to do what is in His word. It is His will and desire to do His word. This allows God, through our declaration in faith to shape, frame, network, coordinate, change, manipulate, and alter our physical, mental, emotional reality (as it is currently understood or experienced) to conform to what He said about it- how it should be experienced or changed.

> "As it is written, I have made thee a father of many nations, before him whom he (Abraham) believed, even God, who quickeneth (*makes alive*) the dead, and calleth those things **which be not as though they were**"(Romans 4:17 em ad).

> "And base things of the world, and things which are despised, hath God chosen, yea, and **things which are not** [the way it should be], **to bring to nought** [to nullify, reverse, or bring to nothing by replacement] **things that are**[the way is currently is]"(1Corinthians 1:28 NJKV)

Talking about Jesus born of flesh and blood into humanity.

> "He Himself likewise shared in the same, that through death, He might destroy him who had the power of death, that is the devil, and release those who through fear of death were all their lifetime subject to bondage. For indeed. He does not give aid to angels, but he does give aid to the seed of Abraham." (Hebrew 3:14-15, NJKV em ad)

Why did Jesus come among us, as one of us. "He who sins is of the devil, for the devil has sinned from the beginning. For this purpose the Son of God was manifested, that He might destroy the works of the devil" (1 John 3:8). Note: remember once you are born-again you are not considered a sinner because your spirit is recreated pure and sealed by the Holy Spirit (stupid human proof as I call it). When you sin, it is in your soul and or with your body, but not your spirit. You are a saint by rebirth, no longer a sinner. The renewing of your mind is about cleaning up the soul.

Remember Mark 11, and the scriptures in Proverbs about death and life in your tongue, and "as a man (or woman this is a gender-neutral term for those who might care) thinks in his heart so is he." Therefore, we must rewire how you think, which controls how you feel, which changes your behavior. Calling something that is only seen in the pages of the Bible as real or true. Saying something is real and true, which does not feel real and is not being experienced as true or real. This is calling it as it *should be*, instead of *as it is*. This is the foundational faith statement to bringing all of the promises of healing (mental, physical, and emotional/mental) or any covenant promise into being, into this reality. God's view is true reality, how it really is or should be experienced. The new tree planted replacing the old is confessing a higher truth over a lower feeling. That confession of higher truth is made in faith, not based on feeling. Accepting Satan's feeling based perspective is accepting a *demonically constructed alternative*, which is *destructive*. Doing this makes Satan's *temporary* reality become a permanent reality, or the tree you want to be uprooted just grew deeper roots.

The Anointing- the power behind the punch

In light of seeing people anointed with oil, the laying on of hands, Paul's handkerchiefs, Peter's shadow, Jesus tassel, and Elisha's mantle from Elijah it is obvious anointing power is transferable in various ways. That is the transferability and tangibility of the anointing of the Lord. It affects people, angels, demons, places, things, in both the physical and the supernatural realms. Faith is a substance and force which activates and is activated by the anointing or empowerment to do specific things above and beyond normal, as well as come against something to destroy or change it. In a much more limited sense, the enemy can anoint those who follow him, but there is no comparison between demonic power and the power of the Holy Ghost. Some are anointed to preach, others to fight, some to be accountants, artistic, or builders. God endues each person with skill and knowledge to perform in excellence whatever he or she is to do. All Satan can do is pervert God's calling on a person and try to get them working for him.

> Moses said to the children of Israel, 'See, the Lord has called by name Bezaleel the son of Uri, the son of Hur, of

> the tribe of Judah; and He Has filled him with the Spirit of God, in wisdom and understanding in knowledge, and all manner of workmanship, to design artistic works, to work in gold and silver... in cutting jewels for setting, in carving wood and He has put in his heart the ability to teach, in him and Aholiab He has filled them **with skill to** do all manner of work.' (Exodus 35: 30-34 NJKV em ad)

One scripture reads about how a group of left-handed men of Israel trained and could sling a stone to strike within a hairsbreadth. Whether it is an anointing for marksmanship or business; work or special task related anointings are referred to as the anointing of Bezaleel, or a Bezaleel anointing. Your anointing in your body, not just your soul and spirit. Remember the bones of the prophet Elijah still retained a saturation of the anointing he had when alive.

When some guys, out to bury their friend, spied an enemy band nearby they hid in the tomb of the prophet and set their dead friend on his bones. When their friend touched the bones, he came alive! Anointing power is residual and transferable. Isaiah is talking about one issue also revealed a purpose and power of the anointing. As you read your Bible be aware of double and multiple complementary, not contradictory, applications of information.

"It shall come to pass in that day that his burden will be taken away from your shoulder, and his yoke from your neck and the yoke will be destroyed because of the anointing oil"(Isa 10:27, NJKV). A burden is a weight or load you carry or which is put upon an animal to carry. A yoke is what you are chained or locked into. Two oxen plowing a field are yoked together that they cannot move apart but only go one direction. They cannot be free unless the yoke is removed or destroyed, neither of which can they do for themselves.

Is the anointing, whether through oil, or the Spirit really for you? Absolutely. Remember Jesus came to destroy the works of the devil. What Jesus did we can also do. This is evidenced by the innumerable miracles which have taken place and are taking place as you read this in people's lives. God is no respecter of persons giving liberally to all who ask. In the Old Testament, the anointing came upon a few people. In Joel God writes of the day He will pour out His Spirit upon all flesh, or all people. That outpouring started on the day of Pentecost around a month or so after the resurrection (over 500 witnesses 1 Cor 15) and ascension of Jesus. The pouring continues today. Peter's first sermon, the first sermon preached after the outpouring started said.

> "In truth I perceive that God shows no partiality…that word you know, which was proclaimed throughout all Judea, and began from Galilee after the baptism which John preached: how God **anointed** (also means to smear onto or cover with empowerment) Jesus of Nazareth <u>with the Holy Spirit</u> and <u>with power</u>, who went about doing good and healing all who were oppressed by the devil, for God was with Him"(Acts 10:34,37-38, NJKV em ad).

The same anointing in Jesus is in and on you. Paul says "I can do all things through Christ (the anointed one and His anointing) who strengthens me" (Philippians 4:13 NJKV, em ad). I pray right now to the Lord that this book and all its contents be anointed with the anointing of Bezaleel. I pray that anointing transfers to be the reader in whatever capacity the reader is called to. I pray the reader according to Your grace, is stirred up in faith and in the spiritual gifts.

Furthermore, I pray for the anointing to be healed and made free from any and all mental, emotional, spiritual, and physiological symptoms, bondages and yokes both in the natural and supernatural, of PTSD or other trauma be upon the reader immediately, and as they work with their caregiver and others. I command in Jesus name, (with the consent of the reader given saying amen at the end of this declaration) every burden and yoke they are under not only be removed but destroyed so as never to return. If you agree with me, this is where you say amen.

CHAPTER 15

Healing the Fractured Soul Part II

"The various characteristics of the dark side can be grouped into some broad categories...Even though these five categories may not account for every possible related issue we face, they can provide the general framework we need to begin the process of understanding our unique dark side... We can use our dark side to serve God's purposes in our life rather than only our unmet need" (McIntosh & Rima, 2004, *Overcoming the Dark Side of Leadership*).

It is the dark side of our human nature, not necessarily the sinful side, but the side which is capable of doing harm to another human being through EIT's, hand to hand combat, or firing from a drone. Then going to bed happier because you won the struggle. You survived. You made the world a safer place. Part of the issue we sometimes face is our acceptability to God and country, or to ourselves.

No matter what happened, know you are loved and accepted by God in the Lord. Be of good cheer; few can do what you are called by God to do. What most run from, you run toward. Feeling joyful that you lived and the enemy did not is ok. You may regret having to do it, or you may not, no problem. Either way, you should not feel guilty or condemn yourself for doing it. Don't accept someone else's guilt trip aimed at you.

In the Bible, the day starts at night. God said the evening and the morning was the first day. In Hebrew culture, shortly after the setting of the sun, the next day begins. For example, in America a days start time is at 1201 am, or one minute after midnight. In the military, we may say 2401 hours, or 0001. Noon is 12 pm or 1200 hours. Generally speaking, the day as we think about it starts when we wake up, say 5 or 6 am, not at 1201am. Our night starts around 9 to 10 pm, or when we lay down to sleep in the evening.

In Hebrew culture, the day starts at 6 pm and ends at the same time it starts, so Tuesday starts Monday night long before 12 am. So, in Hebrew thinking, you lay down to sleep and rest at the beginning of your day for strength for the day. Darkness or average nightfall is the beginning of the day while the daylight is the second half of the day, generally. The criminals on the cross next to Jesus had their knees broken causing them to die quickly. Jesus' knees were never broken, but his side pierced because he already looked dead, and was. This was so no one was hanging on the preparation day for the Sabbath. To keep Jewish law.

For me, it is a mental exercise which I use to reset my mind and body, to think and feel that sleeping is starting my day, a restoring, and or rejuvenating of myself before the demands of work start. I'm just sharing a bit about how I go about the day. Whatever schedule works best for you, you work it. Find your own routine which includes some quiet time to hear from the Lord.

I do my daily devotion at night before I go to bed. I wake up, say good morning Lord or Holy Spirit and hit the ground refreshed and running. I listen and talk to Him even before I am talking to my wife. When I shower I talk to him and, now don't laugh, well ok you can laugh… I hear Him in the spirit best in the shower, alone in the car, and just before laying down to sleep. In these times I am not distracted by work, or someone, or something fighting for my attention. That being said let's do a dry run example day starting just before going to sleep, dealing with recurring nightmares or other thoughts stealing your sleep. For background, we'll say the daily devotion is reading the chapter Proverbs of whatever day it is since there are thirty-one chapters.

> "Soul, I speak to you in Jesus name. The word says God gives me good, sweet, sound and safe sleep. The word says God will sustain me in my sleep and I will wake up,

> from safe sleep. God has given me the spirit of a sound and balanced mind, and that his angels encamp around me and protect me without ceasing day and night, even while I sleep. I have that sound mind, and I will have a sweet, safe sleep according to His promise for God cannot lie. I command every evil spirit to stay out of my mind and dreams; you no longer have permission to torment me.
>
> "I rebuke (which means to beat back violently) you (the enemy spirits), I cast you out of my mind and bind you from returning. Angels, your job as a minister to me is to enforce the word of the Lord which I speak in faith. What I just spoke is in faith. I expect you to execute the word according to Psalm 103 and 91 giving me sound, sweet, and safe sleep, free from torment. Thank you, Lord Jesus, for watching over your word to perform it. Goodnight."

Now the **first time** you pray the prayer (it doesn't have to be the same as the example, make it your own) before you go to sleep, I suggest adding this to it. "Jesus said I can command the physical trees as well as psychological and spiritual trees, to be plucked up, and or dried up from the roots, and bearing no more fruit. I [say your name] command the spirits of (name the issues you want to work on: nightmares, flashbacks, suicidal thoughts etc) connected to these strongholds in my mind be taken captive by the angels, be cast out of my mind. And any trees associated with them be dried up and bear no more fruit forever, in Jesus name.

My suggestion is to write it out on a 3x5 card. Not to be ritualistic but to be consistent. It is a suggestion to help if you're having trouble focusing your thoughts. Expect sweet sleep. If you sleep with a light on, a weapon at hand, or have some other ritual that's no problem. Keep to your routine if you want to. Before this is over you will be comfortable turning them off or putting it away if you want to or not, doesn't matter. What matters is you don't *need* the light on or weapon handy based on fear. If you are a 2nd Amendment warrior, keep a gun under your pillow, or knife - no worries. The idea is doing things, but not based upon fear.

Misfire?

Now you may not believe or feel like you believe a single word you just said. The night might turn into the worst or scariest nightmares you have ever had. Not a problem. These are good signs. Let me explain. If you have demonic oppression joined to your PTSD the spirits of trauma, and paranoia and depression, just to name a few, may not give up so easily. The anointing has overwhelmed them, but sometimes they try to regain their grip through fear, to intimidate you, make you think nothing happened or it just got worse.

When this happens, they are tipping their hand revealing to you that not only physically, or mentally and emotionally are you wounded, but that either they caused it or came because of it to torment you. They don't want to have to leave. If it becomes the worst night ever, that's miserable, but a good sign. You are now in a battle of wills. Will you give up or will you dig in and attack, attack again, and when exhausted attack again- until you win? Should the night turn bad or worse here is the next course of action.

You just woke up from a nightmare. Any counterattack by the forces of darkness is a sign your faith is in action. It is not a sign of failure, keep in the fight, the battle belongs to the Lord, you will win. You may be calling out asking Jesus to give you peace and the Holy Spirit to help you get ahold of yourself; you may be severely rattled. Now you know the root is spiritual the enemy has been found. The anointing and your faith have dealt them a serious blow because they are retaliating in a counter attack. Speak back to them once you get calm, speak to your soul. Some more suggestions or food for thought on things to speak and believe:

"Spirits of fear, guilt, helplessness, and nightmares I refuse to be intimidated by you. I reject you and plead the blood of Jesus over my own soul. I do not have the spirit of timidity; I am not intimidated by you. I have the spirits of power, love and sound mind. I will lay down and sleep peacefully. I am in no real danger; I do not accept the lying spirit which tells me I'll never be free or healed. I speak to the trees of PTSD symptoms both physical and spiritual. I have commanded you be dried up from the roots and pulled up with all the roots and cast out of my mind and into the sea, never to be seen again, obey my words. Dry up, be plucked up, and depart from me."

The next time you lay down to sleep reread the prayer, and add that you will never cease to believe for the sound mind and sleep God promised.

"I speak to you spirits of the enemy. I will never give up believing God's word. Be gone forever. I pray the Lord release His fire of judgment upon you for resisting obeying His word promising, my freedom from you, and all the torments which came with you." You say are gone instead of will be gone; calling it as it *should* be, not as you *feel* it. Try to go to sleep again. Repeat submitting to God and resisting the Devil until satisfied.

You might be thinking hold on, that's great if you believe what you said. But, what if I still don't feel like I believe what I prayed or declared? How can I expect things to work whether they get worse or not if I have trouble believing? Good question with a good answer. First be like the man talking to Jesus who said "I believe. Help me with my unbelief." What he is saying is he believes what Jesus said about believing and receiving and that nothing is too hard or impossible for the Lord. He is also saying he is having trouble believing what Jesus is saying will happen to him. He asked for help to believe, and he got it.

As you declare God's word over your soul, understand the trees both physical and spiritual have roots and reinforcement from days, months or years past, from things you may not even recall. Or depression from others saying how bad it is, or telling you that you may learn to manage your affliction, but will never be free, or maybe never be able to stay married, etc. These things are spoken sincerely by well-meaning people but are not the truth. They are true as far as humanly possible, as far as the senses go. The root may be deep in both realms. You sincerely believed and spoke and were in agreement with the words of well-meaning folks. But in so doing you believed and spoke contrary or in opposition to the word of the Lord. As you change your speech to a confession of faith you have started reversing the old belief or stronghold.

It may seem to have no effect at first, but keep confessing. Remember Biblical confession is the Greek word homologeo (Hom-ol-og-eh-o), which means to say the same thing God says. It is not about confessing sins. To confess the word is to speak what the Word says about a situation only. This brings what is in the spiritual from the divine reality of Heaven into the physical reality of Earth. Confession calls things as they are in Heaven to replace, restore or destroy something in the Earth which God doesn't approve of. God will tolerate what you tolerate because if a human doesn't speak it, it's not going to be done. Remember; all people have the authority on Earth over life and death in their tongue. But, speaking in faith trumps the free will of unbelievers.

Each time you declare the word too your soul you're working at uprooting one belief while planting and watering and growing another. Your seed is in the ground but has not yet grown to produce fruit. Be patient and keep farming. If you do not feel you believe or experience any results, keep farming, the watered and fertilized seed will grow into that new tree and bear fruit. You are destroying one stronghold while building a new and stronger one which is in line with the Word.

If you do not have demonic oppression to deal with, then you will still be applying the word as spiritual medicine to your mind. I do not apologize for my presentation of the influence of the spiritual in our lives because it is the truth from the word of God and personal experiences of too many people to count alive today and since the Resurrection. A problem in modern approaches to mental and emotional health is neglect of the spiritual component, the root.

Our enemy roams about like a roaring lion seeking whom he can devour. He is looking for an opportunity to hurt you on any level and gain a foothold in your soul and body. I believe in every battle, police operations from a traffic stop to a hostage situation, and all intelligence operations spiritual forces are in play, good and evil. Satan's forces not only seek to govern the outcomes of potentially bad situations during a warrior's common duties, they lie in wait. What I mean is before a planned, or high probability of a traumatic event occurs. Demons often are looking to cause or locate a breach in your hedge, any chance multiply suffering.

Example: the next morning

When you wake up, thank God for a good night's rest, even if you didn't have one. Declaring you will not be intimidated by nightmarish attacks of the enemy. They are lying symptoms. A lying symptom is one you continue to experience after you begin your confession of faith. It *was* the dominant reality up until you spoke in faith to them and your situation. Keep confessing the word over and to your circumstances and symptoms, building your faith and replacing what is with what should be.

More examples- "Thank you, Lord, for a good sound, sweet and safe night sleep. Thank you for protecting me from nightmares and flashback. I thank you for your strength as I am healed and have a sound mind of Christ according to your word. Spirits of (name whatever your particular issues may be- maybe make a list) I bind you and command that you will not afflict me today." You can start out praying for the morning, then at noon for the afternoon, then after work for the evening, as well as the before sleep prayer. Just pray for today. Healing and recovery is a day to day process. Each day you may feel differently. Don't worry about tomorrow focus on today. Yesterday is gone forever so don't look back.

Speak the word like you were taking a prescription- 3x a day, or as needed, or once a day, you get the picture. Dr. Lord Jesus prescriptions at the least say, Take As Needed and have unlimited refills. Now the dominant reality is your confession of faith. Anything else is now a lying symptom or replaced reality. Until it is no longer experienced in the physical reality, keep taking your meds. But don't accept it back as the dominant reality. If you accidentally reaccept it by saying for example "I have such and such" instead of "I'm still under attack by such and such lying symptom" then you slipped up.

If or when you slip up and say something you shouldn't say, no problem. Speak to your slip up "I cancel what I such and such or what I just said, and command that seed I spoke to fall onto hard ground and not grow." Now the processes I have been describing are personal actions. Lord Jesus never meant for us to deal with everything alone. Each of us has an individual and collective responsibility we are accountable for. When Jesus sent the seventy and the twelve and later in the book of acts the journeys of Peter and Paul for example- all were in groups of two or more. Fighting the good fight in battle or in recovery is a team effort. When possible seek out groups of trusted fellow ministers of vengeance to encourage you in the Lord, and in general.

Debriefing and Demobilization

After combat operations, or even touching a dead body, the Lord through Moses orders the warriors of Israel (or any person who touched a dead body) a demobilization (demob for short) or decompression period of a week. It categorized the returning warrior or person who touched a dead body, even just to move and bury it, as unclean. Moses is not saying there is anything wrong or evil with the person(s) in this context of unclean. He is saying they are not ready to reintegrate into the community, they need time to process and had to spend this time outside the camp. They are to purify or process their experiences in the company of other warriors, or those of shared experience.

This week of separation from the battle before reuniting with the community was the time to interact with those who shared in the traumatic event. Sharing a burden or testifying of something good with others is a purification process. After this week, the soldiers reintegrate into the general civilian population. The concept and process of group debriefings after traumatic events is ancient, but as vital and relevant today as yesteryear.

During this week, the mental and emotional transition is made to prepare to reenter the civilian safe or green zone- provided by the efforts of the soldier. I hope that the earlier information on blood guilt and what is and is not authorized by the Lord, empower warriors by grace, to increase in resiliency. This initial week prepares the warrior, assumedly guided by seasoned warriors and or professional facilitator caregivers. To start the process of resolution of horrors, help with grief from loss, or closure and reconciliation of survivor's guilt, just to name a few issues.

It is also a time to recognize achievements, bravery, recount heroic acts and good times. This is another reason more warriors should become members of the American Legion, VFW, AMVETS or some such organization. This provides a place to decompress and find understanding and comfort, among new and seasoned warriors. A safe place we fit in while we are readjusting to the routines of the civilian or garrison life. I believe retired warriors have a lot to offer the generations behind them. All of this contributes to reaching the new normal. To fully returning and reintegrating back into society. To begin to enjoy the good of a country you fought and suffered for.

Carrying the Load

Burdens in the Bible come in different forms. That which is put upon you demonically which you don't deserve. That which is your real responsibility to do for yourself or others. And that which comes to you which you cannot possibly overcome alone. Besides comforting others with your comfort, the Bible says a merry heart does good like a medicine. Outsiders to the warrior culture feel the humor we share is often dark and twisted or creepy. So be it. Our coping mechanisms are our own. Other fields such as medical and mortuary disciplines are very similar. God gets it, but outsiders often don't.

Survivors guilt. Each eagle will give its life to save the eagle next to them. I use the symbol or image of an eagle, just as a sheepdog, or dragon slayer. Each portrays a different aspect of warriorhood. Eagles are the natural enemies of snakes. The enemy and their minions are often called scorpions and serpents. We are the natural enemy of the wicked. Your dead comrade would gladly give, or risk his or her life for you, again, the same as you would for them. This is the warrior code.

It's not your fault. You could not have known. Mistakes are sincerely made. You are not God or superhuman. It's still a messed up fallen world; for now. You don't deserve to beat yourself up with what you think would, should, or could have happened differently. There are too many unknown variables. You deserve to live as much as they did. Your value as a single warrior is no less than the value of a married, or married with children warrior.

The immediate impact upon a family may be different, but regardless- it's not your fault. Even if you did make a mistake, armchair quarterbacking after the fact wouldn't help or change it. Honor you're fallen by living and living well. If you must, forgive yourself as the Lord forgives you. If you were dead, watching your left behind comrades feeling guilty about them not being dead or severely injured, or not injured at all when you were. Would you think it strange to accept the offer of coming back to life and them dying or being severely injured instead of you; to make them feel better? Isn't that what is being said? So, the Devil, <u>in your voice, in your head</u> is trying to make you think and say to yourself - "It should have been me." Don't believe it.

It shouldn't have been either of you, but this is the horrid price paid for freedom. The Doctrine of Violence includes risk-reward. If you didn't do what you did, or they didn't do what they did- what price then is paid? What risk becomes a reality instead of a possibility? You are alive, and they are dead or injured. We will never have all the answers until we get to Heaven. Then we will fully understand how and why that happened the way it did. We pray, declare, confess and some still die; some don't get healed, etc. This is life, for now not forever. God didn't will it or cause it, but look around you. His will is often not done for a multitude of reasons. Trust in and listen for the quiet voice of your primary counselor the Holy Spirit. He will help you cope.

LTC Grossman, quoting from a character in another book he wrote, writes about one character feeling lied to about war, its virtues, and honor. Lies he believed until he experienced the horror of war. Then his commander responds to his feeling he was lied to about war and honor.

> "No, my friend, it's not a lie. It's men making the best of a dirty, nasty job that has to be done. There are times when evil comes when darkness falls, and good men must fight. Then we make a virtue of necessity. Pain shared is pain divided. Joy shared is joy multiplied. Every night around the campfire, or with our mess mates over dinner we talk about the battle. Each time we divide our pain and multiply our joy." (Grossman, 2007, p.305)

Believers go to church and fellowship, give testimonies, share problems, hear sermons, and request prayer. This is a form of weekly or more than a weekly meeting. Some go to church prayer in the evening not just sermon in the morning. Then there are bible studies or special support groups sponsored by the church, and volunteering to do food pantry or some other community serving activity. These are venues for sharing, learning, growing, helping others, or coping. Even if you're not a Sunday morning person, no problem. Many military and law enforcement organizations have resources also.

The most successful Christians have daily devotions and or fellowship in prayer with God more than an hour or two a week and or volunteer and participate in some form of activity. Success and the good life is not found sitting at home dwelling and replaying toxic thoughts and feelings which is self-destructive. I have not yet encountered a Christian veteran, intelligence agency, or law enforcement ministry, other than Cops for Christ. We could use more.

Shooting targets are good therapy

There are times a little venting is needed and healthy. However, not everyone can handle your venting, which is a great way to sometimes release it from yourself. Venting on loved ones or bosses etc. is not good. It could come off as abusive or at least confusing. You may even lose your job. Back in my Infantry days, we had a saying; C-4 (powerful explosives) cures everything. Well sometimes, emotionally we want to blow up like C-4. So, let's blow up on a range in a controlled environment at a target who can and wants to take it.

Acknowledge to yourself that you are no less of a man or woman because you are experiencing PTSD while others may not be. Accept that many people will not understand and may even avoid the subject or circumstances with you because it is alien and scary to them. Get to a quiet and safe place where you will not be disturbed. There are two places to vent- on the range at a paper target, or on the Lord who understands what you need to say and doesn't require an explanation. Give it to Jesus; He can take it.

We'll call this the Holy Spirit firing range of a sort, with Jesus as your target; not to destroy but to vent upon. Vent all you got onto Jesus. Let it rip; no holds barred. He can take it. Give it to Jesus, no matter how ugly, mean, venomous, or vengeful, including and especially feelings of betrayal by Him, or lack of understanding His role in whatever you're dealing with. Speak every why, emotion, thought, flashback, night sweats, etc. I am not saying to disrespect the Lord, though you may feel and speak extremely disrespectful to Him in the course of venting, especially the first time. If you do, then ask forgiveness for disrespect, and keep on going. He helps with anger and grieving and understands where you're coming from. Let it out on Him, rather than a spouse, friends or family. He can take it. Jesus would rather take your pain from you, than see you dish it out on someone else, hurting them in the process. It's a tool in the process of restoration.

When you have sent it all downrange - yelled, screamed, cursed, cried, - unloaded your emotional magazine completely. Reload magazine and repeat as necessary. Repent at the end of any disrespect toward God. Acknowledge to Him that His ways, thoughts and judgment, and understanding of the event(s) is right and better. He is all powerful, all knowing, all loving, and all present- He was there. When talking to people, you may struggle with how to say what you want to say. I know for some things I am at a loss for words. With God, you don't have worry about saying it right or sometimes saying it at all. He understands better than you. He was there when it happened. Trust Him without understanding all the why's. Acknowledge to Him that you know He is good and plans no evil toward you. He did not do X to you. Remember Satan did the evil to Job, not the Lord.

If you are having a hard time not questioning the character of God, ask Him for help with that too. Some people here might say cursing at God, really? My pastoral response is yes. Using profanity as you talk to God during extreme emotional, mental, physical, and spiritual anxiety is more common than you might realize in the real world. It is a combination of intense anxiety and spiritual immaturity. Nevertheless, it is a start. It is between you and God and no one else's business. It's not something you should make a habit, or that I would encourage, but the tone of your venting or conversations with God will change as you grow in the Lord and He ministers His peace to you.

Jesus capillary's burst in His forehead, the blood mingling with beads of sweat, while praying in the garden that fateful night. He knew He was about to be betrayed, arrested, falsely condemned, beaten, mocked, shamed publicly, whipped, and crucified. He always knew. It is the prophetic purpose He came be in human flesh for. Jesus sweated blood showing us He understands your extreme emotional and mental stressors. The cursing and foul language that may erupt can be worked on down the road. God isn't concerned about that at this point. Start where you are and don't worry, the Spirit is where you are.

At this moment the Lord wants to start the process of healing. God is less concerned about *how* it is communicated at this point. Jesus is more concerned *that* it gets expressed to and before Him. For more mature Christians there will be less if any foulness while venting. That is because they are more developed or seasoned in a relationship with Him. However, to those who might be looking shocked at my guidelines for venting on the Holy Spirit, in the spirit- how about cutting the wounded person some slack?

Sending rounds down range, laying it at the feet of Jesus your 'target' releases it from you to Him. Trust me; the Lord loves that you are bringing it to Him. He is the only one who really understands it all, better than any of us. Better to vent on God, than get arrested. You get the picture. God loves you even if you don't see or feel it at the moment. The process of healing starts here. We are commanded to give it to God, so send it.

> "God resists the proud but gives grace to the humble. Therefore humble yourselves under the mighty hand of God, that He may exalt you in due time, **casting all your cares** (concerns, anxieties, fears, etc.) upon Him, for He cares for you" (1 Peter 5:5-7, MJVK, em ad).

Communicate what happened (your **event**, your **venting,** is private, intimate between you and God, say only what you're ok with) and how you honestly felt- vulnerable, mortal, frail, terrified, shocked, horrified... to your spouse, close combat buddy, or a person of shared experience. Sometimes our well-meaning spouses have no clue what they're really asking when they sincerely say you can tell them anything. Pray before you speak with loved ones.

Food for thought

There are some books I will quote from briefly which are worth the warrior's time to read. Whether they give the glory to God or not, they represent good advice and counsel helpful for covenant warriors. This is not to say I agree with all the conclusions or theology presented in all these books, I agree with some and not with others. For example, one author sincerely, but incorrectly, lumped the Jewish and Christian God Yahweh, in along with the Muslim god Allah. A mistake many Christians make. A mistake never made by the Jewish community.

> "...the PTSD paradox-the fact that what medical professionals label *symptoms* are also combat survival skills- and how this paradox can create misery after coming home"... "Nagging questions are plentiful, and

we instinctively and immediately engage in trying to solve them without even considering why we're asking them or if they're answerable (or worth answering)" (Hoge C., Col. U.S. Army Ret., 2010 *Once A Warrior Always a Warrior,*p xx, 232).

"Combat veterans need to realize that as they return from the battlefield their families at home have also been in a combat experience of their own...waiting for news, fearing for the individuals' well-being, and hoping no uniformed personnel show up at the front door"(McCoy, William Chaplain LTC (2007) *Under Orders: a spiritual handbook for military personnel,*p237)

"Posttraumatic stress sufferers-not only combat veterans, but others such as victims of sexual assault or natural disaster- stay constantly aroused, as if emotionally and physically prepared to fight or flee at all times"(Armstrong Keith. Best, S. Domenici, P., 2006, *Courage After Fire: Coping Strategies for Troops Returning from Iraq and Afghanistan and Their Families*, p16).

Physical Healing

The same process of speaking the scriptures, taking captive your thoughts, dealing with lying symptoms is used only inserting physically healing scriptures. John prayed we prosper in all things and be in health as our souls prosper. That is another reason I spent so much time on the mental and emotional healing and strengthening. Your psychological and emotional health contribute to your physical healing. If you are an amputee with good prosthetics you may or may not be praying about the maimed being made whole- every body part is included in this. It's no problem. You pray for what you want. Wherever you are content, that is the place your prosperity begins. You are no less a Christian or significant whether you pray and not- the choice is yours.

There are two pieces of legislation which should be passed into law.

One to strip an illegal enemy combatant of their citizenship when caught in the process of planning, executing, or having executed a terrorist act. Then they are tried in a military tribunal instead of civilian court. Regular civilian criminals deserve citizens' rights because their criminal activity or alleged criminal activity is not designed to terrorize, destabilize and contribute to undermining or overthrowing the U.S. government, which is sedition, treason, and or rebellion, or insurrection.

The second piece of legislation would provide that a wounded warrior when possible should have the opportunity to continue their service career. They should have an opportunity to reclassify to another position and complete their twenty years to retirement. Not every soldier or agent needs to pass a PT test if you get my meaning. They will never be deployed in the sense of running patrols or missions, but if you can wheel yourself from a B-hut to the ops center or administrative section... honor them and let them serve as they are able. Don't lose institutional knowledge; as instructors of new recruits is another place many could still serve.

A vet in a wheelchair may not be able to some things, but they can teach classes to new recruits and pass on their wisdom. They have nothing to be ashamed of, and I think it's good for new warriors to see the sacrifice, dedication, and patriotism of wounded warriors. I think it would be inspiring. I also think we owe it to our warriors. It became a different world with your hook instead of a hand. But that shouldn't mean you lose the option to serve.

I know this would mean a revamping of physical requirements and adjustments to promotions procedures. I know to an extent this is dealt with but should be the norm, not the exception. Becoming a law enforcement officer, intel officer, or military service member should be a type of, for better or worse relationship of sorts. They are worth it. They deserve it.

Remember the application principles are the same. Speak spiritual reality over currently experienced physical reality. Lot's of great testimonies, books, and resources available on Sid Roth's investigative show of over 35 years called It's Supernatural. Physical healing is a very commonly taught and experienced. Watch an old crusade by Reinhardt Bonke from Africa from the past 50 years or recently conducted by his successor. Or look up the Brownsville Florida or Azusa street revivals. I could go on and on. As for healing scriptures here are a few more starters.

"With his stripes **we are** healed" (Is 53:5, NJKV).

"by whose stripes **you were** healed" (1 Peter 2:24, NJKV).

I bundled these two together because they both refer to when Jesus was horrifically whipped with a cat of nine tails. The first mention was prophetic about what will happen to the Messiah when He comes. That whole chapter in Isaiah relates to the Lord, and what His sufferings would be when He comes in the flesh, and how that benefits us. All His prophesied suffering happened.

I highlighted the difference in the present and past tense because Peter wrote after the resurrection. Even before the sufferings of Jesus, God credited a future work of the Christ to those who came before Him. It shows how God sees things across time simultaneously and credits Jesus life's work to those before Him, contemporary to Him, and after Him (us). Healing is for today and tomorrow. God described King David as a man after His own heart. David spoke to his soul and unto the Lord at the same time.

> "Bless the Lord, O my soul; and all that is within me, bless His holy name! Bless the Lord, O my soul, and **forget not** all His *benefits*: Who forgives **all** your *iniquities*, Who heals **all** your *diseases*, Who redeems your life from **destruction**..."(Psalm 103:1-4, NJKV em ad)

This is God's general insurance policy of restoration, provision, and protections through covenant. Here is a little more on Psalm 103.

- David speaks to his soul, telling it what to do, how to think. This affects the spiritual and physical trees (dendrites) in his mind.
- Keep the Lord's benefits or covenant entitlements foremost in your mind because they deal with all situations in life, so forget them not.
- There are more benefits in the scriptures for you to search out for yourself.

- Most people know iniquities are sins, and the diseases healed and protected against cover all types of physical, mental, and emotional.
- The Redeems your life from destruction phrase refers to a **constant** protection from ambushes, known and unforeseen dangers, and danger out of your control. This counters Time and Chance. A life redeemed from destruction is not subject to time and chance. Psalm 91 is like an itemized list of all the things destruction in Psalm 103 refers to.

Jesus gives you the same authority and opportunity for the Holy Spirits power to flow through you to do miracles, as it flowed through Him for the miracles. Jesus healed no one Himself, it was the Holy Spirit through Him. We lay on hands, and speak as Jesus did, in faith, and the Holy Spirit will work through you to.

> "And when He had called His twelve disciples to Him, He gave them power over unclean spirits, to cast them out, and to heal all kinds of sickness and all kinds of disease...These twelve Jesus sent out and commanded them, saying...Heal the sick, cleanse the lepers, raise the dead, cast out demons. Freely you have received, freely give" (Matthew 10:1-8, NJKV).

> "Then great multitudes came to Him, having with them those who were lame, blind, mute, maimed, and many others; and they laid them down at Jesus' feet, and he healed them. So the multitude marveled when they saw the mute speaking, the maimed made whole, the lame walking, and the blind seeing; and they glorified the God of Israel" (Matthew 15:29-30, NJKV).

It is the Holy Spirit which is flowing through them to do the works of the Lord. The same Holy Spirit who raised Jesus from the dead. When a fellow warrior is injured, any believer, not just some medic or other emergency personnel, can lay hands on them and speak life and bind the spirit of death. Speak healing and expect a miracle. Again, their free will or words may trump your prayer if its crosswise to the word, or any number of other factors may be at play, which cause the situation to end badly. We still must pray and believe, leaving the end result to God.

You can also speak over yourself before you may be injured. Prepare your mind for taking a hit, but pray and believe you will not take a hit. Remember Isaiah 54:17 that no weapon formed against you will prosper. You may be hit, but death or permanent injury does not have to happen. Speak over yourself "No grave trouble overtakes the righteous, but the wicked shall be filled with evil"(Prov 12:21). The alternative of not trying, not praying, and not believing is conceding defeat with no hope.

> "And always, night and day, he was in the mountains and tombs, crying out and cutting himself with stones… Then they came to Jesus and saw the one who had been demon-possessed and had the legion, sitting and clothed and in his right mind" (Mark 5:5,15 NJKV).

These are excerpts from Mark of the account of a man tormented mentally. He had great strength, couldn't be bound and continuously was hurting himself.

There is no explanation given of how he became this way or his occupation before he became overcome with torment. The same account is in Luke, and another in Matthew, which had two other people instead of one. How did this person get into such a state? I believe a traumatic event took place, and without any help or support system, they became dangerous, crazy, and violent people, through the torment of demons. Nevertheless, he got his life back.

I can't emphasize enough that I'm not saying you are demon possessed if you have mental and emotional problems. I'm saying they may play a part in your torment more often than you suspect. In a western culture on one hand some call upon demonic assistance through fortune tellers, tarot cards, and ouija boards while the other hand acts like there is no spiritual realm with influence in our natural one. When you read these accounts yourself, notice the demons are terrified of Jesus. They know He is the Son of the Highest. Keep in mind they are terrified of the Holy Spirit in you.

CHAPTER 16

Signs, Wonders, and the Three Fears

The blockquote from Mark includes essential testimony of Jesus resurrection. The last chapters of each gospel contain eyewitness accounts of Jesus alive, raised from the dead. Consciously knowing Jesus and is alive today, and always, is the foundation of the entire New Covenant. It is the power of the resurrection flowing into and through believers; the Body of Christ. We are His body on Earth. He is the Head in Heaven. Our authority from Jesus extends from Heaven into the Earth.

"Now when He (Jesus) rose early on the first day of the week, **He appeared first** to Mary Magdalene, out of whom He had cast seven demons. **After that, He appeared** in another form to two of them as they walked and went into the country. And they went and told it to the rest, but they did not believe them either. **Afterward He** appeared to the eleven as they sat at the table", then Jesus says

> "Go into all the world and preach the gospel...And **these signs will follow** those who believe: In My name **they will cast** out demons; **they will speak** with new tongues; **they will take** up serpents; and **if they drink** anything deadly, it will by no means hurt them; **they will lay hands** on the sick, and they will recover"...And they went...the Lord working with them and confirming the word **through the accompanying signs**, Amen".(Mark 16:9-20, JKV, em ad)

The laying on of your hands will heal the sick. You will speak with other tongues, your personal prayer language. You will take up serpents; be in conflict with enemy forces of various kinds. And if you drink, or according to the Greek ingest as to breathe in, drink, be injected with, or eat a deadly (or poisoned) thing it won't hurt you. These promises are for believers. When we act in faith phenomenal signs will be seen.

The Three Fears

There are three good types of fear and one evil type. We've talked enough about the evil spirit of timidity/ cowardice/ intimidation. But, I would be negligent if I didn't comment on the three good ones. Being afraid is normal when bullets fly, the bear steps into your campsite, or some other such event occurs. The fight or flight is part of our natural defense system. That adrenaline and hypersensitivity, hyperarousal, or some call it hyper-awareness is needed in times like these. The strength which saturates our muscles to perform superhuman feats is a physical version and reflection of supernatural power from Heaven.

That is a God-given fear to alert you to danger. Your training is designed to kick in at this time to save your life and the lives of others. Some may freeze, but most will think quicker, and act faster. It is the opportunity in the crisis, which I'll talk about shortly. So, not all fear is bad. The spirit of prudence or reverence in the Bible is also a type of spirit of fear, but not the debilitating demonic kind. Prudence is when you foresee or a problem and plan for it.

Then there is the fear of the Lord, which is reverence and respect for the almighty power of God. Reverence because His thoughts, understanding, and experience are higher than our thoughts, understanding, or experience. Respect, because of His love for us demonstrated in sending Jesus to do for us, what we could not do for ourselves, and what we did not deserve. He sacrificed Himself on the field of Battle across all dimensions simultaneously and defeated all our enemy's, even the part of us which was our own enemy. Jesus loves you so much he fought and died so you could live.

Then there is the third fear. By the terror of the Lord, we persuade men. Some are attracted by His love; others are driven to repentance for fear of Hell. We should all appreciate not having to go to Hell for the evil we have done - all of us. Some have done evil beyond imagination or understanding, but all have gone astray, and the merit system of Heaven permits no amount of evil. None. If you're not saved, get that way... God's desire is all would repent, and none perish, but it's not His choice, it is yours.

One last word on the spirit of Death comes from Peggy Joyce Ruths book and CD on Psalm 91 Workbook (Ruth, Schum, & Tonye). A World War One fighter pilot who had been shot down a few times and survived had been asked how he survived. He talked about pain as his friend reminding him he was alive. His description of the spirit of death was something like a seductive voice telling him all is well, let go. You've done enough; your fight is over. I believe he also mentioned being called to the light. Many report the light.

These types of thoughts are from the enemy. He hung on to the physical pain to live. Hang on to yours if need be. Do not give in to the seduction of the spirit of Death. Never give up; your time isn't up, your job isn't done. You may not be the warrior you once were, but every warrior can pray, share, help themselves, and fellow warriors. *You never retire from significance, you only change the type of significance you bring to the table.* You matter, wounded or not, never forget this. You are loved, even if it's only the brothers or sisters to your left or right. Don't give in the seductions of the enemy.

In thinking about the seemingly never-ending stream of enemies, criminals, and unappreciative people. Don't despair, or wonder is what you do even worth it. Remember there are multitudes who appreciate you, love you, respect you, need you to keep doing what you do. Do it for them. Forget the social and political parasites, keep on keeping on for the Patriots and innocents who depend on you. Sometimes the only reason some die and others live is some gave up internally, and some did not. I'm not judging those who gave the ultimate sacrifice; I honor them all. What I am saying to you is live life abundantly, as best you can. Live well in memory and on behalf of those who cannot.

A Parting Recap

What you believe you can receive. You cannot receive what you do not believe. You can experience instant healing results, many, but not all have. It takes time not to believe one day then start confessing healing or protections then next and always see fast results. Sometimes results take a while because you are uprooting evil trees and planting new trees which need to grow before they bring fruit. God can, and has compressed this time. You can control the development time from seed to bearing fruit by using it more.

If you have faith in healing a headache, then start praying for something bigger. Faith grows from weak to strong to great faith. Some faith is shipwrecked. You will have different levels of faith for different things. You may have great faith for protections and marksmanship, but little for healing.

You can still increase your faith, even if you are not manifesting that gift. To be clear the sick people in the block quote from Mark are all unsaved. They don't have to be a believer to receive if they believe your faith or belief is enough, or give you the authority to believe for them. Christians are expected to build up enough faith to keep themselves and family safe, and healthy. The healing of others is a calling for some people, and a calling to all people at the same time. Any believer can heal anyone else. It is a free gift. There is a multitude of resources teaching on healing more than I go into here.

Some might say I backed down on the power of God to fulfill his promises talking about how some do not receive their healings etc. Not at all. "...but time and chance happen to them all. For man also does not know his time...So the sons of men are snared in an evil time, when it falls suddenly upon them"(Eccl. 9:11-12, NJKV). This applies to unbelievers and believers who do not trust in the redeems their life from destruction clause. Hold fast to your faith, and you will see God's promises fulfilled. Satan looks for opportunities to separate you from your faith because your faith overcomes the world. All men have a measure of faith, but only believers have the God kind of faith, covenant power. Nonbelievers have no covenant. Your faith and covenant trump their natural level of faith and free will.

> "Be sober, be vigilant; because your adversary the devil walks about like a roaring lion, seeking whom he may devour. Resist him (the devil and his ways), steadfast in the

> faith, knowing that the same sufferings are experienced by your brotherhood in the world"(1Pet 5:8-9, em ad). "...and that we may be delivered from unreasonable and wicked men; for not all have faith"(2 Thes 3:2, NJKV).

The demons destroy and use those without faith against the faithful. You are not alone in your sufferings. Isolating yourself is as a sheep straying from the flock and lost. Easy prey for the wolf outside the protective watch of the sheepdogs and Shepard. Get help, get support, get well. You deserve it.

Many Christians who have been through some of the most violent fighting of Viet Nam and other wars, report no PTSD symptoms because of their faith. The stresses and emotional turmoil expressed in the psalms by multiple tour combat veteran King David is worth studying. Again: Post-Traumatic Stress Disorder is **not** a disorder in the sense something is wrong with you. These behaviors are normal reactions in coping with extreme circumstances which caused trauma to your whole being of body, soul, and spirit.

The Chinese character for crisis is often said to be the same character for opportunity. This is not true. The characters which together mean danger are Wei and Ji. Often the principle of crisis and opportunity in Chinese having the same meaning and only one character is not accurate, but the principle of the saying is that in every crisis or there is danger and opportunity.

> "A wēijī indicates a perilous situation when one should be especially wary. It is *not* a juncture when one goes looking for advantages and benefits... Aside from the notion of "incipient moment" or "crucial point" discussed above, the graph for jī by itself indicates "quick-witted(ness); resourceful(ness)" and "machine; device." In combination with other graphs, however, jī can acquire hundreds of secondary meanings... Speaking specifically in the matter under investigation, jī added to huì ("occasion") creates the Mandarin word for "opportunity" (jīhuì), but by itself, jī does not mean "opportunity."(Mair, Victor; Dept. East Asian Languages, University of Pennsylvania)

Ji is part of the word crisis and of a separate word for opportunity. In every crisis you have a decision to make, that is your opportunity before, during, and after a crisis on how you will respond. Being quick-witted or resourceful during either a crisis or opportune situation is a decision you can make ahead of time. Your experiences will run you, or you learn to run them. Be ruthlessly honest with yourself in journaling, praying, venting, sharing, the Holy Spirit will help you work through these things with your caregiver(s). The new normal is good. The new normal is workable and significant. The inside is forever changed, no problem, it's the new normal.

> "War is a dreadful thing, and I can respect an honest pacifist, though I think he is entirely mistaken. What I cannot understand is this sort of semi-pacifism you get nowadays which gives people the idea that though you have to fight, you ought to do it with a long face and as if you were ashamed of it." - C.S. Lewis

Be proud and not ashamed. If you did not do what you did, how many lives would've been lost or hurt? You witness, are exposed to or damaged by some horrific things. Things which are dangerous and morally damaging if not dealt with Biblically. Things morally difficult to do, even though you're authorized by the Lord to do difficult things that are right and necessary. Hold your head up high. Remember, you man the walls protecting the sheep from the wolves, serpents, and scorpions of this world. You are a sheepdog, a bird of prey, a dragon slayer. You are a minister of vengeance.

APPENDIX A

Patton on Prayer, and Soldiering, and Training Letter No. 5, emphasis added

Chaplain, I am a strong believer in prayer. There are three ways that men get what they want; by planning, by working, and by praying. **And any military operation takes careful planning or thinking.** Then you must have well-trained troops to carry it out: that's working. *But between the plan and the operation, there is always an unknown. That unknown spells defeat or victory, success or failure. It is the reaction of the actors to the ordeal when it actually comes.* Some people call that getting the breaks; I call it God. God has His part or margin in everything. That's where prayer comes in. Up to now, in the Third Army, God has been very good to us. We have never retreated; we have suffered no defeats, no famine, no epidemics. This is because a lot of people back home are praying for us. We were lucky in Africa, in Sicily, and in Italy, simply because people prayed. But we have to pray for ourselves, too. A good soldier is not made merely by making him think and work. There is something in every soldier that goes deeper than thinking or working - it's his "guts." It is something that he has built in there: it is a world of truth and power that is higher than himself. Great living is not all output of thought and work. A man has to have intake as well. I don't know what you call it, but I call it Religion, Prayer, or God...

I wish you would **put out a Training Letter on this subject of Prayer** to all the chaplains; *write about nothing else, just the importance of prayer.* Let me see it before you send it. We've got to get not only the chaplains but every man in the Third Army to pray. We must ask God to stop these rains. These rains are that margin that holds defeat or victory. If we all pray, it will be like what Dr. Carrel said [the allusions was to a press quotes some days previously when Dr. Alexis Carrel, one of the foremost scientists, described prayer "as one of the most powerful forms of energy man can generate"], it will be like plugging in on a current who source is in Heaven. I believe that prayer completes that circuit. It is power... I returned to my field desk, typed Training Letter No. 5 while the "copy" was "hot," touching on some or all of General's reverie on Prayer, and after staff processing, presented it to General Patton on the next day. The General read it, and without change directed that it be circulated to the 486 chaplains, but to every organization commander down to and including the regimental level. Three thousand two hundred copies were distributed to every unit in the Third Army over my signature as Third Army Chaplain. Strictly speaking, it was the Army Commander's letter, not mine... Chaplain O'Neal.

Training Letter No. 5

At this stage of the operations, I would call upon the chaplains and the men of the Third United States Army to focus their attention on the importance of prayer.

Our glorious march from the Normandy Beach across France to where we stand, before and beyond the Siegfried Line, with the wreckage of the German Army behind us should convince the most skeptical soldier that God has ridden with our banner. Pestilence and famine have not touched us. We have continued in unity of purpose. We have had no quitters; and our leadership has been masterful. The Third Army has no roster of Retreats. None of Defeats. We have no memory of a lost battle to hand on to our children from this great campaign.

But we are not stopping at the Siegfried Line. Tough days may be ahead of us before we eat our rations in the Chancellery of the Deutsches Reich.

As chaplains, it is our business to pray. We preach its importance. We urge its practice. But the time is now to intensify our faith in prayer, not alone with ourselves, but with every believing man, Protestant, Catholic, Jew, or Christian in the ranks of the Third United States Army.

Those who pray do more for the world than those who fight; and if the world goes from bad to worse, it is because there are more battles than prayers. 'Hands lifted up,' said Bossuet, 'smash more battalions than hands that strike.' Gideon of Bible fame was least in his father's house. He came from Israel's smallest tribe. But he was a mighty man of valor. His strength lay not in his military might but in his recognition of God's proper claims upon his life. He reduced his Army from thirty-two thousand to three hundred men lest the people of Israel would think that their valor had saved them. We have no intention to reduce our vast striking force. But we must urge, instruct, and indoctrinate every fighting man to pray as well as fight. In Gideon's day, and in our own, spiritually alert minorities carry the burdens and bring the victories.

Urge all of your men to pray, not alone in the church, but everywhere. Pray when driving. Pray when fighting. Pray alone. Pray with others. Pray by night and pray by day. Pray for the cessation of immoderate rains, for good weather for Battle. Pray for the defeat of our wicked enemy whose banner is injustice and whose good is oppression. Pray for victory. Pray for our Army, and Pray for Peace.

We must march together, all out for God. The soldier who 'cracks up' does not need sympathy or comfort as much as he needs strength. We are not trying to make the best of these days. It is our job to make the most of them. Now is not the time to follow God from 'afar off.' This Army needs the assurance and the faith that God is with us. With prayer, we cannot fail.

Be assured that this message on prayer has the approval, the encouragement, and the enthusiastic support of the Third United States Army Commander.

With every good wish to each of you for a very Happy Christmas and my personal congratulations for your splendid and courageous work since landing on the beach, I am, etc., etc., signed The Third Army Commander.

APPENDIX B
Founding Documents

The DECLARATION OF INDEPENDENCE
Action of Second Continental Congress, July 4, 1776
The Unanimous Declaration of the thirteen United States of America.

When in the Course of human Events, it becomes necessary for one People to dissolve the Political Bands which have connected them with another, and to assume among the Powers of the Earth, the separate and equal Station to which the Laws of Nature and of Nature's God entitle them, a decent Respect to the Opinions of Mankind requires that they should declare the causes which impel them to the Separation.

We hold these Truths to be self-evident, that all Men are created equal, that they are endowed by their Creator with certain unalienable Rights, that among these are Life, Liberty, and the pursuit of Happiness—That to secure these Rights, Governments are instituted among Men, deriving their just Powers from the Consent of the Governed, that whenever any Form of Government becomes destructive of these Ends, it is the Right of the People to alter or to abolish it, and to institute new Government, laying its Foundation on such Principles, and organizing its Powers in such Form, as to them shall seem most likely to effect their Safety and Happiness. Prudence, indeed, will dictate that Governments long established should not be changed for light and transient Causes; and accordingly all Experience hath shewn, that Mankind are more disposed to suffer, while Evils are sufferable, than to right themselves by abolishing the Forms to which they are accustomed. But when a long Train of

Abuses and Usurpations, pursuing invariably the same Object, evinces a design to reduce them under absolute Despotism, it is their Right, it is their Duty, to throw off such Government, and to provide new Guards for their future Security. Such has been the patient Sufferance of these Colonies; and such is now the Necessity which constrains them to alter their former Systems of Government. The History of the present King of Great-Britain is a History of repeated Injuries and Usurpations, all having in direct Object the Establishment of an absolute Tyranny over these States. To prove this, let Facts be submitted to a candid World. Founding and Influential Documents of American Government

- He has refused his Assent to Laws, the most wholesome and necessary for the public good.
- He has forbidden his Governors to pass Laws of immediate and pressing, unless suspended in their operation till his Assent should be obtained; and when so suspended, he has utterly neglected to attend to them.
- He has refused to pass other Laws for the accommodation of large districts of people, unless those people would relinquish the right of Representation in the Legislature, a right inestimable to them and formidable to tyrants only.
- He has called together legislative bodies at places unusual, uncomfortable, and Distant from the depository of their public Records, for the sole purpose of fatiguing them into compliance with his measures.
- He has dissolved Representative Houses repeatedly, for opposing with manly firmness his invasions on the rights of the people.
- He has refused for a long time, after such dissolutions, to cause others to be elected; whereby the Legislative powers, incapable of Annihilation, have returned to the People at large for their exercise; the State remaining in the mean time exposed to all the dangers of invasion from without, and convulsions within.
- He has endeavoured to prevent the population of these States; for that purpose obstructing the Laws for Naturalization of Foreigners; refusing to pass others to encourage their migrations hither, and raising the conditions of new Appropriations of Lands.

- He has obstructed the Administration of Justice, by refusing his Assent to Laws for establishing Judiciary powers.
- He has made Judges dependent on his Will alone, for the tenure of their offices, the amount and payment of their salaries.
- He has erected a multitude of New Offices, and sent hither swarms of Officers to harrass our people, and eat out their substance.
- He has kept among us, in times of peace, Standing Armies without the Consent Of our legislatures.
- He has affected to render the Military independent of and superior to the Civil power.
- He has combined with others to subject us to a jurisdiction foreign to our constitution, and unacknowledged by our laws; giving his Assent to Acts of pretended Legislation:
- For Quartering large bodies of armed troops among us:
- For protecting them, by a mock Trial, from punishment for any Murders which they should commit on the Inhabitants of these States:
- For cutting off our Trade with all parts of the world:
- For imposing Taxes on us without our Consent: For depriving us in many cases, of the benefits of Trial by Jury:
- For transporting us beyond Seas to be tried for pretended offences
- For abolishing the free System of English Laws in a neighbouring Province, establishing therein an Arbitrary government, and enlarging its Boundaries so as to render it at once an example and fit instrument for introducing the same absolute rule into these Colonies:
- For taking away our Charters, abolishing our most valuable Laws, and altering fundamentally the Forms of our Governments:
- For suspending our own Legislatures, and declaring themselves invested with power to legislate for us in all cases whatsoever.
- He has abdicated Government here, by declaring us out of his Protection and waging War against us.
- He has plundered our seas, ravaged our Coasts, burnt our towns, and destroyed The lives of our people.
- He is at this time transporting large Armies of foreign Mercenaries to compleat the works of death, desolation and tyranny, already

begun with circumstances of Cruelty & perfidy scarcely paralleled in the most barbarous ages, and totally unworthy of the Head of a civilized nation.

- He has constrained our fellow Citizens taken Captive on the high Seas to bear Arms against their Country, to become the executioners of their friends and Brethren, or to fall themselves by their Hands.
- He has excited domestic insurrections amongst us, and has endeavoured to Bring on the inhabitants of our frontiers, the merciless Indian Savages, whose known rule of warfare, is an undistinguished destruction of all ages, sexes and conditions.

In every stage of these Oppressions We have Petitioned for Redress in the most humble terms: Our repeated Petitions have been answered only by repeated injury. A Prince whose character is thus marked by every act which may define a Tyrant, is unfit to be the ruler of a free people.

Nor have We been wanting in attentions to our Brittish brethren. We have warned them from time to time of attempts by their legislature to extend an unwarrantable jurisdiction over us. We have reminded them of the circumstances of our emigration and settlement here. We have appealed to their native justice and magnanimity, and we have conjured them by the ties of our common kindred to disavow these usurpations, which, would inevitably interrupt our connections and correspondence. They too have been deaf to the voice of justice and of consanguinity. We must, therefore, acquiesce in the necessity, which denounces our Separation, and hold them, as we hold the rest of mankind, Enemies in War, in Peace Friends.

We, therefore, the Representatives of the united States of America, in General Congress, Assembled, appealing to the Supreme Judge of the world for the rectitude of our intentions, do, in the Name, and by Authority of the good People of these Colonies, solemnly publish and declare, That these United Colonies are, and of Right ought to be Free and Independent States; that they are Absolved from all Allegiance to the British Crown, and that all political connection between them and the State of Great Britain, is and ought to be totally dissolved; and that as Free and Independent States, they have full Power to levy War, conclude Peace, contract Alliances, establish Commerce, and to do all other Acts and Things which Independent States may of right do. And for the support of this Declaration, with a firm reliance on the protection of divine Providence, we mutually pledge to each other our Lives, our Fortunes and our sacred Honor.

(emphasis added)

The Constitution of the United States

The United States Constitution I felt was too large for this book in conjunction with the Declaration. I do provide two links to a pdf download. However, including the First Amendment and Preamble is worth the space for two reasons. Most people think the actual words 'separation of church and state' are in the Constitution when they are not. Second, the Preamble sets the tone and premise of our American culture and governmental structure. This is the document solidifying We The People as the source authority, through consent, of our duly elected officials and the officials appointed by them. This is what we serve, protect, safeguard, and defend against all enemies foreign and domestic through the sacred service of our men and women in the Military, Law Enforcement, and Intelligence communities- the Ministers of Vengeance.

Preamble

We the People of the United States, in Order to form a more perfect Union, establish Justice, insure domestic Tranquility, provide for the common defense, promote the general Welfare, and secure the Blessings of Liberty to ourselves and our Posterity, do ordain and establish this Constitution for the United States of America.

Article. VII. - Ratification

The Ratification of the Conventions of nine States shall be sufficient for the Establishment of this Constitution between the States so ratifying the Same. Done in Convention by the *Unanimous Consent* of the States present this Seventeenth Day of September in the Year of our Lord one thousand seven hundred and Eighty-seven and of the Independence of the United States of America the Twelfth. In Witness whereof, We have hereunto subscribed our Names. (signatures omitted text only presented, emphasis added)

First Amendment to the Bill of Rights. Ratified 12/15/1791.

Congress shall make no law respecting an establishment of religion, or prohibiting the free exercise thereof; or abridging the freedom of speech, or of the press, or the right of the people peaceably to assemble, and to petition the Government for a redress of grievances.

https://www.constitutioncenter.org/media/files/constitution.pdf
http://www.usconstitution.net/const.pdf

APPENDIX C

Mayflower Compact and Letter from the Vatican

The Mayflower Compact

In the name of God, Amen. We, whose names are underwritten, the loyal subjects of our dread sovereigne Lord, King James, by the grace of God, of Great Britaine, France, and Ireland king, defender of the faith, etc., having undertaken, for the glory of God, and advancement of the Christian faith, and honour of our king and country, a voyage to plant the first colony in the Northerne parts of Virginia, doe, by these presents, solemnly and mutually in the presence of God, and one another, covenant and combine ourselves together into a civil body politick, for our better ordering and preservation and furtherance of the ends aforesaid; and *by virtue hereof to enacte, constitute, and frame* such just and equall laws, ordinances, acts, constitutions, and offices, from time to time, as shall be thought most meete and convenient *for the generall good of the Colonie unto which we promise all due submission and obedience.* In witness whereof we have hereunder subscribed our names at Cap-Codd the 11. of November, in the year of the raigne of our sovereign lord, King James, of England, France, and Ireland, the eighteenth, and of Scotland the fiftie-fourth. Anno. Dom. 1620. (italic and underline emphasis added)http://www.thefederalistpapers.org/wp-content/uploads/2012/12/The-Mayflower-Compact1.pdf

Vatican Letter to President CSA Jefferson Davis

"ILLUSTRIOUS AND HONORABLE PRESIDENT, salutation:

We have just received with all suitable welcome the persons sent by you to place in our hands your letter, dated 23d of September last... in order that the American people may obtain peace and concord, and dwell charitably together. It is **particularly agreeable to us** to see that you, *illustrious and honorable President, and your people,* are animated with the same desires of peace and tranquility which we have...May it please God at the same time **to make** the **other peoples** of America and **their rulers**, reflecting seriously how terrible is civil war, and what calamities it engenders, listen to the inspirations of a calmer spirit, and *adopt resolutely the part of peace...*"

Given at Rome, at St. Peter's, the 3d of December, 1863, of our Pontificate 18.

(Signed) Pius IX"

(http://www.reformation.org/lincoln.html (2 of 9)4/12/2006 4:56:17 PM Assassination of President Lincoln)
and
(http://catholicknight.blogspot.com/2009/02/pope-pius-ix-and-confederacy.html)

APPENDIX D

Southern Secession Declaration Excerpts

Though I used the Declaration of Secession of the State of South Carolina in my example, there are many other declarations. I added these excerpts as examples revealing a spiritual, not just military point. No states cede before the election of President Lincoln. It is business as usual until South Carolina feels they have enough Confederate support, to start the War between the States with a **probability of success**. Then the attack begins encouraging more to officially join the war. Remember, nation (ethnos) shall rise against nation, the demonic divisive spirit of racism is seen at work in our nation, then and now.

Order of Secessions

South Carolina, December 20, 1860; Mississippi, January 9, 1861; Florida, January 10, 1861; Alabama, January 11, 1861; Georgia, January 19, 1861; Louisiana, January 26, 1861l; Texa, February 1, 1861
The attack on Fort Sumter April 12th and 13th 1861
Then joining the war officially comes Virginia: April 17, 1861; Arkansas: May 6, 1861; North Carolina: May 20, 1861; Tennessee: June 8, 1861; Kentucky Ordinance passed by the people in 1861, and finally by Missouri.

South Carolina

But an increasing hostility on the part of the non-slaveholding States to the institution of slavery, has led to a disregard of their obligations…the right of *transit for a slave has been denied* by her tribunals; the States of Ohio and Iowa have *refused to surrender to justice fugitives* charged with murder, and with *inciting servile insurrection* in the State of Virginia...We, therefore, the People of South Carolina...have solemnly declared that the Union heretofore existing between this State and the other States of North America, is dissolved.

Georgia

The party of Lincoln, called the Republican party, under its present name and organization, is of recent origin. It is admitted to be *an anti-slavery party...* The *prohibition of slavery in the Territories* is the cardinal principle of this organization... Such are the opinions, and such are the practices of the Republican party...because their avowed purpose is to subvert our society...To avoid these evils, we resume the powers which our fathers delegated to the Government of the United States...

Mississippi

Our position is thoroughly identified with the institution of slavery-- the greatest material interest of the world...It tramples the original equality of the South under foot... It has nullified the Fugitive Slave Law in almost every free State in the Union, ***It has enlisted*** *its press,* ***its pulpit*** *and* ***its schools*** *against us*, until the whole popular mind of the North is excited and inflamed with prejudice...We embrace the alternative of separation.

Bibliography

Works Cited and Referenced

Allhoff, Fritz(2005)*A Defense of Torture:Separation of Cases, Ticking Time-bombs,and Moral Justification*, International Journal of Applied Philosophy 19:2. ISSN 0738-098X.

Amari, R. (2004). *Islam: In light of history*. Prospect Heights, IL: Religion Research Institute. http://religionresearchinstitute.org/mecca/construction.htm

Armstrong, Karen (1993) *A History Of God*, Ballatine Books, New York

Armstrong Keith. Best, S. Domenici, P.(2006)*Courage After Fire: Coping Strategies for Troops Returning from Iraq and Afghanistan and Their Families*, Ulysses Press, Berkeley, CA

Balandiz, H., & Bolu, A. (2017). Forensic mental health evaluations of military personnel with traumatic life event, in a university hospital in Ankara, Turkey. *Journal of forensic and legal medicine, 51*, 51-56.

Barbar, Benjamin R. (1992) *Jihad Versus McWorld*, The Atlantic Monthly, March issue

Benight, C. C., Freyaldenhoven, R. W., Hughes, J., Ruiz, J. M., Zoschke, T. A., & Lovallo, W. R. (2000). Coping Self-Efficacy and Psychological Distress Following the Oklahoma City Bombing. *Journal of Applied Social Psychology, 30*(7), 1331-1344.

Benight, C. C., & Bandura, A. (2004). Social cognitive theory of posttraumatic recovery: The role of perceived self-efficacy. *Behaviour research and therapy, 42*(10), 1129-1148.

Blacketer R.A.(2010) *No Escape by Deception: Calvin's Exegesis of Lies and Liars in the Old Testament*, Reformation and Renaissance Review, RRR 10.3, 267-289

Bosmans, M. W., Van der Knaap, L. M., & Van der Velden, P. G. (2016). The predictive value of trauma-related coping self-efficacy for posttraumatic stress symptoms: Differences between treatment-seeking and non–treatment-seeking victims. *Psychological trauma: theory, research, practice, and policy*, 8(2), 241.

Bowden, Mark(2003) *The Dark Art of Interrogation: A survey of the landscape of persuasion*, Atlantic Magazine, October, Rawalpindi, Pakistan

Burleigh M.(2011) *Moral Combat; good and evil in world war II*, Harper Collins Publishers, New York, New York.

Cahn, J.(2011), *The Harbinger*, Frontline Charisma Media/Charisma House Book Group, Lake Mary, Florida

Clausewitz, Carl Von C(1812) *Principles of War*, translated and edited: Hans W. Gatzke, September 1942, The Military Service Publishing Company

Caner E. M., & Caner E.F., (2002) *Unveiling Islam An insider's look at Muslim life and beliefs*, Kregel Publications, Grand Rapids MI.

Cantrell Bridget C. Ph.D., Dean, Chuck (2005) *Down Range: To Iraq and Back*, WordSmith Books, Seattle, WA.

Cole D(2008) *Whether Spies Too Can Be Saved*, Journal of Religious Ethics. Inc. JRE 36.1:125-154

Collins, Gary R.(2007) *Christian Counseling third edition; completely revised, expanded, and updated*. Thomas Nelson, Nashville TN

Dietz, R. S., & McHone, J. (1974). Kaaba Stone: Not a meteorite, probably an agate. Meteoritics & Planetary Science, 9(2), 173-179. Dr. Clinton T.,

Davidson D LTC (1983) *Nuclear Weapons and the American Churches: Ethical Positions on Modern Warfare*, Army War College (U.S.) Strategic Studies Institute University of Michigan digitized 2006. The Just-War Criteria: A Contemporary Description p19-35

Department of the Army (2005) *Religious Support Handbook for the Unit Ministry Team*, Training Circular No. 1-05 [TC 1-05], HQ Dept. Army, Washington D.C. 10 May

Entwhistle, David N. (2010) *Integrative Approaches To Psychology and Christianity*, Cascade Books, Eugene, OR

Fogleman, Ronald R.(Gen. ret.) (1995) *The Fifth Dimension of Warfare*, Information Operations, Volume 10, Number 47; Remarks as delivered by Gen. Ronald R. Fogleman, Air Force chief of staff, to the Armed

Forces Communications-Electronics Association, Washington, April 25, 1995. Public Domain

Firth, J (2012) *History of Plague Part 1 The three great pandemics*, Journal of Military and Veterans Health, April, vol 20, iss 2, p11-16

Goldstein, L. A., Dinh, J., Donalson, R., Hebenstreit, C. L., & Maguen, S. (2017). Impact of military trauma exposures on posttraumatic stress and depression in female veterans. *Psychiatry research, 249*, 281-285.

Grossman D. LTC (ret) (2007) *On Combat*, PPCT Research Publications

Grotius, H. (2012). *On the law of war and peace,* Batoche Books 52 Eby Street South Kitchener, Ontario,N2G 3L1, Canada

Hawkins, R. (2009) *The Quick-Reference Guide to Biblical Counseling*, Baker Book, Grand Rapids MI.

Ferrajão, P. C., & Oliveira, R. A. (2014). Self-awareness of mental states, self-integration of personal schemas, perceived social support, posttraumatic and depression levels, and moral injury: A mixed-method study among Portuguese war veterans. *Traumatology, 20*(4), 277.

Floyd, Scott (2008) *Crisis Counseling: A Guide for Pastors and Professionals*, Kregel Publications, Grand Rapids, MI

Forsyth D, Zyzniewski L, Giammanco C (2002) *Responsibility Diffusion in Cooperative Collectives,* Personality Social Psychology Bulletin, 28: 54 p2

Goldstein, C.S. (2012) *Just War theory and Democratization by Force: Two Incompatible Agendas*, Military Review: The Professional Journal of the U.S. Army, p2, September-October

Hartley G., Karinch M. (2005) *How To Spot A Liar*, Careers Press, Franklin Lakes, NJ

Hoge C. U.S. Army (Col Ret) (2010)*Once A Warrior Always a Warrior*, Globe Pequot Press, Guilford Connecticut

Hagee, John (2007)*In Defense of Israel*, Frontline publishing, A Strang Company, Lake Mary Florida

Hayward, J. (2010). The Qur'an and war: Observations on Islamic just war. *Royal Air Force Air Power Review, 13*(3), 41-63.

Hernandez, Sonny. (2016) http://christianfighterpilot.com/2016/06/07/the-2016-afrc-chaplain-corps-conference-disaster/#more-35237

History Channel retrieved from http://www.history.com/topics/history-of-ptsd-and-shell-shock

Horn, T. R., & Putnam, C. (2012). *Petrus Romanus: The Final Pope is Here.* Crane, MO: Defender.

Hoyt, S. F. (1912). The etymology of religion. *Journal of the American Oriental Society, 32*(2), 126-129.

Huntington S. P.(1985)*The Soldier and the State; the theory and politics of civil-military relations,* Belknap Press of Harvard University Press, Cambridge, Massachusetts

Israeli War (1967) http://history.state.gov/milestones/1961-1968/ ArabIsraeliWar67

Jackson, John Paul (2013)*Needless Casualties of War,* tenth printing, Steams ministries international, Flower Mound, Texas

Jacknedoff R. *(2009)The natural Logic of Morals and of Laws, BROOKLYN LAW REVIEW,* Vol. 75:2, p383-407

Jarrett, T. (2008). Warrior resilience training in Operation Iraqi Freedom: Combining rational emotive behavior therapy, resiliency, and positive psychology. *US Army Medical Department Journal*, 32-39.

Johnson, James Turner(2008*) Thinking Comparatively About Religion and War,* Journal of Religious Ethics, 36:1, 157-179

John Jay,(1794) Retrieved from https://supreme-court.laws.com/john-jay

Kanel, Kristi (2007) *A Guide to Crisis Intervention third edition*, Thompson/ Brooks and Cole, Belmont. CA

Kollar (1997) *Solution-Focused Pastoral Counseling: an effective short-term approach to getting people back on track*, Zondervan, Grand Rapids MI.

Koppl R.(2005) *Epistemic Systems*, Professor of Economics and Finance Fairleigh Dickinson University, September, Madison, NJ 07940, USA

Kurtz L(1998) *Encyclopedia of Politics and Religion*, ed. Robert Wuthnow. 2 vols. (Washington, D.C.: Congressional Quarterly, Inc.), 783-789

Leaf About Retrieved from http://drleaf.com/about/

Leaf Caroline Dr. (2009) *Who Switched off My Brain? Controlling toxic thought and emotions,* revised edition, Thomas Nelson Publishers

Littlepage, K (retrieved 2013)*The Impact of Historiography: Piracy and Religion from 1590 to 1660*

Luban, D(2008)*Unthinking the Ticking Time Bomb,* July, http://lsr.nellco. org/georgetown/fwps/papers/68/

Maher, D.E.(2008) *The Rhetoric of War in Tibet: Toward a Buddhist Just War Theory*, Political Theology, 9.2, 179-191.

Mair, Victor H., (Essay) Professor of Chinese Language and Literature Department of East Asian Languages and Civilizations University of Pennsylvania, Retrieved from http://pinyin.info/chinese/crisis.html

McDonald, M. (2017). Haunted by a Different Ghost: Re-thinking Moral Injury. *Essays in Philosophy,* 18(2).

McShane T.W. Col. (2012) *In Search of the Good War: Just War and the Realpolitik in Our Time,* Military Review: The Professional Journal of the U.S. Army, p9, September-October

McCoy, William Chaplain LTC (2007) *Under Orders: a spiritual handbook for military personnel,* Eden publishers, Fort Leavenworth, KS

McIntosh, Gary L., & Rima, Samuel D., (2004) *Overcoming the Dark Side of Leadership, The Paradox of Personal Dysfunction,* Baker Books, Grand Rapids, MI

McMinn, Mark R. (1996) *Psychology, Theology, and Spirituality in Christian Counseling,* Tyndale House Publisher, Carol Stream, IL

Michaelsen, J. (1982). *The beautiful side of evil.* Harvest House Publishers.

Military Chaplain, (2010) *The True Story of the Patton Prayer,* Volume 85, Number Three, Fall 2010, (The original article was published in The Military Chaplain, October- November 1948, volume XIX, Number 2.) ISSN-0026-3958

Mitchell, James, E. Ph.D. (2016) *Enhanced Interrogation: Inside the Minds and Motives of the Islamic Terrorists Trying to Destroy America,* Crown Publishing Group, New York

Murray K (2012) *John Heckewelder's "Pieces of Secrecy" Dissimulation and Class in the Writings of a Moravian Missionary,* Journal of the Early Republic, 32, Spring

Musashi, M. (2003). *The book of five rings: A classic text on the Japanese way of the sword.* Shambhala Publications.

Naifeh, J. A., Ursano, R. J., Benfer, N., Wu, H., Herman, M., Benedek, D.M., ... & Aliaga, P. A. (2017). PTSD symptom severity and sensitivity to blood, injury, and mutilation in US army special operations soldiers. *Psychiatry Research,* 250, 78-83.

Nazarov, A., Jetly, R., McNeely, H., Kiang, M., Lanius, R., & McKinnon, M. C. (2015). Role of morality in the experience of guilt and shame within the armed forces. *Acta Psychiatrica Scandinavica, 132*(1), 4-19. doi:10.1111/acps.12406

Newberg, A. B., Wintering, N. A., Morgan, D., & Waldman, M. R. (2006). The measurement of regional cerebral blood flow during glossolalia: a preliminary SPECT study. *Psychiatry Research: Neuroimaging, 148*(1),67-71.

O'Driscoll C(2008) *James Turner Johnson's Just War Idea: Commanding the Headwaters of tradition,* Journal of International Political Theory, 4(2), 189–211, Edinburgh University Press

O'Neill, J. H. (1971). The True Story of the Patton Prayer. *Review of the News,* 6. Reprinted in The New American 12 January 2004, https://www.fpparchive.org

Parco J.E., Levy D.A.(2010) *Attitudes Aren't Free, Thinking Deeply about Diversity in the US Armed Forces,* Air University Press, Maxwell AFB, Alabama

Pfaff T., Tiel J.R. (2004) *The Ethics of Espionage,* Journal of Military Ethics 3(1): 1-15

Penn State (2006) Retrieved from https://www.pennmedicine.org/news/news-releases/2006/october/language-center-of-the-brain-i

Poster History of Uncle Sam (2017) retrieved from http://time.com/4725856/uncle-sam-poster-history/

Putnam, C., & Horn, T. R. (2013). *Exo-Vaticana: Petrus Romanus, Project LUCIFER and the Vatican's Astonishing Plan for the Arrival of an Alien Savior.* Defender.

Renner, Rick (2007) *Dressed to Kill: a Biblical Approach to Spiritual Warfare and Armor,* Published by Teach All Nations, Tulsa Oklahoma

Riggs, S. A., & Riggs, D. S. (2011). Risk and resilience in military families experiencing deployment: The role of the family attachment network. *Journal of Family Psychology, 25*(5), 675.

Ritov, G., & Barnetz, Z. (2014). The interrelationships between moral attitudes, posttraumatic stress disorder symptoms and mixed lateral preference in Israeli reserve combat troops. *International journal of social psychiatry, 60*(6), 606-612.

Rivera, G.(2017) Retrieved from https://www.youtube.com/watch?v=EcWbuBPNtPw

Schaeffer, Francis A *A Christian Worldview Vol 5 Christian Manifesto*

Secessions (n.d.) Retrieved from http://www.libs.uga.edu/hargrett/selections/confed/dates.html http://constitution.org/csa/ordinances_

secession.htm#South%20Carolina https://www.civilwar.org/learn/primary-sources/declaration-causes-seceding-states

Sennett J.E.(1998) *The Analytic Theist; an Alvin Plantinga reader,* William Eerdmans Publishing Company, Grand Rapids Michigan

Shay, Jonathan (1994) *Achilles in Vietnam; Combat Trauma and the Undoing of Character,* Scribner publishing, New York, NY

Shay, J. (2014). Moral injury. *Psychoanalytic Psychology, 31*(2), 182.

Sherman N.(2010) *The Untold War: inside the hearts, minds and souls of our soldiers,* W.W. Norton and Company, New York, New York

Stone, G. R. (2007). Government Secrecy vs. Freedom of the Press. *Harv. L & Pol'y Rev., 1,* 185.

Stone, Perry (2013)*The Code Of The Holy Spirit,* Charisma Books Charisma Media/Charisma House Book Group, Lake Mary, Florida

Syse, H. (2010) The Platonic Roots of Just War Doctrine: A Reading of Plato's Republic, Diametros nr 23, marzec: 104-123

Tick E. (2005) *War and the Soul healing our nations veteran form post-traumatic stress disorder,* Quest Books Theosophical Publishing House, Wheaton, IL

Training Letter No. 5 Retrieved from https://www.mca-usa.org/wpcontent/uploads/2017/04/TMC Fall 2012 web.pdf

Vermetten, E., & Jetly, R. (2018). A Critical Outlook on Combat-Related PTSD: Review and Case Reports of Guilt and Shame as Drivers for Moral Injury. *Military Behavioral Health, 6*(2), 156-164.

Washington, George. (1796) *Farewell Address,* September, 19, 1796, p.22

Watkins C.B. (2005) *Christian War Ethics and the Just War Philosophy,* Christopher B. Watkins, published 2003, updated 2005

Watson R. (2013) *The Ethics of Domestic Government Spying,*

Wright H. Norman, (2001) *The Complete Guide to Crisis & Trauma* Regal Publishing, Ventura, CA

Yehuda, R., & Hoge, C. W. (2016). The meaning of evidence-based treatments for veterans with posttraumatic stress disorder. *JAMA psychiatry, 73*(5), 433-434.